The Fundamental Ideas of Christianity

Being the Gifford Lectures on Natural Theology
delivered to the University of Glasgow
in Sessions 1892-3 and 1895-6

PUBLISHED BY

JAMES MACLEHOSE AND SONS, GLASGOW

𝔓ublishers to the 𝔘niversity.

———

MACMILLAN AND CO., LTD., LONDON.

New York, - - The Macmillan Co.
London, - - - Simpkin, Hamilton and Co.
Cambridge, - - Macmillan and Bowes.
Edinburgh, - - Douglas and Foulis.

———

MDCCCXCIX.

John Caird.

The Fundamental Ideas
of Christianity

By
JOHN CAIRD, D.D., LL.D.
Late Principal and Vice-Chancellor of the University of Glasgow

With a Memoir
By EDWARD CAIRD, D.C.L., LL.D.
Master of Balliol

VOL. I.

Glasgow
James MacLehose and Sons
Publishers to the University
1899

GLASGOW: PRINTED AT THE UNIVERSITY PRESS
BY ROBERT MACLEHOSE AND CO.

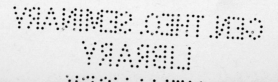

PREFACE

IN writing the following memoir, I have been assisted by very valuable suggestions and criticisms from Professor Jones, of the University of Glasgow. I have also received much help from him and from Mr. Robert MacLehose in revising the proofs of the Gifford Lectures.

I have to offer my best thanks to friends of my brother who have intrusted me with many of his letters.

E. C.

BALLIOL COLLEGE,
  October, 1899.

CONTENTS

CONTENTS.

LECTURE IV.

LECTURE V.

LECTURE VI.

LECTURE VII.

LECTURE VIII.

MEMOIR

I HAVE undertaken with much hesitation to write
a short sketch of my brother's life, as an introduction to his Gifford Lectures. In doing so, I
have to remember that he was a man of much
reserve, which even after his death I am bound
to respect; and that for a long time my relations
with him were so close and intimate, that it is
probably impossible for me to see him as others
saw him. Also his life was uneventful, and the
materials in the way of correspondence which are
at my disposal are not large.

John Caird was born at Greenock, on the
Clyde, on the 15th December, 1820. He was
the eldest of seven brothers, one of whom died
in infancy, and the others still survive. His father
was John Caird, partner and manager of the
firm of Messrs. Caird & Co., engineers. He was
educated in the schools of Greenock, and, in par-

ticular, he received his first classical training from Dr. Brown, a teacher of the old school, a man of much vigour and individuality, full of enthusiasm for the Classics, and of contempt for any training not based upon them, and a profound believer in the power of the "taws." Of one of his pupils who had considerable success in life, Dr. Brown is recorded to have said, "That's because I thrashed him well." In spite of the severity of his discipline, Brown's half-conscious humour, the energy he threw into his profession, and the lively interest he took in those whom he had taught, awakened strong feelings of regard in many of. his pupils.

At the age of fifteen, John Caird was withdrawn from school to enter his father's office, and in the next eighteen months he was passed through several departments of the engineering works, in order that he might have a practical acquaintance with all the details of the business. At the expense of some wounds and bruises, he acquired some facility in working with mechanical tools, and at the same time he also gained some knowledge of mechanical drawing. But he soon became conscious of the need for further education, and I have found a letter of his, written in

1837, in which he urges his father to send him for a year to the University of Glasgow to pursue mathematical and other studies, and promises that if his request is granted he will endeavour to the utmost to profit by the opportunity. Having received his father's consent, in Session 1837-8 he attended the Mathematical and Logical classes in the University, and took prizes in both. His main object at this time was simply to qualify himself to be a better manager of an engineering business, and in this he was so successful that his father is recorded to have said that "John was worth any two of his assistants." During the year spent at the University, however, other interests had begun to take hold of his mind, and as I gather from his correspondence with an intimate friend, Mr. Allan Park Paton, of Greenock, he devoted some part of his time to reading and writing poetry. Some specimens of his verses are preserved, which have the usual merits and defects of such youthful effusions.

In 1838, he returned to work in the foundry; but the death of his father in September of the same year, and shortly after of his uncle, James Caird, who was at the head of a firm of chain-makers and smiths, led to the termination of his

connection with the engineering business. During
the year 1839, indeed, he superintended the chain-
making works, but towards the end of it circumstances rendered it necessary for this business to be
disposed of; and for a short time he was in doubt
as to his future career. The experience which
he had acquired, and the credit he had gained
for energy and ability, led to his being offered
the post of a manager in a mill in Greenock;
but the growing interest in academic studies which
had been awakened in him during the year at
College made him reluctant to follow such a
career. And certain early religious impressions,
which were deepened by the deaths of his father
and uncle, led him to look to the Church as
the profession which he would prefer to all others.
It may be mentioned also that he had already
shown some indications of that power of public
speaking which was his most prominent gift.
As soon, therefore, as it became clear that he
possessed sufficient pecuniary means to enable him
to do so, he resolved to pursue his studies at the
University. He had allowed his Classics to become somewhat rusty, and had consequently some
hard work in preparing himself for the University
classes; but the interval between school and the

University was not lost. He had, I think, gained from his business training something of that practical directness of intellect, and that reverence for scientific truth, which were among his most prominent characteristics.

For the next five years, from 1840 till 1845, he threw his whole energy into study, and his career at the University was exceptionally brilliant. He took several University prizes, among others, one for poetical composition, and one for an essay on Secondary Punishments, on which he spent much pains, even visiting many prisons in order to verify his facts. He stood first in the classes of Moral and Natural Philosophy, and in all the Divinity and Ecclesiastical History classes; and though he had not much turn for languages, he also distinguished himself in Latin and Hebrew. He formed intimate and lasting friendships with a few other students, who like himself were destined for the Church, among whom I may mention especially Duncan Weir, afterwards Professor of Hebrew in the University of Glasgow; Archibald Watson, afterwards minister of East Parish Church of Dundee; Robert Graham, afterwards minister of Kilbarchan; and John Paisley, afterwards minister of the Parish of Garelochhead, all of whom died

before him. But during these years he seems
generally to have been in a somewhat depressed
state of mind, feeling much his loneliness at
College, and always eager at every opportunity to
escape from it to his home in Greenock, or to
have one of his younger brothers to visit him. In
a letter to a friend with whom he corresponded
much during these years (Mr. James Williamson,
of Greenock), he speaks repeatedly of " the heart-
and home-sickness, the inevitable depression and
anxiety which have been ever the attendants of
my student life." " Believe me, my dear friend,"
he says on one occasion, " if I do meet with
success in after life, it is dearly purchased by
the racking and feverish anxieties of a student's
life, by its often sad forebodings of the future,
and by its many hours of loneliness and labour."
This depression had little or nothing to do with
any intellectual doubts or difficulties, of which I
cannot find any trace. He had been brought up
in a circle into which any idea of scepticism as
to the doctrines of the Christian faith had hardly
entered ; and his philosophical studies, which were
at that time mainly in writers like Reid and Stewart,
while they exercised his powers, were not such as
to affect his intellectual or moral life very deeply.

When he passed into the Divinity Hall the noise of the "Non-Intrusion" controversy, which was then in the air, while it disturbed the student's intellectual peace, rather distracted him from deeper questionings as to theological subjects. So far as I can gather from the imperfect records that remain, my brother came from the University with his faith in the general body of what is called evangelical doctrine quite undisturbed. But in his earliest preaching he showed a tendency to dwell almost entirely on what he then regarded as the essentials of religion, on those practical aspects of it which are the most useful and effective themes of the pulpit, and to pay less attention to questions of doctrine. This tendency, even from the earliest times of his ministry, awakened a certain suspicion as to his 'soundness,' which was not founded upon anything positive, but only on what was described by some people as a 'want,' *i.e.* a want of specific dogmatic statements in relation to articles of the Calvinistic system, which he did not disbelieve, but in which he saw no special practical bearing. And, indeed, it was always a characteristic of his preaching to dwell on the ethical meaning of Christianity as all-important, and everything else as subsidiary. But in later times, when the comparative quiet of a rural parish enabled him to make deeper studies in philosophy and theology, he came to attach more and more importance to the system of doctrine as embodying the Christian view of man, and his relation to God.

In 1845, after the conclusion of his studies in Divinity as well as in Arts, he took the Degree of M.A., and was almost immediately ordained as minister of the parish of Newton-on-Ayr. In that parish he remained only for 18 months, when he accepted a call to Lady Yester's Church in Edinburgh, a charge which he held until near the end of the year 1849. During this time his power as a speaker had become known throughout Scotland, and drew crowds to hear him, not only in his own church but wherever he preached. His style was less chastened, and his thoughts less weighty than they afterwards became; but he spoke with an earnestness and vehemence, with a flow of utterance, and a vividness of illustration, which carried his hearers by storm. No one could be less of a mere actor, but when he was deeply interested in any subject it was natural to him to give to his thoughts a kind of dramatic expression. When he had time, he wrote his discourses carefully and committed them to memory, but often in Edinburgh the pressure of parish work rendered this impossible, and he was able only to write down a few notes. And sometimes when this was the case, he spoke with more force and effect than when he had carefully prepared. Gifted with a voice of great compass and flexibility, which seemed to adapt itself to the expression of every feeling, never hesitating for a word, and himself completely lost in the idea he was expressing, he held his audience in his grasp. Sometimes, indeed, in the vehement torrent of speech, he lost control of his utterance, as he would not have done at a later period, and his voice rose too high—but those who heard him were generally too much moved to be critical.

What he preached was simply, as I have indicated, the Christian faith as he had received it, in its most practical aspect. If in the form in which he presented it there was a shade of difference from what was common at the time, it lay in the fact that he dwelt less upon doctrines about Christ, and more upon the idea of identification with him as a living person ; less upon atonement by his death, and more and more upon unity with him. If there were some even at that time who accused my brother of 'not preaching

b

Christ,' the charge was the exact reverse of the truth. It might rather be said that he never preached anything else, and that the idea of the sympathetic realization of Christ's life and death, and of Christ's union with man, was the one theme upon which all his preaching turned. " I am never weary," he writes to a friend at this period, " of recurring to the thought of the personal nearness, the mysterious yet most familiar sympathy, the profound and unerring wisdom, the mingled majesty and tenderness of that divine yet gentlest of Consolers. If Christianity had no more than this, this one so beautiful, so real and wonderfully suitable provision for the deepest yearnings of the heart would be to me proof sufficient of its divine origin. I have all the certainty of moral evidence that this is the true specific for all the unrest and manifold distractions of man's inner life, . . . 'the peace of God that passeth all understanding, keeping our heart and mind through Christ Jesus.'"

In a sense, this predominance of the idea of Christ never ceased to be characteristic of his preaching ; but in later days he was more occupied with the idea of the unity of the divine and the human, as he conceived it to be manifested in Christ, and with the further results of this idea in the moral and intellectual life of man. But at this time it was not Christianity as a system of thought, or as a principle for the explanation of human life and experience, that took the most prominent place in his mind, but simply the image of Jesus Christ as a Divine Being, who had given Himself to man that man might give himself to God.

I have been favoured with the following account of his ministry in Edinburgh, by the Rev. Dr. Macmillan, of Greenock, who was at that period a student in the University there.

The three years of Dr. Caird's ministry in Edinburgh were among the most fruitful of his whole life. He himself, I have reason to believe, loved to look back upon that period as a time of highly quickened intellectual and spiritual life. Owing to the great reputation he had acquired by his faithful performance of pastoral duty, and by his remarkable eloquence in the pulpit in his previous charge of Newton-on-Ayr, the Town Council of the Metropolis unanimously elected him to be the minister of Lady Yester's Church in the south side of the city. At this period he was only twenty-six years of age, and his youthful appearance added greatly to the profound impression which his oratorical gifts produced. He seemed to have dispensed with the slow, gradual training by which other members of his profession reach maturity, and to have all at once acquired the full mastery of his remarkable powers. The church to which he was appointed, though territorially important, was not one of the principal or fashionable charges of the city. In consequence of the great growth of Edinburgh in recent years Lady Yester's Church has become obscured by new streets and buildings; but even in those days it did not occupy a prominent position, or obtrude itself upon the notice of the passers-by. It had to be sought out with some diligence in its quiet corner. There were no special architectural features to distinguish it, having been built in the plain useful style which at that time characterized nearly all the Scottish churches. The interior was somewhat dark and dingy, and the building itself altogether was destitute of any special attraction for the vagrant worshipper. A good steady-going congregation attended regularly the ordinary services of the church up to the time of the vacancy.

But when the new preacher came, the place seemed all at once to have been changed by magic. The very external appearance of the church seemed to brighten with a sunshine of its own. Instead of being hidden in a secret nook, Lady Yester's Church became at once the most prominent place in Edinburgh. Long before the hour of worship on Sunday morning streams of people might be seen enlivening the quiet streets leading to it; and when the service began, not an inch of standing room could be found within the crowded building. The deep dark galleries and sombre pews were lit up with a sea of faces; and every eye was fixed upon the massive pulpit in eager expectancy. A profound silence fell upon the multitude when Mr. Caird appeared. Mounting the stairs with slow and dignified step, robed in the usual black gown and bands, he sat down for a few minutes

in the pulpit. Then rising he reverently began the
service by giving out a portion of a Psalm to be sung
by the congregation, reading the whole of it in quiet and
measured tones. His eager, youthful face seemed shaded
with thought; and his long black hair, brushed back
from his forehead, lent a striking prophetic look to it.
After a comprehensive prayer, remarkable for its beauty
and felicity of expression and fervour of manner, he read
a chapter from the Old and New Testament with much
dramatic force, bringing out the meaning in a way quite
unusual at the time, and fitted to arrest the most careless
attention. When he announced his text, a great gleam
of brightening countenances, as if a sudden sunbeam
had entered the church, ran electrically throughout the
crowd, and every one settled down into a profound
listening attitude. Without manuscript or note before
him, the preacher began by laying out his subject in a
manner so distinct and methodical that every one present
could grasp it as a whole; and then proceeded to unfold
and illustrate it with wonderful freshness and power.
Carefully composed and committed to memory as was
his theme, he spoke as if with pure spontaneity the
thoughts that arose within him at the moment. Profoundly impressed himself, his words rang out strong and
fervent, emphasized by the most appropriate gestures.
Standing back from the pulpit board, brushing his long
hair from his forehead, his eye kindling with a dusky
yet piercing light, "orb within orb," he poured forth a
succession of impassioned sentences which fairly carried
you away. There was no pretence, no studied unnatural
effect, but the fire and rapture of native eloquence.

Now and then there was an unexpectedness in some
allusion or illustration which was very effective; but his

periods were usually connected together, alike by the links of logical sequence and by the unity of feeling and of philosophic and poetic growth. Whatever of dimness had attached to one's ideas of Scripture was dissipated as mist by sunlight, and all was clearly and definitely evolved from one root or central thought. Occasionally he used a striking metaphor which shone in his subject like a stained-glass window; and often a short pithy sentence full of simple meaning, with an electric touch, went straight to the heart, and opened up a whole long vista of thought and feeling. With a long and highly-wrought peroration, in which he seemed to exhaust all his oratorical powers, he brought his discourse to a conclusion; and the loud sob of the audience indicated how profoundly they had been thrilled and strained in the course of its delivery. His sermons, which reached from the first, and uniformly maintained, a high level—far above the average—were more religious than theological, more practical than devotional. They were distinguished for their philosophic breadth, and their intense sympathy with all the struggles and sorrows and sins of humanity. They ranged over a wide and varied field of subjects. Starting from the familiar evangelical truths, they touched all the experiences of ordinary life, and brought the gospel into harmonious relation with all that is beautiful in art, and ennobling in philosophy and history.

Situated not far from the University, in a quarter of the town affected by the students connected with theology, art, and medicine, Lady Yester's Church soon attracted this class of hearers, who showed by the regularity of their attendance, and the sacrifices which they made to be present, how greatly they valued the privilege. During the three years of Mr. Caird's incumbency, the Edinburgh

students had very exceptional advantages. The Scottish
Metropolis at that time was indeed entitled to be called
"The Modern Athens." Never before or since has there
been such a galaxy of great men among the professors of
the University; men of European reputation, who have
left their enduring mark upon our literature, philosophy,
and science. Sir William Hamilton, Christopher North,
Aytoun, James Forbes, Syme, Christison, Simpson, Gregory,
Bennett, all shed lustre upon this one seat of learning at
the same time; and the students, stimulated by the teaching of such professors, and by the new ideas of science
and philosophy which were beginning to dawn upon
Scottish minds, heralding the mighty revolutions in thought
which belonged to the age later on of Darwin, were in
the most favourable mood to be benefited by such preaching as Mr. Caird supplied. The religious mind, too, was
quickened by the throes of the Disruption which had
scarcely yet passed away, and the ecclesiastical atmosphere in Edinburgh was surcharged with potent elements
that were well fitted to quicken the spirit and stir up
enthusiasm. Mr. Caird, who never identified himself with
religious controversy, but lived in a calm region of his
own, came into this vortex of stimulated life and energy,
and by his marvellous preaching imparted to it a healing
and ennobling influence. On the Sabbath day he directed
the quickened thought of the students and his other hearers
into the highest channels, and showed to those who were
being taught the wonderful generalizations of science and
philosophy, that God was the highest generalization—that
Jesus Christ and Him crucified was the keystone of the
arch of human knowledge, in whom all things consist or
hang together.

After nearly three years of this life, my brother,

who had been working at the utmost tension from
the time of his father's death, began to feel that
the strain of managing a large parish, making congregational visits, and at the same time preaching
every Sunday to crowded audiences, was more than
his strength could bear.   And after some hesitation,
he accepted, towards the end of 1849, the charge of
the parish of Errol, in Perthshire.   There he remained
for the following eight years, living for the most part
a very retired life, doing the work of his parish with
much energy, but enjoying, one might say, for the
first time in his life, the opportunity for independent reading and reflection.   The comparative
leisure of a rural living gave him opportunity to
undertake many studies in literature and philosophy
in which he felt himself to be deficient, and to
think out many questions which had arisen upon
his mind in the course of his work, but which he
had not hitherto been able to consider.

During his ministry at Errol, the quiet of his
life was only broken in upon by two events.   One
was the opening of a Girls' School of Industry, on
the building, furnishing, and other equipment of
which he spent much time and pains between 1853
and 1856.   His motives in making the effort to
establish this school are very well explained in the

following letter to an intimate friend who had
been a member of his church in Edinburgh
(dated March 14, 1854):

" The school is for the industrial training of girls.
Young girls in this parish and neighbourhood, as
soon as they can earn a penny, are set to work at
handloom weaving or coarse field labour. There is
no existing means of female education apart from
the common parish school. The result is, that
girls grow up utterly ignorant of the commonest
sorts of household work, are unfit for domestic service, even of the rudest kind, still more unfit to
manage their own houses when they marry. They
have no habits of personal neatness, no taste for
order, cleanliness, domestic comfort ; they never
aspire to anything beyond the mere eking out of
their coarse, scanty, comfortless life, and their only
pleasures are sensual indulgence and scandal.
What a life ! I declare that, with every effort to the
contrary, I seldom return from a day's visiting in
our village without feeling my moral tone lowered
by breathing in such an atmosphere. What must
it be, without education, or elevating influences of
any sort, to have to breathe in it continually ? I
am determined to do something to help them.
And so this school is to be got up as a probable

means of elevating socially one most important
class, the girls of the labouring poor. It is to be
built with some attention to taste and beauty in
the structure and grounds, that even these external
influences may second the more direct teaching and
training within doors. In the establishment will
be given, besides the usual branches, instruction in
sewing, knitting, cooking, laundry work, dress-
making, etc. In short, we shall do our best to
open up higher and less demoralizing sorts of industry for the girls of the poor, qualifying some to
become good domestic servants, some to be school
mistresses, and many to be better managers of
their own homes, so as to introduce some approach
to neatness, taste, and comfort among our sordid,
degraded, Scottish poor."

The funds for this school were mainly raised by
my brother himself, partly by subscription, partly
by appealing to congregations in Edinburgh and
Glasgow, and other towns in Scotland, and partly by
a bazaar in Errol. I have myself an indistinct
remembrance of hearing him plead for this object,
with more than his usual force and eloquence, in a
church in Glasgow. He was soon able to meet the
necessary expenses, and had the pleasure of seeing
the school opened, and filled with scholars early in

1856. In March of that year, he wrote to the same friend as follows : " As to the school, I know you will rejoice with me to learn that it has succeeded beyond my most sanguine expectations. We opened only four weeks ago, and already our numbers are about 100, quite as many as the school can comfortably hold. What is better, our operations are giving universal satisfaction among the parents and parishioners in general, and every dissentient voice is silenced. The schoolroom is a very beautiful one, and when our playground is dressed up and the arrangements completed, I think our school machinery will be such as few parishes can boast of. I attribute our success mainly to our having been most fortunate in the selection of a teacher, a most sensible, quiet, firm, self-possessed sort of person, who manages to combine great strictness of discipline with a rare power of attracting the children to her, and so making them work out her plans, not out of constraint, but out of regard to her wishes. The cooking and sewing operations are not yet begun, but most of the children come from a considerable distance, and in a week or two we will be prepared to dine about fifty of them (with a plate of soup and a bit of bread, for a penny) in our soup kitchen. Detachments of the elder girls

are to take the management of the culinary
department in succession, keeping the kitchen tidy,
preparing and cooking the soup, arranging the
table, and attending to the younger girls at table.
You have no idea how manifest an improvement
is already beginning to show itself in the bearing and demeanour of the children.   Moreover,
our teacher sings very nicely, and we are already
training the children to help us on Sunday in church.
. . . The children have all donned a somewhat
quaint-looking apron, which gives the school, with its
rows of tidy forms and smiling faces, a very orderly
and pleasing aspect.   Pray forgive me for running on
in this garrulous way, but I can scarcely help myself,
for my head is quite full of it ; and you have no idea
what an additional chance this new spoke in my
parish wheel has given to my work.   Much of the
success is, I daresay, to be attributed to novelty ; still
the school supplies so obvious and manifest a want
that I have little doubt as to its ultimate and
permanent success."

The school continued to be a great interest to my
brother as long as he was in Errol, and, as I hear
from the present minister of the parish, is to this day,
" in a most flourishing condition, and has been a
very great blessing to the locality."

The other event to which reference has been made, is that in 1855 he was invited to preach before the Queen at Balmoral, and that Her Majesty was pleased to command that the sermon which he delivered should be published. The text was, " Not slothful in business, fervent in spirit, serving the Lord," and the sermon was published under the title, *Religion in Common Life.* Its theme was the necessity of carrying the religious spirit into all the ordinary practice of life, and the hollowness and worthlessness of any religion that wastes itself in feeling, in zeal for orthodoxy, or in the formalities of worship, and fails to consecrate the whole secular existence of man. In some sense, this sermon strikes the keynote of much of his later preaching and writing. For there was no thought on which he more constantly dwelt than that of the unreality of the hard divisions which are often made between one part of life and another, between faith and reason, between the church and the world, between the religious and the secular life in any of its forms. To break down such walls of separation, or to show their relative character, and the organic, or more than organic unity of life, is the theme of at least half of his later writing on theological or philosophical subjects.

As an illustration of the predominant thought of the sermon, I may quote the following letter written nearly at the same time, in which my brother first expresses the difficulty which he felt so strongly in his own case, of bringing his thought near enough to life, and then adds a few words upon the general question. " The greatest or one of the greatest difficulties that beset me, as a ghostly adviser of others, is the extreme unpracticalness of my sermonizing. It seems to me on reflection as if almost all I write were mere idealities. I spin out a leading thought or idea, with what seems a logical air of reasoning, into its various ramifications ; but when I get to the end of it and pick up a newspaper, I often feel shocked at the sort of transition from the theoretical man and woman in the sermon, to the intense homely reality of the people and affairs that are talked of in the newspaper. And then I begin to wonder if people who know life do not think my thought that of a mere dreaming essayist ; and if that be all—if they are merely sometimes pleased with the essay, and think I have worked out the idea tolerably well— what is the use of the whole affair ? I might as well have been a scribbler of magazine articles, where literary effect is the only end aimed at. . . . I don't like going into general society, indeed, to be honest,

I shrink from it, with a distaste a monk might envy ; but if I thought that ignorance of the world's ways rendered my talk ineffective and useless, I would either conquer the hermit in me, or take to some other line of work. . . . The difficulty you talk of is a most real one : I mean that of bringing principles to bear on the common trials and petty anxieties of daily life.   Theoretical affliction and submission in a book, or in our solemn and sometimes formal words in prayer, are a very different thing from that homely rugged, hard-featured thing that meets us in the face, when we come down from the clouds to the world of realities, the world of headaches and heartaches, of coarse, uncongenial contacts and intercourses.   But this is our trial, and the trial which, since the age of persecution is passed away, is perhaps the most common and the most difficult to which a Christian is subjected.   I know no help for it but perseverance and prayer.   It is the old thought of great principles and small duties and trials, and I need not descant upon it to you.   But I am quite convinced that Christian advancement consists in nothing so much as a habit, acquired by long effort and after many struggles and failures, of bringing high religious motive and feeling to bear on the common incidents of life.   Don't you envy that state of mind where this has ceased to be a work of effort and conscious toil, when duty becomes a delight, God's presence constantly realized without endeavour, and so His service perfect freedom?"

The sermon speedily ran through many editions, was spoken of by Dean Stanley as "the best single sermon in the language," and contributed to make its author known as a preacher in England as well as in Scotland. It was the first thing he had published; and but for the command of the Queen—who shortly after appointed him one of Her Majesty's chaplains for Scotland—he would not, as I gather from his letters, have been willing to publish it. Indeed, at this time he seemed almost oppressed by a sense of the defects of his own education, and of the need of greatly extending his knowledge of life and philosophy, before he could publish anything. "I shrink," he wrote shortly before, "without more reading and thought than I have yet had the opportunity of undertaking, from the attempt to seek a wider scope for my thoughts than my own pulpit and parish can afford me." But he was doing his best to make good the defects of which he was conscious. In particular, he eagerly studied the writings of Carlyle and Ruskin, the former of whom had a very deep influence upon him. He also read extensively in English theology, and was greatly interested in the writings of Newman and Pusey, and generally in the movement of which they were the leaders. He had, indeed, no sympathy, then or at any time, with sacerdotalism, and still less, if possible, with the tendency to make religion centre in the Sacraments. But in spite of this, he felt the attraction of the fresh stirring of religious life in the Church of England ; and the controversies to which the movement gave rise caused him to reflect more deeply than he had hitherto done on the relation of Authority and Reason. Also, he was greatly interested in the effort after greater ' beauty of holiness,' greater attention to fitness and perfection of form in the expression of religious feeling. From the beginning of his ministry, he had felt a strong desire to modify the somewhat bald and prosaic form to which Puritanism had reduced the service of religion in Scotland. And the movement to improve the architecture of the churches, to devote greater attention to the musical training of choirs and congregations, and generally to elevate the æsthetic character of church worship, found in him a constant and active supporter.

Still more important, perhaps, as a step in intellectual progress was the fact that he began the study of the German language and literature, and to bring his mind into contact with the theological and philosophical thought of Germany. He had for some time been sedulously reading the translations of the German orthodox theologians which were then beginning to be issued, and he was gradually drawn on from them to an interest in the writings of Schleiermacher, and, at a somewhat later period, of other German philosophers and theologians. I am not able to say how much he had done in this direction before he left Errol. He had at any rate begun a study which influenced him more and more as he advanced in it during the years that followed.

One point has already been indicated which it is necessary always to remember in order to understand his mental development both at this time and afterwards. He was not one of those who are early led by doubt to philosophical inquiry, and for whom any ethical and religious convictions which they attain, are deeply affected almost from the beginning by reflexion. Though he had a natural bent to philosophy, and eagerly studied logical and ethical subjects as they were presented to him at the University, it cannot be said that such studies had hitherto influenced him very deeply. The years during which he was at the University were, on the whole, years of philosophical barrenness. Hume had awakened Kant from his dogmatic slumbers, but he had been less successful in his native land, where a philosophy of 'Common Sense' protected men from unsettling thoughts, and, as it were, consecrated the *status quo*. There was then in this country no very powerful stirring of thought, no very potent philosophical influence, with the doubtful exception of Coleridge; and religious controversy was generally concerned with quite other matters than the metaphysical basis of theology. Dr John Macleod Campbell had, indeed, for a moment troubled the waters by his attack upon some of the principles of Calvinism, and had perhaps loosened the hold of the strict system of Election and Predestination upon the religious life of Scotland. But the immediate effect was to produce a tendency to regard those doctrines as too mysterious for discussion, rather than to awake a thorough examination of the assumptions on which they are based. Perhaps this was one of the reasons which caused my brother in his earlier ministry to turn away from discussion of doctrine, and to dwell almost exclusively upon the ethical aspects of Christianity, and particularly on

the idea of unity with Christ—leaving the dogmas
of Theology to rest on the basis on which they
were supposed to be secured by the words of
Scripture, as interpreted by the tradition of the
Reformed Churches.

At Errol, however, he began to be dissatisfied
with this attitude and to seek for some more distinct
rationale of the faith that was in him. The craving
to make things clear and intelligible to himself
was very deep in his nature. I do not think that
his faith was ever seriously shaken; it was too
closely bound up with his life, and wrought into
all his habits of mind by years of pastoral work,
to be so shaken. But after this period, he constantly seemed to feel that an uncritical, unreasoned,
and unexplained faith was insufficient. And,
almost unconsciously at first, he seemed to be
looking in every direction for ideas which might
light up those parts of the Christian system that
seemed to him obscure. At a later time, the
critical reaction of reflexion went somewhat further
and carried him to the rejection or modification of
many of the elements in the then commonly
received views of Christian doctrine. But I think
that it may fairly be said, that his philosophy, as
it grew to clearness in his mind, seemed rather to

confirm and deepen his faith in Christianity, by rendering its most mysterious doctrines luminous, and showing how its principles serve to explain the life of man and of the universe, than essentially to disturb or change it. This, however, is to anticipate what was, in the main, a later development.

During the eight years of his ministry in Errol, he had frequently preached in various parts of the country, and there was a growing demand for his services in aid of any important movement, charitable, educational, or religious. And after the first few years of rest in Errol, his clerical friends began to urge upon him the duty of again accepting the charge of some urban congregation, where his powers as a preacher would find a better field of exercise. As early as June 1855, he wrote in a half humorous spirit, to a friend who had informed him of some movement in Edinburgh that might lead to his being offered the charge of one of the most important churches in that city : "If you have ought of the cat-like love for familiar haunts and old well-known corners, of which I am conscious among very strong developments among my own bumps, I pity you just now very much, in your ejection from said haunts into all the unkindly felicities of a new

home. It takes a long time before one's tendrils
gather round and fix themselves on new objects,
and the moss of quiet memories collects—the only
thing of the sort a tidy housekeeper could not
sweep away—on the unfamiliar habitation. People
would call this sentimentality, but I daresay it is
to some people a more real thing than roast beef.
" And yet, O most cruel lady! you seem to hint
at such a dissevering of roots and sweeping away
of soft moss as with a sacrilegious housemaid's
brush for me. Be the day far distant when any
such vile necessity shall come. Every peeping
geranium and fresh budding rose among the beds
I have just been 'planting out' under my window
seem to look reproachfully in my face at the very
supposition. Health, strength, soundness of lung
and throat and a long incumbency to the minister
of ——— ! "

For the present he refused to consider such
offers ; but at the end of the following year,
he was strongly urged, especially by his friend,
Dr. Watson, then a minister in Glasgow, to accept
the charge of the Park Church, which was being
built to meet the needs of the rapidly extending
West End of the city ; and about the same time
he received an intimation that a similar offer was

shortly to come from St. George's Church, Edinburgh. After some hesitation, my brother resolved to accept the Glasgow charge. His main reasons for the decision are explained in the following letter :—

"You will be surprised to learn that I was already informed of the St. George's movement. I heard about it yesterday from Mr. Stevenson. . . . I wrote him a hurried reply, telling him, as I now tell you, that I have been in some perplexity for a few weeks past, about a similar invitation from the Glasgow people to accept the charge of their new church. In many respects the Glasgow position is one to my mind. The congregation is unformed, and so would be likely, when it is formed, to consist, not of those who tacitly submit to a man because he becomes minister of the church they occupy, but of those who would come to the church because they expected benefit from my way of teaching. It is, moreover, a church unconnected with the Presbytery—I mean not a Parish Church— and I hate Presbyteries ; but in St. George's I should be forced to attend them. My work in Glasgow, again, would be mainly preaching and congregational visiting. Now, in Edinburgh, I felt that in addition to this the pressure of a large parish which

I could not, and would not, neglect, was too much for me ; and if I undertook it again I fear it would speedily be with the same result—retirement once more to the country.   Even as it is, I believe that in Glasgow I shall have an assistant to help me, both in my public and private duties.   The Glasgow church, finally, has been got up by men interested in the welfare of the Old Church, and at great cost, so that I do not know but that in point of duty they have a claim to any little support I can lend them.   All things considered, therefore, though I am sorely reluctant to have my roots shaken and loosened once more, I am tending to the conclusion that I should accept the Glasgow invitation. . . . I may mention, but only for your private information, that one other and minor reason for my preferring Glasgow is that I need not go there for nine or ten months hence, the church being only in process of building ; and this time at present is almost necessary for the getting up of a volume of sermons which I am just beginning, but which, slow and laborious work as it is, would be quite impracticable amidst the engagements of St. George's."

My brother's life in Errol, though monotonous, had been so peaceful, and had given him so much time for study, that he was very loath to exchange its quiet for the anxiety and hurry of a town charge. He had also formed very close ties of friendship with members of his congregation, which made it hard for him to leave them. Of this he speaks to a friend (in December, 1857) :—

"I have for weeks been going round from morning to night to the houses of my poor people here, and discovering even in the humblest of them a depth of feeling for which I had scarcely given them credit. But it is sad work parting, and there is a sort of half reproachful tone in their kind wishes for my future which makes this transition especially painful to me. And then to think that another chapter in one's brief history is closing, and that a few, a very few more, and all will be over! Don't wonder, my dear friend, if I have not much heart to write about anything else just now."

He preached his first sermon in Park Church on the last Sunday of 1857. And in June of the following year he was married to Isabella Glover, daughter of the Rev. Dr. Glover, of Greenside Church, Edinburgh, a union that added greatly to the happiness of his after life.

Of his ministry in Park Church I am not able to say much. The congregation was not one which required a great deal in the way of pastoral care, and he had therefore more leisure to devote himself to preaching and preparation for it. "For me," he declares (in November, 1858), "I am writing away hard enough in my small way, but whether with much profit to myself and others I cannot perceive. The mere intellectual work is, I fear, but too apt to overlay the deeper aim of thinking and writing for the pulpit; and I have an uneasy suspicion sometimes that there would be truer self-abnegation in giving myself to outward pastoral work, and less, or less elaborately, to that of solitary thought and sermonizing. On the other hand, perhaps no man can be true or useful to others unless he is first true to himself and to whatsoever gift, little or great, God has given him. But I don't see my way clear in the matter." His sermons by this time had become richer in thought and more weighty in expression; his style was somewhat chastened of its early exuberance, and his speaking showed more self-command and restraint, without as yet losing any of its force—though perhaps it might be somewhat less attractive for a popular audience. He still felt that his essential vocation was preaching, and not long before, after an illness, he had written to a friend:

" I have now quite got rid of the effects of indisposition, and resumed my work, greatly delighted, I confess, to get into the pulpit once more. Many false motives mingle but too often with one's pleasure in preaching, and as the corruption of the best things is always the worst, a minister's work may become a very degrading one ; still, if prosecuted in a right spirit, it is surely the noblest sort of work on earth. And I am sure you can easily conceive how intensely interesting, how almost necessary to one's existence it becomes. If God were to lay me aside from this work, I should pray and strive, I hope, for grace to submit ; but the fresh zest with which I have returned to it at present makes me feel how very different a thing, apart from this vocation, life would become."

In another letter his view of the matter is less hopeful :—" I am sure you are right in thinking that a minister ought to be, if he has it in him, the thoughtful and thought-inspiring educator of his people. But in what conceivable position can he fill this office in our day and country? Among a rural auditory the head can only be reached through the feelings, and except for ideas of the broadest and most palpably material sort, the teacher in such a position has no scope. In a civic auditory, such as an Edinburgh congregation, the capacity of thinking is often very little greater, and when it does exist, the horrible spirit of church bigotry and narrow-souled orthodoxy is now so rampant, that any sort of teaching that does not bear the broad stamp of orthodox mintage in tone and language is apt to be looked upon with a very suspicious eye. 'This is not the *simple* Gospel,' as if simplicity in religion, any more than in learning, meant always going over the well-conned A, B, C; or preaching the Gospel, harping perpetually on 'old news.' I have sometimes in my day-dreams let my mind picture to me a preacher's Paradise: a quiet, not very numerous but thoughtful and earnest-minded people, bringing each successive week thought to meet thought, and ready to reciprocate every real feeling, and to carry away and embody in the practical discipline of a holy life every hint, suggestion, principle, that had aught of truth and reality in it. But I must not run on at this rate, else my letter will become a sermon."

The general character of my brother's preaching in Park Church may be gathered from the volume of sermons mentioned in one of the letters quoted above, which was prepared mainly during his last year at Errol and published early in the first year of his ministry in Glasgow. Generally speaking, it is marked by the characteristics of his earlier preaching; but there are in it traces of more mature thought and of wider views of the meaning of Christianity. There are perhaps two points which distinguish it from the common run of sermons preached at that time in Scotland. In the first place, there is throughout a persistent effort to break down all artificial boundaries between religion and ordinary experience, and, by every resource of image and comparison which the writer can command, to re-translate the terms of dogmatic theology into the language of common life, and to bring out its essential ethical meaning. As in the sermon on " Religion in Common Life," he wars against every form of piety that keeps religion for Sundays, or hides it in a mystery, or identifies it with peculiar feelings, practices, or beliefs, so in this volume of sermons he is continually striving to reach a distinct realization of the real moral value of each of the articles of the Christian system.

Another characteristic of these sermons is the ever-recurring thought of the greatness of the possibilities of human nature. The consciousness of the manifold intellectual and moral experience of which man is capable, of the infinite sadness of his common

sorrows and the infinite sweetness of his common
joys—the feeling of humanity and sympathy with
ἡ σύμπασα τοῦ βίου τραγῳδία καὶ κομῳδία—was
perhaps the deepest thing in his nature, and the
main source of his power as an orator. For qualities peculiar to the few, for the tastes and characteristics of special classes of men, for things away
from the general experience, he had little appreciation—sometimes, indeed, a kind of repulsion. But
no one had a more constant feeling of the wonder
of ordinary human life, and the pathos of its
transitory happiness in the ever near presence of
death ; and few were more easily moved to action
by a tale of distress, or more careful, when so
moved, to keep their left hand from knowing what
the right hand was doing. And, on the other hand,
it was equally natural for him to dwell upon the
contrast of the chances and changes of man's destiny, with the possibilities of his nature and the
infinite importance of the moral issues of his life.
Many of the sermons read like variations on the
great theme of Pascal : " Man is but a reed, and
the weakest in nature ; but he is a reed that thinks.
It does not need the universe to crush him ; a
breath of air, a drop of water will kill him. But
even if the material universe overwhelm him, man

would be more noble than that which destroys him, because he knows that he dies, while the universe knows nothing of the advantage it obtains over him." It may, indeed, be said that pulpit oratory is too apt to dwell on this contrasted view of life, and so to lose hold of reality in the search for antithesis. And it is no doubt true that public speaking in all its forms is obliged to a certain extent to paint in black and white, in order to make its distinctions visible to the popular eye. But the danger of such rhetorical antithesis is removed, or greatly lessened, when it is accompanied, as it always was in my brother's case, by a persistent effort to make the contrast intelligible.

I may introduce at this point a description contrasting his earlier and later manner of preaching, for which I am indebted to Dr. Story, who is his successor as Principal of the University of Glasgow.

You wish to have my "earlier recollections" of Dr. Caird as a preacher. It is not easy to summon these to come back across the abyss of fifty years. It was when he was minister of Lady Yester's, and I a lad not yet at College, that I first heard him, in 1849. But the impressions of these youthful days are clear in outline still, and the recollections more vivid than many of later date. After he went to Errol, he used to preach, occasionally, in Edinburgh, in St. George's sometimes, oftener, I think, in Greenside, to congregations always as large as the

church would hold. I remember well my first sight of
him, in Lady Yester's: A slim young man, pallid in complexion, with a mane of long jet-black hair, which he had
a way of throwing back from his forehead in the fervour
of preaching, as if he felt its weight—a dark eye capable
of quick varieties of expression, and a voice of singular
flexibility, rich in tone, wide in compass. He began the
service with an air of reverence and solemnity that arrested
attention; and his prayers were marked with an order in
arrangement and beauty of diction, specially noticeable in
those days. The sermon was of course, as always in
Scotland, the centre of interest, and as a work of art and
exhibition of rhetorical power, struck the youthful listener
then—and the conviction has never suffered change—as the
highest effort in that kind that even the Scottish pulpit
could display. Chalmers, to judge by the popular accounts
of him, must have been more overwhelming, more absolute
in rugged power; but his rough voice had none of the
musical inflexions and polished force of Caird's, and his
style had none of his literary grace and felicity. When
Caird got into the full flow of his declamation, one was
carried off in the impetuous torrent, whether one would
or not. The fire of the eye, the rapidity of the gestures,
the resonance of the voice, the sacred passion of the
orator, were not to be withstood. However dull and un-
emotional you might be, you felt the magnetic contagion,
and were "taken captive of him at his will." After those
years, 1849–52, I did not hear him again until he had for
some time been settled in Glasgow. A certain change had
meanwhile passed on him. The old charm and power
were there, but the tremendous oratorical force was re-
strained. The sermons were read. To the thoughtful
hearer they were, no doubt, better worth the hearing.

They were, as of old, eloquent, but the eloquence was less exuberant, and the substance and the theological tone of the preaching were different from the earlier type.

The year 1862 brought a great change in his life. I have already said that in Errol he had begun to think more about the philosophical basis of his creed, and this tendency to reflection had become still stronger in the intervening years, so that, even in his sermons, he often introduced a partial discussion of the doctrinal aspects of Christianity. When, therefore, the Chair of Theology in the University of Glasgow became vacant, he was urged by some of his friends to become a candidate for it; and, after much hesitation, and with many doubts of his capacity for its duties, he did so. He was unanimously elected to the office by the University Court; but, by arrangement with the previous professor, Dr. Hill, he did not take up his duties until after the Christmas vacation. His motives in undertaking the work of an academic teacher are indicated in the following letter (dated November 24, 1862): "As for myself, you divine my present state of mind. I know not whether to be glad or sorry; satisfied or alarmed. It was only after long hesitation, and much conflict of mind, that I

d

applied for my new post. I think I acted more
in deference to the advice of others, to whose
judgment I defer, than on my own convictions.
. . . If I let them rise, I know that I would
at this moment be the victim of all sorts of wistful,
regretful feelings; for it is no light thing to
give up a kind of work that, with all its worry
and anxiety, has been very congenial work, and
to enter upon a new career for which I am inadequately prepared. And there is, apart from
that, the mere fact that it is the closing of one
chapter, and the opening of a new one in a book
that contains but few at the most, and that will
soon be closed. . . . But I do not let myself
dwell on these things; my path is now clear,
and I must act in the 'not backward are our
glances bent' spirit. Moreover, to tell the truth, I
am for the present precluded from almost any
thought but work; for, you know, I was appointed
to the Chair only a few days ago, and without a
scrap of MS. in readiness, I am called to lecture after
the Christmas holidays. . . .

"In many respects, if I had time to think, I know
I should feel the position of theological teacher of the
future teachers of our church to be a very noble one,
well worthy of the devotion of a man's whole life and

energy. God help me. I am profoundly conscious
of weakness and unworthiness, but I shall do my
very best ; and if I fail it will be a sign that my place
and work lie elsewhere, and I shall try to bear
my disappointment meekly. . . . It is very kind
of you to warn me of the censorship to which, in
common with every man who ventures to think
or speak one word out of the routine jargon that
stands for thought and faith with so many, I am
subjected. I must lay my account with that, but
I shall not needlessly provoke it. I have not the
shadow of a wish for notoriety, not certainly
for notoriety of that kind. My only desire is
to work out of sight, and do my share of the
world's work, quietly and usefully."

Later he writes (January 14, 1863), "I would
gladly write to you a long story at present, but I
write after a hard day's work, and with the prospect
of a six o'clock beginning of another to-morrow.
I am in the sad position of being obliged, on the
most important and difficult questions, to run off
the merest superficialities, without time for matur-
ing my views. When I manage to get a day
beforehand with my lecture, the next at once
suggests modifications which imply the throwing of
my last night's lucubrations into the fire. And all

this with the responsibility of guiding others! Oh
for summer and the green fields, and a month's
quiet musing!

"I am very glad that you liked my Introductory
Lecture, and also that you thought of telling me
so. I like approbation, as who does not? when
I can trust it. But oh, the odiousness of vulgar
admiration of the popular preacher! Right glad
am I, for one thing, to have done with *that*. . . .
The lecture is not what you think it, and I won't
publish it separately. It was got up after my
appointment, to meet a special emergency; and
though, of course, I believe in it myself, yet I might
afterwards, as my knowledge increases and convictions mature, regret having stereotyped my crude-
ness. This note, I fear, looks very like what it is,
the last maunderings on the verge of unconsciousness. Good night!"

The Introductory Lecture referred to in the
above letters was characteristically devoted to an
assertion of the possibility of treating theology as
a science, and the repudiation of all defences of
religion on sceptical principles, and especially of
that recently made by Mansel on the basis of the
Hamiltonian philosophy. Such an agnostic apology
for Christianity, in which security for the faith was

sought in the incapacity of man to criticise it, seemed to my brother like calling in the devil to protect the sanctuary.[1] He had indeed, at an earlier period, rested for a moment in the evasion of Leibniz, that a thing might be above reason, without being contrary to it ; but he soon discovered that such a distinction meant nothing.[2] As this Inaugural Lecture strikes the key-note of his later teaching, it may be desirable to give a short account of it.

He begins by pointing out the relation of Theology, as the Philosophy of Religion, to the physical and natural sciences, showing the difference of their methods, but maintaining the claims of the former to be in the highest sense scientific knowledge. He repudiates " the false opposition between personality and law," and the inference that religion has to do with that which is arbitrary. " The signs of the highest personality are not to be sought in the manifestation of mere will, but in the manifestation of will under the guidance of intelligence—that

[1] Verachte nur Vernunft und Wissenschaft,
   Des Menschen aller höchste Kraft,   .   .   .
   So hab' ich dich schon unbedingt,
says Mephistopheles of Faust.

[2] Cf. the *Introduction to the Philosophy of Religion*, p. 71, where he shows that this distinction is really a subterfuge.

is, of will acting rationally and regularly, of will
acting by law. When we consider the idea of
personality more carefully, it will be seen that it
manifests itself as mere will only in the weakest
and most childish natures, in persons whose ideas
are unprincipled, governed by no plan or rule, with
respect to whose actions we can form no calculation ; for you do not know what whim may seize
them, what fallacy mislead them, into what vagary
their inconsistent life may fall. But the more wise
and thoughtful a man becomes, the wider the reach
of his foresight and the range of his knowledge, the
more fixed and consolidated his principles of action,
—with the greater confidence can you predict what
he will say and do; for the more numerous become
the data on which your calculations are based.
And the highest activity, the nearest approach to
infallible uniformity of conduct would be attained,
if the agent became, what no human person is,
perfectly wise and good."

The lecturer then goes on to deal with the objections of those who hold that God, as an infinite
and absolute Being, is beyond the reach of knowledge. "Nature manifests mind, but can we rise
above nature, and know the infinite mind of which
it is the expression? Is the supernatural accessible

to human intelligence?" Sir William Hamilton, in his modified revival of Kantian principles, had propounded a doctrine as to the relativity of knowledge, from which Mansel drew the theological inference, that by the necessary laws of thought we are precluded from knowing God. " To think is to relate and to condition, and therefore thought, by its essential nature, cannot grasp the Absolute and the Unconditioned." By a train of thought, which has become more familiar since the time when he spoke, the lecturer shows that the view of the Infinite and the Absolute, upon which Mansel proceeds, reduces it to indeterminate being, and that such being is the opposite of the real Infinite. " God, the highest of all beings, should be one, of whom not the fewest, but the greatest number, of qualitative limitations can be predicated. He is the Being in whom are all conceivable powers, excellencies, good and great qualities in their highest perfection. . . . The conclusion, therefore, to which by such considerations we seem to be led, is, that the intellectual impotence with relation to divine things, of which so much has been made by this school of thinkers, is no real impotence. It is the impotence of thinking about nothing. If this philosophy be true, it is the apotheosis of zero; the highest type of religion would be sheer vacuity of mind, and of all human beings the idiot would be the most devout." He then goes on to show that, on the principles of Mansel, we would be precluded, not only in the present, but for ever, from the knowledge of God.

"For the disability which this philosophy supposes is one that pertains to us not as *human* beings, but as *finite* beings—not as defective creatures, but simply as creatures. It is therefore a disability which applies to all finite and created beings, which would only cease by our ceasing to be finite. . . . The creature, on this view, must be transformable into the creator before it can know the creator. And the awful conclusion is, that the Father of the Universe is shut out from communication with His children, and they from Him.

"In conclusion, let me say that it is not in the spirit of this philosophy that I desire to teach. Humility is wholesome, but not the humility that teaches us to abjure our birthright, or to court the Master's approval by telling Him that we have hid His talent in the earth. It is well to study and learn the limits of human knowledge, but it is not well or wise to prescribe ignorance as the remedy for presumption. The self-sufficiency of reason it is well to check; but it is not therefore necessary to prevent its vagaries by a self-imposed banishment from the presence of God. . . . Man is a mystery to himself; how can he think to comprehend God? The commonest phenomena of nature, the lowest manifestations of life, of which the physiologist takes note, include secrets which human science cannot penetrate : shall we expect to find everything patent in the manifestation of the eternal life of the heavens? But, all this admitted, it does not follow that because we cannot know all, our partial knowledge is not therefore to be trusted ; that because human intelligence cannot comprehend God, it can have no real knowledge of Him ; because it cannot 'find out the Almighty to perfection,' it can never know Him at all. Hopeless and universal indeed would be our ignorance, if that can never claim to be knowledge which is not perfect knowledge. In that case, we are not only incapable of knowing God, but also our fellowmen and ourselves. For who will contend that he has fathomed the depths of a single human heart, or that the philosophy of the human mind contains for him no insoluble problem? If, then, we feel that we *do* know something of our brother, though we cannot know all, we conclude that our knowledge of God may be real, though it cannot be exhaustive. 'He hath given us an understanding to know Him that is true.' . . .

"It is to this knowledge, in so far as it admits of a systematic or scientific development, that I have been called, however unworthily, to act as your guide. It is no simple or easy task. The office of the theologian, though not higher, is, I am well aware, one involving intellectual exercises far more severe and subtle than those of the preacher. He may be a fluent or eloquent speaker who has no analytic power to trace and to expound those principles which lie at the root of all language, which are involved in all accurate speech. The instinctive sharpness of the special pleader may be utterly dissociated from the power to investigate the laws of thought, or to develop the dialectical principles and rules which are involved in the act of reasoning. And in like manner, higher in one view though the qualifications of the preacher of the truth may be, yet it is quite possible for a man to feel and declare in apt and impressive words the truths of the Gospel, who is destitute of the power scientifically to analyze and defend them. To the theologian appertains the duty, not simply to state and enforce the truths and duties of religion, but to investigate the sources and extent of our religious knowledge, to point out the evidence on which our belief of it rests, to define and verify each separate conception or doctrine, to show the manifold relations of different truths, and to mould all the separate elements into a consistent and systematic form. All this, to be done well, implies something rarer than the rhetorician's art. To such a task, never did any one approach with a more anxious and depressing sense of inadequacy than that with which I now undertake it. I come to it fresh from parochial work, the weekly exigencies of which left me little or no leisure for research, or for studies that could not be immediately utilized. In those high researches in which we shall be engaged, I shall often be only feeling my own way on a path where I am but a few steps in advance of those to whom I act as guide. The views of divine truth to be submitted to you will, in form at least, be as the sheaves which a reaper has brought back from the harvest field, as the spoils of a wrestler but just released from the conflict. But be that as it may, to Him who is the Revealer of the Word of Truth, which is to be our daily study, to Him who is the Giver of all light and life, Himself 'the Light of all our seeing,' I commend myself and you. And filled with the profoundest sense of in-

adequacy, yet with at least that preparation which
arises from the most ardent love and enthusiasm
for the study, I begin my work."

The attitude taken up towards science and
philosophy in this lecture was, at the time, a new
thing in the Theological Halls of Scotland, and it
provoked a good deal of comment, partly un-
friendly. Theologians were startled by the appeal
to reason as the final arbiter of truth; and
the philosophical followers of Hamilton, then
numerous in Scotland, were irritated by the
uncompromising rejection of Mansel's use of the
' philosophy of the Conditioned,' as a defence of
religion. Beyond a few letters in the newspapers,
however, no public notice was taken of the lecture;
but at this time, and for many years after, there
was an atmosphere of suspicion attached to my
brother's name in what are called ' religious circles.'
He was frequently accused of Rationalism, of
Socinianism, and even of darker heresies than
these. But none of these charges ever found expression in any definite proceeding before the
Church Courts, till a much later date (1874), when
a futile attack was made upon him in the Presbytery of Glasgow, for a sermon, now printed in the
volume of *University Sermons*, on "the Guilt and

Guiltlessness of Unbelief." On that occasion, he refused to make any defence, or give any explanation; but when his principal accuser attempted to justify his withdrawal of the charge, by asserting that in re-delivering the sermon, my brother had modified the passages objected to, he, for once in his life, wrote to the papers to state that "the sermon preached in Dundee, on the newspaper report of which the charge of heresy was based, and the sermon preached in Edinburgh, on a report of which, it seems, the charge is to be withdrawn, are word for word, the same." Gradually in his later years such reports died away, as a result mainly of the great changes of opinion, within and without the church, which he, among others, had a considerable share in causing.

The truth is that such suspicions were awakened and partly justified, not by any special assertion of his that could be called heretical, but rather by the new tone of his teaching and the unfamiliar point of view from which he spoke. In a sense he was more orthodox than many of his assailants; for he sought to find an intelligible meaning in doctrines, which for them had become a dead tradition, or an incomprehensible mystery. But this new attitude of mind could not but puzzle and irritate those who were accustomed to identify truth with a traditional creed that neither developed nor changed; and to whom the re-interpretation of old doctrines, with all the subtle changes of matter and expression which it involved, seemed to disturb and unsettle all the terms of the so-called " Scheme of Salvation." The real question, however, was not one of heterodoxy or orthodoxy, but of the introduction of a freer movement of thought, which broke through the limits of both, and substituted for the mechanical repetition of formulas, the natural and ever changing expression of a growing spiritual life. Such a movement can hardly be resisted by the ordinary weapons of controversy, because it does not affect any special dogma or substitute its opposite for it, but rather alters the whole way of looking at doctrinal statements. Just because it involves a greater revolution than any change of specific articles, because it involves in a manner the denial and restatement of them all, it is hardly perceptible from day to day, even to those who are the instruments of it, and not perceptible at all to the general public. But he who measures the change in the religious ideas of the country during the last fifty years, can see that it has more importance than if one of the parties in any of the great controversies of the past had converted their opponents. Something more has happened than any shifting of dogmatic formulas, and it has happened in many cases without any such shifting. The bones, so to speak, may seem to remain the same, but they have been clothed, or are gradually clothing themselves, with the living tissue of a new organic structure. It is to this kind of change in the general ethical and religious attitude of the new time, that my brother's work contributed most. His mind was in some ways strongly conservative, and hardly, and with difficulty, separated itself from anything that was hallowed by the associations of the past; but his persistent desire to make things intelligible, and to fertilize his most cherished beliefs by fresh thought and improved expression, made him a suggestive and stimulating teacher of the religious teachers of Scotland, and did much to fill their minds with the new ideas that are gradually changing the world, and especially the religious life of modern Europe.

My brother's strength was very much strained during his first session, as he had passed directly from the care of his church to his professorial duties; and, indeed, for a time had to attend to both together. And, as he states in a letter quoted above, he had no lectures written, and no time to make special preparations for teaching, before his academic labours began. It is true that during previous years, his studies in theology and philosophy had been becoming more and more thorough, but the care of the Park Church had left him few intervals for such work. Now, how-ever, he was able to devote the long six months' vacations to a course of systematic reading, especially in the history of doctrine, and subse-quently in the general history of religion. And in connection therewith he also very greatly extended his philosophical studies, with, of course, a special view to the criticism of religious ideas. I may perhaps be excused for speaking of myself at this point, as I can hardly discharge my task without mentioning my intimate association with my brother during the years which followed. Being a good many years his junior, I had long looked up to him as an elder brother, had been much assisted by him in my earlier years of study, and had generally spent a considerable part of my vacations in his house. I had gradually, I may say, grown into his friendship, and after 1866, when I became a professor in the University of Glasgow, I was

in constant, and, during the session, almost daily
communication with him, for a period of twenty-
eight years. Many a discussion have we had on
subjects of philosophy, theology, or University
affairs, during walks in the country, in his smoking-
room, or in summer evenings while strolling up and
down in front of the University and looking down
upon the lights of Glasgow. Such a friendship,
made more intimate and confidential by the natural
tie of brotherhood, by many common studies, and
by a general sympathy of mind, which was the
deeper that it was united with many partial
differences in our points of view and habits of
thought, is one of the most sustaining and inspiring things in life. It made it possible for us
to give to each other continually the benefit of
the freest criticism, without a risk of misunderstanding; and the thought of each other's
appreciation was to us both one of the strongest
encouragements to effort : at least it was so with
myself, and I believe it was so with him. The
main difference between us was, that while I could
hardly dissociate from philosophical study any of
the convictions I had attained, philosophy was for
him—at least in any form that strongly influenced
his inner life—a later acquisition. It was at Errol

e

that he first seriously turned his thoughts to the subject; it came to signify more and more to him during the years that followed; and when he entered on his duties as a teacher, he felt the necessity of making his studies in this direction as thorough and comprehensive as possible. What he sought in philosophy was primarily to make faith intelligent and intelligible. The words of Anselm, which he subsequently used as the motto to his *Introduction to the Philosophy of Religion*, might be held to express his permanent attitude on this subject: *negligentia mihi videtur, si post-quam confirmati sumus in fide, non studemus quod credimus intelligere.*[1] But he did not, like Anselm, undertake this search for a *rationale* of faith with any scholastic presupposition that reflection could not modify the doctrine with which he started. At the same time he had a confidence, which did not lessen with time, that such modifications could not touch anything which was really essential to religious life, or to Christianity. His life as a pastor and preacher had given him a deep and, I may say, an unshakable conviction of the general truth of the Christian view of life,

[1] It seems to me a failure in reasonable conduct, that one who is confirmed in faith should not seek to understand what he believes.

of its adaptation to human nature, and of its
capacity of supplying a key to the practical difficulties of human experience. In his sermons for
the Park Church, as well as those written subsequently, there is no theme to which he more
frequently recurred. He was, therefore, completely
emancipated from that fear of reason, which seems
to hang so often like a weight upon the most
spiritually-minded of the orthodox clergy. He
was prepared to sacrifice everything that would
not stand the test of criticism ; but he had an
assurance, deeper than could be felt by any one
who had not gone through a similar experience,
that such criticism would be fatal only to the
'wood, hay, and stubble' that had been built by
unskilled hands upon the foundation of Christ,
and not to the stones of the temple, still less to
the foundation itself. Perhaps he did not realize
—I say this only to indicate a difference between
us which was never completely settled in all our
discussions—how great must be the transformation
of the creed of Christendom, before, in the
language of Goethe's well-known tale, the hut
of the fisherman can be transformed into the altar
of the great Temple of Humanity.

As to his success as a teacher of Theology, I

think it best to allow his pupils to speak ; though
I will not deny that in the following testimonies,
some allowance may be made for the loyalty and
gratitude of students to a professor who has
opened up for them a new sphere of thought.
From many such testimonies to the power of his
teaching, I select the following. In the *Scotsman*
for August 1st, 1898, an old student writes :

It is nearly forty years since Dr. Caird resigned his
brilliant ministerial prospects to become Professor of
Divinity in the University of Glasgow. At that time there
were not wanting wiseacres who shook their heads over
the appointment, distrusting the influence over young
preachers of one whose orthodoxy they suspected, won-
dering whether the brilliant rhetorician would prove a
close reasoner, and whether the masterly preacher would
prove a successful teacher. All these fears were soon
falsified. Many a minister can tell how his first real
abiding interest in theology dated from the hour when the
new Professor of Divinity began to expound it ; how, in his
hands, the old doctrines became full of human interest.
The mind of even the most commonplace divinity student
was stimulated, and his enthusiasm kindled, by the apt
criticism, the high and reverent speculation, the personal
influence of a teacher, who was himself a student, bringing forth from day to day from his treasury things new as
well as old. . . . Students who went to his class under
the idea that they would only have to listen to oratory,
were speedily disillusioned. Dr. Caird soon proved himself
to be a severe reasoner, as well as a brilliant illustrator.
In his hands, theology glowed with life, and his students

found they had as a teacher, not merely one who was in touch with modern thought, but who was himself making it. . . . One feature of his teaching was the entire absence of the dividing of Christianity into many separate doctrines; and it may be truly said that few professors have put their mark so convincingly upon so many ministers of the church, without making them adherents of any peculiar or limited school. So far as practicable, the Chair was made one of pastoral as well as of systematic theology, and there are not a few occupying now the pulpits of Scotland, whose first clear ideas of what a sermon ought to be, and of the dignity and responsibility of their calling, came from Dr. Caird.

I am favoured with the following estimates of his work as a Professor by the Rev. Dr. M'Adam Muir, of the Cathedral, Glasgow, and the Rev. Dr. Strong, of Hillhead Parish Church, Glasgow, both of them former pupils.

Dr. M'Adam Muir writes:

It is not too much to say that attendance at Dr. Caird's class marked an epoch in the life of every one of his students. To many of them it meant a complete revolution in their way of looking at things, upon all of them it produced a profound influence. It was a time of special agitation in the theological world, and excellent people not unfrequently warned us to beware lest we should be "unsettled" by the new Professor. There are those who can thankfully bear witness that, instead of unsettlement, they found in his teaching stability and confirmation. His object, we came to learn, was not so much to instil his own particular views into our minds

as to make us think for ourselves. A course of lectures
might be fragmentary and unfinished, but the conclusions
might safely be left for us to work out at leisure. His
method might be utterly different from the ordinary method,
but it was full of life and suggestion. One thing which
could not fail to strike us was his fairness in stating the
case of opponents. He presented as clearly, as sympa-
thetically, the argument which he sought to controvert as
that which he sought to establish. While fearless and
open, he was at the same time singularly wise and judi-
cious in the statement of his opinions. He would never
wantonly wound the conviction, or even the prejudices, of
the earnest. He disliked negative teaching : he was constructive, not destructive ; he contented himself, as a rule,
with enunciating truth, leaving the error to die of itself.
He did not, for example, enter into the details of the
Sunday Question or of Subscription to the Westminster
Confession, which, in consequence of the utterances of Dr.
Norman Macleod and Principal Tulloch, were evoking
very keen feeling, but he incidentally laid down principles
which sufficiently indicated his own position and guided
us to take up our own. During his delivery of the Gifford
Lectures, it was no uncommon thing to hear it said, "How
remarkably Dr. Caird's views must have been modified !"
as if he were in his later days building up the Faith which
formerly he had destroyed. The teaching was practically
the same as that which he gave to his students. The
change was in public sentiment rather than in him, a
change which he himself had materially helped to bring
about. The reader of the Gifford Lectures will rejoice in
the spirituality, the thoughtfulness, the eloquence by which
they are distinguished ; he may understand the enthusiasm
with which we heard the earlier lectures when the views

embodied in them were comparatively new. So far as I can remember, Dr. Caird never had reason to complain of inattention : all were interested alike by the matter and the manner. He indulged in no rhetorical declamation, but the power of the orator continually revealed itself. The language always so felicitous, the voice always so exquisitely modulated, lent an indescribable charm to his instruction. I can never forget his reading of Shelley's *Arethusa* :

> Arethusa arose
> From her couch of snows
> In the Acroceraunian mountain,

and, though it is almost too sacred to mention, I am sure my fellow-students will bear me out in saying that the brief prayer which he daily used left upon our minds an impression of devoutness to which we can hardly find a parallel. No novelty of thought, no stateliness of diction, touched us so much as the man himself. We regarded him with what I believe to have been an altogether unique combination of reverence, affection, and confidence : a reverence, an affection, a confidence which did not cease when we were no longer under his immediate influence, but continued to deepen to the end; and his memory will remain to us as that of one of the greatest, simplest, and best men whom we have ever known.

Dr. Strong writes :

Though it is now more than thirty years since I was a student under Principal Caird, my recollection is still most vivid of the style and substance of his teaching, and of his magnetic influence on me and on many of my fellow-students. His coming to the Divinity Hall was truly a time of awakening among us. Whispered conversation, surreptitious reading of books and newspapers, once so common, now suddenly ceased. We listened to the lectures, full of interest in his fresh presentation of what had been to us hitherto but dry and antiquated doctrines—charmed with Dr. Caird's lucid and illustrative style—set thinking, even the dullest and most careless among us, while he mercilessly dissected some familiar theory, or supported a received doctrine by arguments and analogies to us most novel and striking.

Dr. Caird's object as a professor was twofold. On the one hand, to make us think clearly—to give us a rational apprehension of divine truth; and, on the other hand, to render us apt expositors of that truth—able to teach others also—to make them see what was visible to our eyes. He did us an invaluable service in keeping us steadily at work. In the oral examination on his lectures to which we were daily subjected, as well as in the weekly essay which we were required to write, and which he openly criticised, sometimes to our confusion, he compelled our attention and brought home to us our own ignorance or misapprehension. But he was withal a generous critic, and whether we happened to agree with him or not, he was ever ready to recognize and commend any attempt at serious thinking, any evidence of diligence or power.

Dr. Caird was the first, so far as I know, to invite, and even to insist on, some attempt on our part to preach *extempore*; for he used to say that ordinary congregations could hardly be expected to listen patiently to a man "glowerin' at a paper." The effort was often painful, and the result ludicrous, but it gave a wonderful stimulus to latent powers in the students; while the suggestions offered by the professor at the close of the hour, as to the proper treatment of the special text or subject, were to many a revelation of what a sermon ought to be.

In these his earliest lectures on theology, our revered professor gave us in outline very much what in his latest (Gifford) lectures he has treated more fully. His aim from first to last has been the same—to place theology on a rational basis—to bring our thinking on the greatest of all subjects into line with our thinking on other subjects of serious import—thus to give theology a philosophic or scientific basis, and to harmonize, if not to identify, natural and revealed religion. There are not a few among us to-day who owe to him our first clear idea as to the place and meaning of Christian doctrine—our first definite conception of what and how, as ministers, we ought to teach. Nor can we ever forget the spirit of devoutness and reverence which by word and example he ever inculcated. We cherish, and are the better for, the dear memory of one, indifferent to wordy theological warfare, and to vulgar worldly ambition, because he lived among the things unseen and eternal.

As to the matter of his teaching, it is obvious from the introductory lecture that he was greatly influenced by the idealistic philosophy. In fact, as he often maintained, it is in some form of that philosophy that one who would defend theology, as a form of scientific knowledge and not merely as a supernatural revelation, must find his weapons. At first he was mainly interested in the Kantian proof of the relativity of knowledge of the objective world to the consciousness of self—a principle which, however, he carried out to its consequences, irrespective of

the limitations within which Kant confines it.   Subsequently, his thoughts turned more and more to
the Hegelian development of this principle, and
its application to theology.   He was interested in
Hegel mainly by two things : first, by the thorough-
ness with which he carries out the idealistic principle, and, secondly, by the strong grasp of ethical
and religious experience which is perhaps Hegel's
greatest characteristic.   To the first of these points
my brother continually recurred.   As he would have
nothing to do with sceptical defences of religion, so
he spoke almost with contempt of the various half-
way houses that have been built between the position
of Kant and a thorough-going Idealism, as also
of the many attempts of modern theologians to
evade the open field of thought, and to fall back
upon some moral, or æsthetic, or religious faith,
which is not to be explained or criticised by reason.
Above all, he distrusted the policy of writers who
use the weapons of Idealism to defend the faith,
and then attempt to repudiate the aid of Idealism.

As to the second point, I have already said that
it was the ethical meaning of Christianity, and
especially the idea of self-identification with Christ,
which had been the main theme of his earliest
preaching.   And this characteristic of it did not

alter in later days, except in so far as his increasing study of philosophy led him more and
more to generalize the principles of Christianity,
and to follow them out in their wider application
to life and thought. In like manner, in his lectures
to students as in his subsequent writings, it was
always the ethical bearings of principles that most
strongly interested him, and on which he spoke
with most force and originality. He was drawn
to Hegel, therefore, most of all, because he seemed
to find as the basis of all Hegel's speculation a close
and living perception of the facts of the moral and
spiritual life. It has often been said that Hegel
twisted the doctrines of Christianity to suit his
dialectic, and it is certain that the result of his
treatment did not leave them quite unchanged, but
gave them a new interpretation ; as, indeed, every
process of thought that is of any value must in
some way transform the data with which it starts.
Still there is, I think, considerable evidence[1] that
the Hegelian dialectic was not generalized independently and then applied to Christian doctrine,
but was rather itself reached in the first instance,
by carrying back into its logical presuppositions the

[1] I have tried to give some of his evidence in my volume on *Hegel*
(in Blackwood's " Philosophical Series "), p. 25 *seq*.

Christian doctrine of the relations of the divine and
the human.   At any rate, any one who reads my
brother's *Introduction to the Philosophy of Religion*
must feel that, for him at least, the language of
religion and philosophy, the words of Scripture and
the dialectical evolution of thought, passed into each
other without any consciousness of a break or in-
congruity ; and that it was as the philosophical
interpretation and explanation of the latter that the
former had its strongest hold upon him.   He no
doubt admitted and maintained, that the half-meta-
phorical language of ordinary thought is inadequate
to express spiritual relations, and in his *Introduction*
he attempted to explain the grounds, nature, and
extent of this inadequacy ; but he was not led
by this into that abstract separation or opposition
of truth in philosophy to truth as it exists for
the ordinary religious mind, which is perhaps the
greatest danger of imperfect speculation upon religion—of any speculation that has an insufficient
grasp and appreciation of the facts speculated about.
If he committed an error it was rather that he
followed Hegel in believing that the whole structure of dogma, as it has been developed by the
Church, could be re-interpreted by philosophical
reflection, without any essential change.

I find a difficulty in dealing with the often-made assertion that my brother was a Hegelian, because, in view of the many interpretations of that philosophy, it is difficult to know what the critic means by the charge. He was undoubtedly very deeply influenced by Hegel, and believed himself to be in the main interpreting his thought. In fact, if the question had been put to himself, he would perhaps have said that he was a mere popularizer of the thoughts of greater men, of whom, among the philosophers, he would have put Hegel first. But he seldom quotes Hegel, and never uses his thoughts without impressing something of an individual stamp upon them, or at least giving to them a new expression. He was entirely with Hegel in his trust in the powers of the human intelligence ; and would have said in his language that " The hidden being of the Universe has no power in itself that could offer resistance to the courageous effort of science." [1] He was without fear of scientific and philosophic criticism, and believed that any doubt awakened by it would end in revealing a deeper basis of truth. He followed Hegel also, as I have said, in refusing to seek safety for religion in any

[1] Hegel's Address at the opening of his Lectures in Berlin, in 1818. *Werke*, vi., p. xl.

of the cities of refuge that have been opened for
it since the days of Kant: in feeling, in the moral
consciousness, or in some special form of an æsthetic
or religious intuition, which is to be regarded as
above reason and exempt from criticism.   But if
Hegelianism is, as some tell us, the resolution of the
life of the world into "some spectral woof of impalp-
able abstractions, or unearthly ballet of bloodless
categories"; if it is the substitution of the theory
of reality for reality itself; if it is a system that
resolves man into a mere modus of the divine, or
God into the poetic substantiation of an abstraction
—and all these things have been said of Hegel; if
it even means a denial of the substantial truth of
the ordinary Christian consciousness, and the substitution for it of a philosophical theory, then my
brother was not a Hegelian.   In fact, there is not
one of these views which he has not repeatedly
attacked; and his *Introduction*, so far as it is not
directed against Materialism or Agnosticism, might
be described as an attempt to show that all of
them are erroneous.

The idealistic philosophy, as it has presented itself
from Kant onwards, and especially in Schelling
and Hegel, is essentially a philosophy of evolution.
Hence it has given a great stimulus to historical

researches ; and the study of it naturally led my brother to dwell more and more on the history of doctrine, and subsequently on the general history of religion. His class lectures, so far as they were not devoted to the metaphysical basis of religion, generally took the form, of a critical history of the development of dogma in the Church, in which he attempted above all to show that ecclesiastical controversies have contributed to the evolution of truths which were beyond the issues recognized by the contending parties, and that the Church has had a growing life of thought in which nothing was lost. Taking this view of ecclesiastical history, his severest strictures were directed against that prevailing school of modern times which treats the dogmas as a sort of false excrescence upon Christianity, produced by the influence of Greek philosophy, and which seeks to get rid of them all by a return to the primitive Gospel of Jesus. He held that such a view was directly opposed to the conception of Christianity as containing in it a principle of universal religion: a principle, therefore, which was able to assimilate all elements of thought and life, whether derived from Greek, or Jewish, Latin, or German sources, and to make them the means of its own development. He main-

tained that Christianity is a religion not revealed
once for all, but one which has been ever growing
and showing greater powers, the more new elements it
has absorbed. And it was, of course, involved in this,
that the development of doctrine is still advancing,
and in a freer and fuller manner than during the
early Greek and the Scholastic age, when it was
hampered by a mechanical belief in authority. Nay,
he would have allowed and contended that it has
to submit to a transformation and new birth through
idealistic philosophy, if it would maintain itself in
the modern world.

These convictions are expressed, among other
places, in a lecture delivered at the opening of the
new University Buildings on Gilmorehill in 1870,
which he described as "A Plea for a Scientific
Theology," and which ends with the following words :

"Let us then rise to the true dignity of our vocation as scholars and theologians ; and that will we
do only by absolute, unreserved, self-denying loyalty
to truth. Reverence even for the most sacred of
books does not require that we refrain from ex-
amining into its credentials, and into the evidence
and rational significance of its contents. Still less
does reverence for the theologians of the past imply
that we abstain from subjecting their opinions to

t of minute and careful examination—from

 best lights of philosophy, science, logic,

their construction of the teaching of

d refusing to accept at their hands a

sition which is not so justified. It is

ance to hold that the theological inquirer

 day is in a better position than they for

struction of a true theological system. We

t presume to be wiser or better men than

 because we can profit by their labours, and

see a little further by their help. We have means
and appliances at our command, too, which no
earlier age of inquirers has possessed. Philological
and historic criticism has in our day made great
advances. Inquiries into the authenticity and
structure of ancient documents, the limit of their
authority, and the principles of their interpretation,
are now conducted in a far more thorough, sifting,
and, at the same time, more liberal, tolerant, and
truly scientific spirit, than in former times. Physical
science has in many directions made vast strides
since the latest of our Creeds and Confessions were
constructed, and so enabled us to remodel our views
of the conditions of inspiration, and the limits of
Scripture teaching outside of the province of moral
and religious truth. Finally, the complexion of a

f

theological system depends greatly on the
sophical and logical method and c
thought which we bring to its const
surely we may hold, without presump
logic and philosophy of our day are in
that contentless scholastic logic and bar
inalism, which cumbered the earth when most
traditional creeds and systems were being
May we not, then, enter on our labours w
unhopeful spirit? Need we fold our hands as
work of the theologian were ended, and that ever-
growing progress and freshness of results, which is
the stimulus and reward of intellectual labour in
every other sphere of thought, were here no longer
possible—as if the last stone had been already
placed on the temple of truth, the last sheaf
gathered from the Master's field? No, it is not so.
Long has the Church's labour been ; but the great
living temple that has been slowly rising through
the ages is still far from complete ; and where, on
its stately walls and uprising towers, hands that can
work no more have left off to build, we are now
called to resume and carry on the noble task. The
field where generations of reapers have gathered in
such rich results is still waving luxuriant with a
perennial harvest of thought ; and still to the

youngest and latest come of His servants, the Master's voice is calling, 'Go thou also into the vineyard.'" [1]

The same idea is expressed more fully in the *Introduction to the Philosophy of Religion*, and illustrated in the last chapter of that work by the relation of Christianity to pre-Christian religions. The book ends with the following passage, which I quote at length, because it shows very definitely the general outcome and tendency of my brother's way of thinking :

"What, however, we are here specially concerned to notice, is that the idea of organic development is in no way inconsistent with the claim of Christianity to be regarded as a religion of supernatural or divine origin. There would be some reason for the recoil of Christian feeling from this idea, if it implied that there is nothing more in Christianity than a combination of pre-existing elements, or that its originality consists merely in the reproduction, in a collective form, of ideas contained in the religious and in the philosophical and ethical systems of the ancient world. . . . But such a view of the origin of Christianity is not more historically

---

[1] *Introductory Addresses*, delivered at the opening of the University of Glasgow, Session 1870-71, pp. 41, 42.

improbable than it is inconsistent with a true idea
of organic development. . . . For in organic development, the new, though presupposing the old,
involves the introduction of a wholly original
element, not given in the old.   Hence we are not
to conceive that Christianity could be elaborated
out of pre-Christian religions and philosophies, any
more than that life could be elaborated out of
inorganic matter.   To apply this principle to
religion, is to assert a relation between Christianity
and the earlier stages of man's spiritual history ;
indeed, unless we suppose the human race to have
been annihilated, and a new race, out of all connection or continuity with the former to have been
created as the receptacle of the new religion—
without some such monstrous supposition, we must
think of Christianity as essentially related to the
antecedent course of man's spiritual life, and related
to it in the way which rational spiritual life by its
very nature involves.   But the connection of Christianity with the past, which we here assert, is a
connection which at the same time involves the
annulling and transmuting of the past by a new
creative spiritual force.   To assert it, therefore, is
to hold that Christianity neither borrows nor repro-
duces the imperfect notions of God, be they what

they may——pantheistic, dualistic, anthropomorphic, monotheistic——in which the religious aspirations of the old world had embodied themselves. In the light of this idea, we can perceive these imperfect notions yielding up, under the transforming influence of Christianity, whatever element of truth lay hid in them, whilst that which was arbitrary and false falls away and dies. If, for example, the old pantheistic idea that 'the things that are seen are temporal,' and that beneath all the passing shadows and semblances of things, there is an enduring substance, a reality that is 'without variableness or shadow of turning'——if this idea comes to life again in the Christian consciousness, yet the new Pantheism does not, like the old, suppress, but rather elicits and quickens the individuality, the freedom, the moral life of man. If it says, 'The world passeth away and the lust thereof,' it says also, 'He that doeth the will of God abideth for ever.' If the antagonism between good and evil which gave Dualism its meaning and power, survives in the Christian view of the world, yet the new Dualism, unlike that of the old religion, is consistent with the belief not only in the ultimate triumph, but also in the sole and absolute reality of good. If it asserts that 'Sin hath entered into

the world, and death by sin,' yet it declares that,
'All things work together for good to them that
love Him,' and that a time is coming when 'God
shall be all in all.' If Christianity claims as its
own that idea which anthropomorphic religions
foreshadowed—that man is the image of God, and
that he is capable of rising into a divine fellowship
and of being made partaker of a divine nature;
yet, in contrast with the old religions, it raises the
human without limiting or lowering the divine,
and sees in all earthly goodness a reflexion of the
nature of God, without making the nature of God
a reflexion of the weakness and imperfections of
man. Lastly, if Christianity contains, in common
with monotheistic religions, the idea of a God
elevated in His absolute being above the world,
unaffected by its limits, incapable of being implicated in its imperfections, it yet enables us at the
same time to think of God, not merely as an
Omnipotent Power and Will above us, but as an
Infinite Love within us. It sees in our purest
thoughts and holiest actions, God Himself 'working
in us to will and to do of His good pleasure.'
It tells us that our 'bodies are the temples of His
Holy Spirit,' and it sets before us a human life as
the fullest expression and revelation of the nature

and life of God.　Thus, whatever elements of truth, whatever broken and scattered rays of light, the old religions contained, Christianity takes up into itself, explaining all, harmonizing all, by a divine alchemy transmuting all, yet immeasurably transcending all—'gathering together in one all things in heaven and earth' in its 'revelation of the mystery hid from ages,' the revelation of the One who is at one and the same time, Father, Son, and Spirit; above all, through all, and in all."

My brother's lectures were thus throughout inspired by the idea of development, and therein lay both his orthodoxy and heterodoxy.　A considerable mass of MS. lectures exist, but not in a form suitable for publication, except so far as the substance of them has been absorbed into his *Introduction to the Philosophy of Religion*, and his *Gifford Lectures*.　But one sees that he persistently endeavoured to fill the mind of his students with the conviction that truth in theology is not expressible in a definite number of dogmatic statements, but is a growing body of thought, which puts forth new powers in the minds of those who receive it, and is continually ripening to fresh issues.　Nor was he unaware—though it may be thought by some that he did not fully allow for

it—of the greatness of the transformation which
such a process of evolution brings with it. He
clung very closely to the forms of the past, even
while he was showing the power of the spiritual
principle that had produced them to transmute
them and give them a new significance.

During his tenure of the Chair he did not take
any great part in the general business of the
University ; but there were one or two occasions
on which he exercised his influence. In 1868
he proposed that the degree of D.D. should be
conferred on Dr. John M'Leod Campbell, who had
been deposed from the ministry of the Church of
Scotland, in 1831, for teaching the doctrine of
Universal Pardon, *i.e.* for maintaining that the
mercy of God was not limited to the elect,
according to the strict doctrine of Calvinism.
In this case it may fairly be said, that the heretic
has in the long run converted the Church ; for
though there has never been any definite act of
the Churches of Scotland withdrawing from the
positions of the Calvinistic system, the whole
doctrine of Election has been allowed to fall into
the background, and it would be difficult to find
many congregations in Scotland, outside of the
Highlands, where it is still preached in the strict

form which once was common. Older men may
remember times in their youth when they puzzled
themselves about the way to attain assurance as
to their own election, or whether such assurance was
possible ; but for all who are open to the influence
of thought, the controversy has passed into another
stage, in which both the assertion and the denial
of such doctrines seem equally irrelevant. Perhaps,
in the style of preaching which is now most common,
the change has been almost too thorough, as it has
taken the direction of a practical kind of discourse
that leaves out all reference to deeper theological
questions. And there are some still living, who,
without being believers in Election or Reprobation,
are not sorry that they were educated in a time when
the pressure of Calvinism forced them early to begin
to think of great questions as to the nature and
destiny of man.

My brother rejoiced much to be the means of
partially removing a stigma which, by the sentence of
the Church, had been left on one of the most pure
and saintly of men, who, in his book on the Atonement, had refuted the coarser views of that doctrine,
as it were from within, and by the aid of their own
presuppositions. Of course the University did not
mean by conferring a degree on Dr. Campbell to

express any sort of agreement with his special views,
but only to recognize the merit of his work as a
theologian.   But the occasion drew forth many testimonies to the greatness of his influence upon religious
thought, notably one from Dr. Ewing, the Bishop
of Argyll and the Isles, who published in the
Glasgow Herald of May 3, 1868, a letter to my
brother, in which he spoke of the act of the
University as significant of a great change in the
religious life of Scotland, and a recognition that
" Revelation is not a mystery superadded to the
mysteries of Nature, but a key given to us to
unlock those mysteries ; that it is a Revelation
which commends itself to our reason and conscience, producing faith as the result of this, and
not demanding faith on the ground of authority."
Dr. Ewing then goes on to dwell on the light
which Dr. Campbell had thrown upon various
aspects of Christian doctrine.   In his answer, my
brother writes (May 8, 1868) : " I heartily agree
with what you say as to Dr. Campbell's teaching,
and its influence on modern theological thought.
It is a most hopeful thing that in Scotland, where
views of the Atonement based on shallow forensic
metaphors have been so long prevalent, the power
of a book which starts from the fundamental idea

of the Fatherhood of God should have been so widely felt, and the substantial truthfulness of its teaching so widely recognized. At the same time, I am bound to add, that the degree to which you refer, though it may indicate the rise of a wiser and calmer tone of thought as to matters theological than once unhappily existed in this country, is not to be regarded as indicating in the body from which it emanated, any acceptance of Dr. Campbell's theological views. In proposing to the Senate to confer this degree on him, I was obliged to rest my case simply on his recognized position as one of the most able and original theological writers of our day. And in proof of this, I cited testimonies to the great merit of his book from various authorities in England and Scotland. . . . On the whole, I think there was but one opinion among my colleagues, that we did honour to ourselves in honouring such a man, a man of so much wisdom and thoughtfulness, and of so pure and blameless a life."

Dr. Dickson, who succeeded my brother as professor of Divinity, communicates to me the following reminiscences :

Of his main work as Professor—the teaching from the

Chair—I had no personal knowledge, for I never had the
privilege of hearing him lecture. . . . But the power
and stimulus of his teaching needed no other witness than
the manifest excitement in the College Courts—the keen
interest of the students, as suddenly quickened as it was
steadily maintained—the enthusiasm of the moment passing
into abiding gratitude for an impress that with many moulded
their future. Not a few of the ordinary students of the
Church of Scotland continued in regular attendance for a
fourth session, which the General Assembly had ceased to
require; and the students belonging to other Churches,
especially the United Presbyterian, in considerable numbers
took classes in the Divinity Hall. In Session 1872-3, if I
am not mistaken, half the prizes in the Hall were carried off
by these Nonconformist students.

Soon after becoming Professor, Dr. Caird entered with
hearty sympathy into a proposal originating with his colleague, Dr. Weir, for the revival of the Degree of B.D. on
such a footing that, under the existing circumstances of
the Churches and the Universities, the examinations conducted by the Faculty of Theology should be open not
only to the students completing their studies in the Divinity
Hall of the University of Glasgow, but to graduates of
the University in Arts who had taken their theological
course in extra-mural Halls recognized by the University
Court, without insisting on any condition of further
attendance; and he had the satisfaction of seeing this
liberal arrangement brought into operation by the Faculty
when he was at its head, and crowned thereafter with
such success that, during the first thirty years of its working (1866-1896), upwards of 300 candidates have received
the new Degree, and of these nearly as many have presented
themselves from the extra-mural Halls as from that of the

University. Whatever other benefit may have accrued to theological study from the gentle stimulus of the Degree, it is pleasant for any one who has lived through the stormy conditions of the ecclesiastical atmosphere of Scotland during those thirty years, to recall the comparative calm within the University, which enabled it to contribute such an *eirenicon*.

Dr. Caird also took a special interest in remodelling the regulations for the D.D. Degree. He felt strongly the evils incident to the earlier mode of bestowing it as a matter of favour on private or personal grounds; his position rendered him specially liable to be beset by the importunities, if not of postulants in person, at any rate of their impulsive friends. He was zealous for the honour of the University; he desired that its honorary degrees should be conferred on academic grounds, and should mark contributions to theological literature, of which the University was in a better position to judge than of the discharge of professional duties coming less directly under its cognizance. Accordingly he welcomed a suggestion to give to the Degree a more special character by placing it on the basis of proceeding from M.A. or B.D. to D.D. by undergoing a higher examination or sending in a thesis. The new system underwent a probation of many years : the higher examination, though it led to numerous inquiries, resulted only in two Degrees conferred on that ground (viz., on Professor Orr, now of the United Presbyterian College, and on Dr. M'Kichan, of the Free Church Mission at Bombay); the requirement of a thesis, which involved incidentally no small correspondence, yielded in many instances such excellent fruits as went far to justify the expectations formed from it; but in others its practical working fell short of those ideals; and a few years ago the Regulations, while substantially retained, were, with the Principal's assent, modified into their present form.

During his tenure of the Divinity Chair he took little part in the ordinary business of the Senate, partly because of the claims and attractions of his professional studies, partly because he had entire confidence in his friend Dr. Weir bringing, as Clerk of Senate, to the conduct of affairs a rare knowledge of the history and constitution of the University, a singularly clear and calm judgment, and a devotion to duty in which its interests were safe. But there was one matter into which he threw himself with zeal, and in which he rendered signal service—the movement which issued in the new buildings at Gilmorehill. He was from the outset an active and not a merely ornamental member of the Subscription Committee—regular in attending its meetings, and ready always to respond to the frequent calls that he should lend personal aid to the deputations that sought to enlist the sympathy of leading citizens. How much of the substantial outcome was due to his special cooperation no one now can tell; but it cannot be doubted that the mere presence of one who held so unique a place in the knowledge and esteem of all the citizens was a potent element of prevailing intercession. This part of Dr. Caird's work, little known probably outside of the Committee (of which few members now survive), in helping to build the very walls within which he was afterwards to reign, ought certainly not to be forgotten.

Before passing from the Hall stage of his work, I should not omit to mention the peculiarly warm interest which he took in his students—his unfailing readiness to aid them with his counsel, the genial sympathy with which he entered into the spirit of their social life, and the steady friendship with which he followed the fortunes of those

who had most favourably impressed him, always willing to
bear testimony to their merits and to remember their special
claims when patrons or congregational committees asked
his opinion or desired his recommendation. Nor did his
interest in the Hall cease with his tenure of the Chair; he
was always desirous to be informed of the names and distinctions of the students whose work had most commended
them to my colleagues or myself; and many, not only of
his own students, but of their successors year after year,
have had more reason than they themselves were often
aware of, to be grateful for the Principal's interposing a
seasonable word on their behalf.

In 1871, after the University removed from the
old College in High Street to the new buildings on
Gilmorehill, my brother took the opportunity of re-
viving the University Chapel. At an earlier time
there had existed a regular service for the students,
conducted by one of the professors in the Hall of
the University; and after that ceased, sittings for
the students had been reserved in one of the City
churches. On the removal of the University to
the new site, my brother proposed that the services
should be revived, and that ministers of all denominations of the Christian church in Scotland
should be invited to assist. He himself undertook
the principal charge of the arrangements of the
Chapel, not only during the time when he was
professor of Divinity, but during the whole time of

his connection with the University. He successively invited to preach before the University the
leading ministers of the Church of Scotland, the
Free Church, the United Presbyterian Church, and
of other less important denominations. In particular,
he invited several of the clergy of the Episcopal
Church in Scotland to take part in the services,
and gave them the option of using their own
Liturgy. Among others, Bishop Ewing consented
to preach, but was prevented doing so by the
objections of the then Bishop of Glasgow. Sermons
were, however, preached by various eminent clergymen of the Church of England, by Jowett, Stanley,
the present Bishop of Ripon, and others ; and
also by clergymen of the Church of England in
Scotland, who do not own the authority of the
Scottish bishops. My brother attached considerable importance to these services, as bringing the
students together for worship independently of the
special communion to which they might belong,
and practically teaching them to regard the points
on which they were divided as of comparatively
little importance. It was supposed at first that
the movement would encounter opposition from
the sectarian spirit of some members of the
churches ; but as a matter of fact no such objec-

tion was taken to it, except in the one case I have mentioned, and from some quarters it received high commendation. In particular, a letter was sent to my brother signed by Dean Ramsay and many of the most influential clergy of the Scottish Episcopal Church, thanking him for his liberality in asking members of their communion to preach and conduct the services in the University Chapel, and stating that they "gladly hailed this proposal, as tending to encourage a more kind and friendly feeling between bodies of Christians in this country."

My brother had always been in the habit of preaching for ministers of other churches than his own, whenever invited to do so; and after the institution of the Chapel services in the University he did so very frequently. He was no churchman, in any exclusive sense; he had, indeed, almost a horror of ecclesiastical politics, and, so far as possible, avoided attending Presbyteries and other Church Courts; and he was almost indifferent to the causes of disagreement between the main denominations into which the Christian church is divided. He was, of course, loyal to the Church of Scotland, and he was in favour of the principle of an Established Church. In a lecture

on the " Universal Religion," delivered in 1874, he
says : " The ideal of a Christianized social state
would be one in which Church and State would be
no longer opposed as separate organizations, but
would pass into each other, and become identified
in that body politic in which each member lived,
suffered, rejoiced, in the life, and suffering, and joy
of all the rest." But apart from this ideal kind of
Erastianism, I do not think I remember his expressing any antagonism to other denominations than
his own ; and if he ever spoke severely, it was of
some exhibition of ecclesiastical bigotry in his own,
or any other communion. Sometimes such divisions
seemed to him rather a subject for humorous treatment ; and I remember that once when addressing
a United Presbyterian congregation, he gave them
almost more liberality than they desired, by declaring that he would not take the trouble to cross
the street in order to convert a man from their
denomination of Christians to his own.

In 1873, Dr. Barclay, the Principal of Glasgow
University, died. He was a man of great vigour
and individuality of character, though in his last
years his energy was weakened by repeated
attacks of illness. He had a somewhat brusque
manner of address, and his lion-like growls at

anything that displeased him might sometimes scare those who did not understand him ; but his unpretending simplicity of character, his humorous directness of utterance, and his geniality and kindliness of nature, endeared him to his colleagues, and to none more than to my brother, with whom he had very close relations of friendship. I still remember the thrill of emotion with which my brother spoke the last words of the funeral sermon, which was preached in the University Chapel. " Farewell, dear and honoured friend ! We shall never see thy face, nor hear thy well-known voice again—never till the eternal morning dawn. Be it ours to preserve the recollection and walk in the steps of him, and of all the good and wise who have trod before us the narrow path of duty. May we so live that when life reaches its close we too may look backward, feeling we have not lived in vain, and onward with the same tranquil heart and the same trust in God, to that which lies beyond the veil."

The appointment to the Principalship is in the hands of the Crown ; but on this occasion a petition was sent in by all the members of Senate, begging that the office should be conferred upon Dr. Caird ; and on the recommendation of Mr. Bruce, then

Home Secretary, he was appointed by Her Majesty to succeed Dr. Barclay, on March 7, 1873. My brother's own feelings regarding it, and his pleasure at the unanimity with which his colleagues had spoken in his favour, were expressed shortly after in the following letter (dated April 7th).

"I am very busy, finishing the duties of my former office, whilst beginning to learn the duties of the new. I am very sorry to give up teaching, for it had become a second nature, and my intercourse with the students and sympathy with their work were a daily delight to me. But my colleagues requested me to offer myself for the vacant office, and sent up a memorial to the authorities, signed by all of them, so I felt I had little choice left in the matter. This fact is a proof to you of what I am happy to say is the case, that we have, in our Senate, so far as my experience goes, always been a unanimous body; I trust my new relation to them will be no interruption to the harmony.

"The Senate have, I believe, the power to require the Principal to teach some subject not embraced in the regular curriculum, and I shall ask them to exercise this power in my case, so that my connection with the practical work of the University may not cease. Besides, there are various ways,

such as preaching in the College Chapel on Sundays,
delivering addresses on public occasions, etc., in
which I may still be of use to the students. In
short, I shall try to console myself for having to
give up a position for which I was better gifted,
I fear, than for the somewhat ornamental office to
which I have been transferred. The old Principal,
though his tastes and tendencies were different
from mine, and his age put a wide gulf between
us, was a man for whom I had both respect and
liking. I saw much of him in his hours of weakness
and trouble; he had a very kindly feeling to me,
and so his death makes a great blank. I would
fain have escaped from speaking of him in public,
but I had to preach, with a sad heart, what is
called a funeral sermon."

Among the various tokens of good will from
the divinity students he was leaving, my brother
was especially pleased by an address which he received from the Nonconformist students who had
attended his class, sometimes in almost as large
numbers as the students of the Church of Scotland.
It is worth while to quote the words which he
used in responding to this address, as they express
more fully than he has done anywhere else, his
views as to the work of his Chair.

The greatest drawback to my recent preferment is that it cuts me off in a great measure from the work of teaching, and from my connection with the divinity students. For now a good many years past that work has been my daily delight. Not only are the subjects pertaining to the Chair of Divinity thoroughly congenial to me; not only have I felt a deep and growing interest in the great questions of which it is the province of the theological professor to treat, but that interest has been greatly vivified by seeing it reflected in the minds of the students. Many a thorny and intricate problem has been made easier to me by seeing the manner in which it was grappled with by young, acute, and enthusiastic minds. Many a subject which familiarity had begun to deprive of its first interest has had fresh interest rekindled in it, in my own mind, by witnessing the new zest which it awakened in yours. I think I can honestly say that many of the happiest hours of my life are those which I have spent in the class-room; and looking back over the past ten years, and the succession of students who have attended the Divinity Hall, it is a source of pleasure and of pride to me to reflect that I cannot recall a single instance in which there has been any interruption of the most kindly and harmonious relations between the students and myself.

Of course, as a minister of the Established Church I could not fail to feel a special interest in that part of my class which was composed of those who were to be its future clergy. But, gentlemen, I do not utter words of course when I say that it has been a great delight to me to find, year after year, and of late years in increasing numbers, members of other communions enrol themselves among my students. I have felt a peculiar gratification in this, inasmuch as, whilst the other and major part of the class attended mainly as part of the prescribed course of study, and because they could not help it, in your case the attendance was spontaneous; and this was a manifestation of your early adherence to the Voluntary principle which I for one should be the last to take exception to. I could always be sure that you came to the Hall—I would not be so vain or presumptuous as to say, attracted by my poor prelections—but at any rate from real love of the subject, and from a desire, in addition to the teaching of the able and learned professors who constituted your regular instructors in theology, to gain any slight, increasing insight and information which might be derived from hearing the same subjects treated of by a different mind, and from perhaps a somewhat different standpoint. Moreover, I have also felt gratified by your presence in the Divinity Hall, because it seemed to me in no slight measure to conduce to that mutual respect and kindly feeling between the future ministers of the various Churches which it ought to be every good man's aim to promote, and to subvert the hideous spirit of ecclesiastical jealousy and rancour which it ought to be every good man's aim to put down. If the recollections and associations of college days go with us through life, and if, as I myself feel, the friendships which are formed then are through all the future years sometimes the most abiding; then surely, when church divisions or ecclesiastical discussions and conflicts shall range you in opposite ranks with your former fellow-students, it should serve in some measure to infuse a gentler, sweeter, and kindlier spirit into those inevitable differences, to reflect how you once paced side by side the courts of the old College, or sat together on the same benches, and participated in the same studies, ambitions, and generous rivalries of the Divinity Hall,

I shall take leave to add that I have felt a special gratification in your presence in the Divinity Hall, for this further reason, that it seemed to me to furnish at least an approximation to the true conception of a theological seminary. I cannot presume to speak for others, and there may be some here who won't agree with me, but I have never been able to see why theology should be studied in a different way and under other restrictions than science and philosophy. I think it seems to betray a distrust of truth—it has the appearance of conscious weakness in the adherents of any definite theological system—when the professors of science and of philosophy appeal only to the force of reason, while the teachers of theology must needs teach starting from foregone conclusions. Theology is the queen of the sciences, but she abdicates her imperial place when she submits to any other bonds than those imposed by God's word and God's truth. It is at least an approximation towards her glorious liberty and greatness, when theology is taught side by side with other sciences in a great seat of learning, and when the students who repair to the Divinity Hall are the very same students, the same in character and complexion, under no greater restrictions or limitations, of church, or school, or sect, than the students who study philosophy, literature, and science. For these and other reasons which I need not enter upon at present, I feel the deepest gratification in the movement which you have originated, and in the kind and generous and flattering terms you have been pleased to address to me. I shall only say, in conclusion, that there are no friends in the world in whom I have a deeper interest, for whom I feel a stronger affection, and in whose prosperity I feel greater pride, than those students with whom I have been associated in the studies in the Divinity Hall.

My brother had not before his election taken much part in general University business; in fact, he considered himself to have no capacity for details of finance and administration, and up to the date of his appointment as Principal, he showed considerable distaste for them. But, as Chairman of the Senate, and also—in the absence of the Lord Rector who was seldom present—of the University Court, he had to make himself thoroughly acquainted with all matters of importance that came before either body. Also, as the one official of the University who was not identified with any special interest or department of study, he was constantly appealed to by all parties, and had often to mediate between them. I think I may say that during the rest of his life, he thoroughly identified himself with the University, and grudged no labour that was needed to promote its improvement in any way. He was as impartial as any man with strong convictions could well be, and generally withheld his own opinion, and kept his mind open for the consideration of anything that might modify it, till he had heard all that was to be said by others. He strove much to be fair to all parties, and was inclined to give the utmost toleration, consistent with order, to the

expression of all views, even those most opposed
to his own. It is impossible, and is not part
of my task, to give a history of University politics
during the time when my brother was Principal,
yet anything short of this could hardly show the
extent to which he devoted his time and thought
to any important movement connected with the
University. They were years of great agitation
in University life, during which, in the University
Council and elsewhere, violent attacks were made
upon the Senate, which, till the passing of the
University Bill, was entrusted with the principal
control of the finances and the general administration of the University, as well as with the regulation
of the teaching and discipline. And the professors
themselves were much divided as to the policy to
be adopted. After the appointment of the University Commission, and the reconstitution of the
University Court, with increased power and increased representation both of the graduates and of
the civic authorities, there was much discussion as to
the various ordinances passed by the Commissioners,
and frequent collision of interests and opinions,
in the Senate, the Court, and the General Council
of the University. In most of these matters my
brother sought, so far as possible, to act as

moderator, and to avoid identifying himself with any party, and only expressed his own opinion when the question seemed to him vital. It was not without severe self-control that he was able, as he did at least in the majority of cases, to maintain the balance and avoid being carried away by his personal sympathies. He did not pass through these years without many hours of severe mental anxiety, and often he suffered greatly from loss of sleep when matters of importance were weighing on his mind. This trouble grew with advancing years, when his power of throwing off the burden of the day sensibly diminished, and he also found it more difficult to come to a decision in cases where there were conflicting reasons. Yet his self-command was such that, to those who saw him in public, he almost always seemed quite clear and calm.

One of the functions of the University Court is to elect new professors, except in a few cases where the appointment is reserved for the Crown; and as Chairman, the Principal had often to take a leading part in such elections. In fact, he considered this as perhaps the most important part of his duties, and he took endless pains to inform himself as to the merits of the candidates, and to guide the Court to a right decision. Especially where the subject of the Chair was one on the qualifications for which he felt himself able to form a clear and definite opinion, he was immovable in his resolution to carry the man he approved, and threw all his energy and influence into the scale. It cost him a good deal to do this ; for he was not one who loved conflict with others, or rejoiced in victory over them. But he felt that to get really strong men for the teaching of the University was more than any measure of reform in its machinery that could be devised.

Without going into disputed questions in the recent policy of the Scottish Universities, it would be impossible to indicate all the subjects in which he especially interested himself ; but I may mention one or two points which have now got beyond the reach of controversy. He felt a deep interest in the movement for the higher education of women, and took every opportunity of pleading publicly for the extending to them all the privileges of the University. He was unwearied in the discussion of the well-worn commonplaces as to the capacity of women for such education, and its importance to them. Perhaps I may venture to recall the fact

that many years ago, before my brother was
Principal, I had the pleasure of voting with him
in the Senate, in a minority of two, in opposition
to a proposal to petition Parliament against some
Bill that favoured the admission of women to
medical degrees. The debate about the education
of women generally, as well as about their medical
education, gradually wore itself out in the long period
between 1867, when the first steps in the direction
of such education were taken in Glasgow, and 1889
when the University Bill was passed ; and the
clause in that Bill empowering the Commissioners
to open up all degrees in arts and medicine to
women was accepted as settling the matter, without, so far as I know, a dissentient voice. My
brother did all in his power to bring about this
result, and also took a great part in the subsequent
negotiations which led to the incorporation of Queen
Margaret College with the University.

The University of Glasgow has always had close
relations with the City, and throughout its history
has received steady support and aid in every
difficulty from the Municipality, and from the leading merchants and business men of the community.
In particular, its removal to the new buildings in
1870 was made possible by the munificent contri-

butions of the citizens; and since that date, it
has received many gifts and bequests from individuals.   In fact, it is to the City mainly that the
University owes its having been able to keep pace
to some extent with the growing scientific and
educational demands of the new time; and the
re-constitution of the University Court, which makes
the Provost and another representative of the Town
Council its members, has also done something to
make the connection more intimate.   My brother
always regarded it as of the utmost importance to
maintain the good feeling that ought to accompany
such an alliance between the University and the
great City of which it is a part, and his long
friendship with many of the leading men of business
and civic officials rendered it easier for him to do
this.   Especially his readiness to respond to calls
upon his time, and to speak for civic objects, or
on great civic occasions, must have done much to
make the City take pride in its University, and
interest itself in its credit and success.

His position as Principal separated him in
some degree from the general body of the
Professors, and except on one occasion, when he
undertook during an interval the duties of one of
the Theological Chairs, he never directly took part

in the regular instruction of the students. But he endeavoured in other ways to bring himself into relation with them, especially by preaching, several times in each session, in the University Chapel, and generally conducting its devotional services, even when other clergymen preached. He was also in the habit of delivering a regular address to the students at the opening of each session, on some subject connected with the studies of the University or with studies, such as those of History or Art, which he desired to introduce into it ; or again on the life and character of some prominent writer, who might be regarded as a representative of such studies—on Spinoza, Bacon, Hume, Butler, Galileo, etc. The most important of these have been collected in the volume of *University Addresses*, published last year, a volume which also contains specimens of the less formal addresses which he gave at the close of the Graduation ceremonies with which each session ended. In these he usually chronicled the benefactions made to the University during the year preceding, took notice of any important changes in the history of the University, especially of the death or retirement of professors and the election of their successors, and concluded with some advice and exhortation to graduates and under-graduates in reference to some aspect of their academic life. These addresses did at least something to cultivate in the students that feeling of corporate unity, which, owing to circumstances, and especially to the absence of anything like the collegiate life of Oxford and Cambridge, has generally been less strong in the Scottish Universities than in England. A good many events happened during his tenure of office which tended in the same direction : the institution of the Students' Representative Council, the building of the Union, the foundation of new University Societies in connection with the principal studies of the place ; and in all of these he took a lively interest. He had much to do with the efforts made, and generally made successfully, to enlist the services of the students themselves in the maintenance of order in the public ceremonies of the University.

Of his relations to his colleagues in the Court and Senate, it is hardly for me to speak, but many members of these bodies have spoken for themselves. The Principal in a Scottish University is a *primus inter pares*, and he can only act with effect if he gains their support and confidence. And the colleagues he had were many of them men of whom any University might be proud. To name only those who are no longer living, and of whom it is possible to speak more freely, there were among the Professors that embodiment of τὸ καλόν in all its senses—Edmund Law Lushington,

> Wearing all that weight of learning,
> Lightly like a flower;

John Nichol, the best of lovers and haters, whose ardent and aspiring genius is only inadequately represented to those who did not know him by the fine literary and poetic work which he has left; Duncan Weir, the strong and modest teacher and wise counsellor, who, if he had lived to prepare for publication the lectures he gave to his pupils, would have been recognized as one of the greatest Hebrew scholars of the day; Allen Thomson, known in his time as one of the best anatomists of the country, and one of the most sagacious counsellors in the affairs of the University; John Veitch, the editor of Sir William Hamilton's works, who varied his vigorous prelections on Logic by sympathetic studies of the life and history of the Scotch Borders; James Roberton, whose great legal and historical learning were not more remarkable than his genuine kindliness of nature; George MacLeod, distinguished alike as a surgeon and a teacher; James Thomson,

h

in whom scientific originality was combined with singular simplicity and beauty of character ; and William Leishman, eminent as a physician and writer on medicine, and full of practical wisdom in the business of the University. Of others no less eminent who are still living, and who, like these, were his friends and mine, I may not speak ; those who have been students of the University during the last twenty years will easily supply their names. But I think I may say that the teachers of the whole period of his Principalship did not fall short of the best traditions of the University, and that most of them were united in strong feelings of friendship with its head. Nor could any one have felt a more personal interest in their success, or a deeper sense of the honour of presiding over them, than he.

As to his general conduct of the business of the University, and, in particular, his relation to the University Court, the Senate, and the University Council, which consists of the general body of graduates, I am favoured with the following communication from the Rev. Professor Dickson. After speaking of his addresses to the University and his services in the University Chapel, Dr. Dickson proceeds to say :

These public functions, wherein he was known to all, were far from being the whole, or even the most onerous and important of his services to the University, although there were probably some who measured his work mainly by these occasions, and deemed his position otherwise one of dignified leisure, occupied only with those congenial studies of which the world gladly at intervals received the ripened fruits. His office was no sinecure; from his daily life the cares and responsibilities of business were never absent, although they were but little, if at all, known to the general public. They knew, indeed, that he had the duty of presiding in the meetings of the Council, the Senate, and the Court; but, except in the case of the former, which met but seldom, the proceedings were neither open nor reported, and none but the limited number of members present had means of ascertaining either how much that duty involved, or how it was done. In the Council, which had to deal frequently with questions of University policy on which strong differences of opinion emerged and fell to be discussed by numerous speakers within time-limits practically fixed by the convenience and patience of members, the Chairman had the delicate task of reconciling freedom and order; and none could have brought to it more dignity, fairness, and tact, good-natured tolerance towards at times diffuse or irrelevant talk, and firmness, when necessary, in maintaining the authority of the Chair. In the more important fields of the Senate and Court his presence was more essential and indispensable. Other members might come and go; but he remained at his post, as a rule, from the outset to the end of sittings which often lasted for several hours. Others might absolve themselves from such business as less immediately concerned them; to him nothing academic could be foreign, and he had to make himself conversant beforehand with the bearings of the questions to be discussed. These questions—although I was at one time a member of the Court, I speak mainly from my experience of the Senate—were varied, often complicated and difficult of solution, giving rise to sharp differences of opinion and of action; and, if I may venture to say so, even in that august body there might emerge tendencies to oblivion of the standing orders and to digression or desultory talk, which called for the Chairman's intervention. He brought to the Chair a rare combination of qualities which made his rule as generally acceptable as it was efficient— knowledge of the business to be done, and experience in the conduct of University affairs, a quick appreciation of whatever might be urged on either side, impartiality, unfailing courtesy, and geniality. He was not a mere umpire; he had a vote as well as a casting vote. The former he was often content to give in silence; if he saw fit to justify it, or if he was called to exercise the latter, he stated tersely his reasons. Whether one might or might not agree with his views in any particular case, it was impossible to doubt that they had been formed, and were urged, in what seemed to him the highest interest of the University.

Nor was the action of the Principal confined to these courts in which he presided. Great part of the work of the University was done, or at least prepared, in Committees, of which several were standing, while others were appointed for special purposes as occasion required. Of most of these the Principal was a member in virtue of his office, or by special selection; he was in the habit of regularly attending their meetings, and often took an active part in their work. In the important Committee charged with the management of the Library, of which I was Convener, we seldom missed his presence and counsel throughout the five and twenty years of his reign.

Let me only add that these five and twenty years were by far the most eventful in the history of the University, for they witnessed, over and above the routine of its daily life from session to session, all the discussions raised and changes initiated by two Universities' Commissions (one of Inquiry in 1876, another Legislative and Executive in 1887)—the prolonged concomitant agitation of all manner of academic grievances, real or alleged—the strenuous warfare long waged between extra-mural and intra-mural interests—the vehement assaults on the administration of the Senate, and the transference of its patronage and financial and executive powers to the Court—new privileges claimed for, and conceded to, the students in the recognition of their Representative Council—the recasting of the whole system of Degrees in Arts, with its introduction of manifold options—the adjustment of the marvellously complicated Ordinances, almost every clause of which had to be fought over in Council, Senate, and Court—the debates over tests and degrees in the Faculty of Theology—the fuller equipment of the Faculty of Law—the creation of a new Faculty of Science—the disposal of questions emerging in the Faculty of Medicine as to the affiliation of Colleges, the relations of clinical to systematic teaching and of the University with the Western Infirmary, and the requirements of the Medical Council—the provision of new Chairs and Lectureships, and the relative development of technical, tutorial, and laboratory instruction—last, but not least, the admission of women as students, and its conditions, whether generally or with special reference to the position of Queen Margaret College.   In all of these questions, at most of their phases, Principal Caird was not merely an interested onlooker watching the movements of the great machine entrusted to his care, but an influential agent in shaping and controlling its course. As he loved the University, of which he was proud as an alumnus, and which in its turn was proud of him as its chief, he lived and laboured for it; and to him above all as *pars magna* belongs the honour of pervading and inspiring its newer life at Gilmorehill.

Up to the time of his appointment as Principal, he had published nothing but Sermons and Addresses. In addition to the volume published in 1858, of which I have spoken, he contributed a number of Essays (which were sermons slightly modified) to *Good Words* in 1863; and during his Principalship, he from time to time published a number of the Sermons and Addresses which he delivered to the University, especially two on " The Unity and Progressiveness of the Sciences," which are included in the volume of *University Addresses*. He also printed various sermons preached on public occasions, among which I may mention a Lecture delivered in Westminster Abbey, on " The Universal Religion," in 1874; a sermon on " Mind and Matter," preached before the British Medical Association in 1888; a Funeral Sermon for Principal Barclay in 1873, and two Sermons contributed to the volume of *Scotch Sermons*, published in 1880.

Most of his leisure during his Principalship was, however, given to studies connected with the philosophical basis of theology. In 1878-9, he was appointed to the "Croall Lecture" in Edinburgh, and gave a course upon this subject, which, with considerable alteration, he published in 1880 as an *Introduction to the Philosophy of Religion*. In 1888 he contributed the volume on *Spinoza* to the series of Blackwood's "Philosophical Classics." He had also on various occasions given lectures on the "History of Religions," two of which, on Brahmanism and Buddhism, were published in 1882.

Of the *Introduction to the Philosophy of Religion*, after what has above been stated as to his professorial teaching, I need not say much. It is an attempt to work out the idea of the essential rationality of Religion as against Materialism and Scientific Agnosticism ; and also against that kind of Agnosticism which arises when the claims of Religion are based upon authority, or even upon the immediate intuitions of feeling. It proceeds, generally following the lines of Hegel, to criticise the ordinary arguments for the being of God ; to show wherein consists the real necessity of religion ; to trace the development of the religious consciousness, and to exhibit the relation of morality to religion. Finally, it deals with the application of the idea of evolution to religion, and illustrates this theme by considering the relation of Christianity to pre-Christian religions. In a review written immediately after its publication, the late Professor T. H. Green gives a very fair estimate of its contents, with some important criticisms. His general account of the book is that " it represents a thorough assimilation by an eminent Scottish theologian, who is also known as a most powerful preacher and teacher, of Hegel's philosophy of religion. At the same time, it is quite an original work— original, if not with the highest kind of originality, which appears but once in a century, yet with that which shows itself in the independent interpretation and application of a philosophical system very remote from our ordinary ways of thinking. An Englishman to whom the language and prolix technicalities of Hegel's writings—or rather of that ill-organized compilation of notes of lectures in which alone his doctrine is preserved—form a hindrance to profitable study, will here find the essence of what he had to say on the most interesting of subjects, presented by a master of style." Green, however, goes on to bring against my brother, and perhaps, through him, against Hegel, the charge of too directly identifying, or at least appearing to identify, thought and reality, in a way that does not leave room for their relative difference. In spite of this objection, Green expresses his entire agreement with the fundamental principle of Hegel's idealism, that "the world in its truth or full reality is spiritual," and that "on any other supposition its unity is inexplicable." I venture to think the censure thus indicated is not valid against Hegel; and also that it is not valid against my brother, except in so far as he does not always guard sufficiently against a possible misunderstanding of the unity in question, the unity of thought and reality, as if it were simple sameness. On the other hand, I think that Green himself, in this article (as in some passages of his *Prolegomena*), has lost hold of a truth, of which elsewhere he is one of the most effective exponents, when he allows that "such a knowledge of the spiritual unity of the world, as would be a knowledge of God," is impossible to us. *That*, in any case, is a doctrine against which my brother's whole argument is directed, and he could not understand how Green should maintain it, consistently with his own principle that "the world in its full reality is spiritual." The conviction that God can be known, and is

known, and that in the deepest sense all our knowledge is knowledge of Him, was the corner stone of
his theology. " Religion," he declares at the end of
the first chapter of the *Introduction*, " by its very
nature contains, and must ever contain, an element
of mystery, but a religion all mystery is an absurd
and impossible notion. Finite intelligence cannot
be the measure of the infinite. The realm of truth
is inexhaustible, and the highest human intelligence
at its furthest point of progress and of spiritual
knowledge must still see stretching away before
it the region of the unknown, the unfathomable
depths of that Being before whom the befitting
attitude must ever be that of humility, of reverence,
of awe, and aspiration. But it is obvious that
these emotions owe their existence and their
strength to the fact that their object is contemplated as something more than the unknown; and
that we must conceive of that in Him which lies
beyond our knowledge, as, though unknown, *not* un-
knowable. . . . In the presence even of finite
excellence, we may be conscious of feelings of deep
humility and silent respectful admiration; and this,
too, may be reverence for the unknown. But that
which makes this reverence a possible and a wholesome feeling, is that it is reverence not for a mere

blank inscrutability, but for what I can think of as an intelligence essentially the same as my own, though far excelling mine in its range and power: and the salutary humility which possesses me in the presence of such minds arises from the fact that I know, and can appreciate, the thing they are, and that I see in it that which dwarfs my own petty attainments. In like manner, the grandeur that surrounds the absolute, the infinite reality beyond the finite, can only arise from this, not that it is something utterly inconceivable and unthinkable, but that it is for thought or self-consciousness the realization of its highest ideal of spiritual excellence. The homage rendered to it is that which is felt for a being in whom 'are hid all the treasures of wisdom and knowledge.' "

The little book on *Spinoza*, in Blackwood's " Philosophical Series," was somewhat marred by a miscalculation. After my brother had completed his MS., he found that he had written it on too large a scale for the series. He was therefore compelled to mutilate it by omitting the life of Spinoza. As it stands, the volume contains, besides careful studies on the predecessors of Spinoza, a very full and thorough examination and criticism of the Ethics. I do not know any

book upon the Ethics where the task is more
adequately performed. My brother had always
been drawn to Spinoza by strong sympathy with
the main tendency of his thought. In his sermons,
from "Religion in Common Life" onwards, we
found him combating the tendency to make hard
and fast divisions between different aspects or
elements of human life—between the secular and
the sacred, between the church and the world,
between the moral and the religious life. And
when he became a teacher of theology, he reacted
in the same way against the fixed division set up
between philosophy and theology, faith and reason ;
and made it his endeavour to show that a faith
which has not reason implicit in it, is a dead faith.
Now in Spinoza he seemed to find the great philosophical corrective of this tendency " to split the
world in two with a hatchet." Some writers have
treated Spinoza as the representative of a Pantheism in which all finite being is submerged ; others
have seen in his *Deus sive Natura*, a denial of all
divinity but nature, and in his twofold attributes,
an anticipation of the popular scientific dualism
of the day. What my brother saw in him was
the great opponent of all theories that divide God
from the world or the world from God ; and so,

in the language of Schelling, tend " to make nature godless, and God unnatural." He saw in him a philosopher inspired with the great idea that the distinctions of the finite world which are recognized by the ordinary consciousness, though they have their meaning and value, are none of them absolute ; that there are none of them which the unity does not embrace and explain. In other words, he saw in Spinoza the great teacher of the organic view of the world, as a real unity through all the distinction of its parts and as maintaining its identity in all their change and conflict. At the same time, he admits the defects of Spinoza's logic, and particularly, the one great defect, that while his demonstration of the *relativity* of all forms of the finite is complete, his way of showing the *reality* of those forms, as attributes and modes of the infinite substance, is arbitrary and inadequate. Thus there is a kind of excuse for those who assert that, according to Spinoza, all is lost in God but nothing is found in Him ; that He is not a living God who manifests Himself in and to His creatures, but a characterless substance, of which nothing can be said but that it *is*, and that it *alone* is.

This balanced view of Spinoza's philosophy is

summed up in the following paragraph : " The last word of Spinoza's philosophy seems to be the contradiction of the first. Not only does he often fluctuate between principles radically irreconcilable, but he seems to re-assert at the close of his speculations what he had denied at the beginning. The indeterminate infinite, which is the negation of the finite, becomes the infinite which necessarily expresses itself in the finite, and which contains in it, as an essential element, the idea of the human mind under the form of eternity. The all-absorbing, lifeless substance, becomes the God who knows and loves Himself and man with an infinite " intellectual love." On the other hand, the conception of the human mind as but an evanescent mode of the infinite substance, whose independent existence is an illusion, and which can become one with God only by ceasing to be distinguishable from God, yields to that of a nature endowed with indestructible individuality, capable of knowing both itself and God, and which, in becoming one with God, attains to its own conscious perfection and blessedness. The freedom of man, which is at first rejected as but the illusion of a being who is unconscious of the conditions under which, in body and mind, he is fast bound in the toils of an inevitable necessity, is reasserted as the essential prerogative of a nature which, as knowing itself through the infinite, is no longer subjected to finite limitations. The doctrine of a final cause or ideal end of existence, which was excluded as impossible in a world in which all that is, and as it is, is given along with the necessary existence of God, is restored in the conception of the human mind as having in it, in its rudest experience, the implicit consciousness of an infinite ideal, which, through reason and intuitive knowledge, it is capable of realizing, and of the realization of which its actual life is the process. At the outset, in one word, we seem to have a pantheistic unity in which nature and man, all the manifold existences of the finite world, are swallowed up; at the close an infinite self-conscious mind, in which all finite thought and being find their reality and explanation."[1]

On the other hand, as the writer goes on to contend, there is a point of view from which " the contradictions under which Spinoza's thought seems ever to labour can be regarded as the accident of an unconscious struggle after a deeper principle in which they are solved and harmonized. In the light of that principle we can speak with him of an indeterminate and infinite unity, in

[1] Spinoza, p. 303 *seq.*

which all finite distinctions lose themselves, and with him we can see that there is no paradox in the assertion that 'he who loves God, does not desire that God should love him in return.' We can discern, at the same time, a profound meaning in those apparently mystical utterances in which he seems to gather up the final result of his speculations—'God loves Himself with an infinite intellectual love'; 'God in so far as He loves Himself loves man'; 'the intellectual love of the mind to God is part of the infinite love wherewith God loves Himself'; 'the love of God to man, and the intellectual love of man to God, are one and the same.'" [1]

In the last ten years of his life, my brother's mind turned to the idea of writing a book, in which the principles laid down in the *Introduction to the Philosophy of Religion* should be applied to the main doctrines of Christianity, and the attempt made to show that each of them is the expression of a truth which can be rationally explained and vindicated. He had already made some studies in this direction when he was chosen by the Senate to be Gifford Lecturer for Session 1890-91. In that Session he delivered twelve lectures, in which he attempted to show the truth

[1] Spinoza, p. 314.

of the Christian ideas of God, and His relation to the world. It was for him, as I have already indicated, no unwelcome limitation that, by the terms of the Gifford Bequest, he was called on to discuss the subject without reference to any authority but reason. Owing to various causes, he was not able to lecture during the two following years, in which the Gifford Lectureship was held by the late Professor Wallace; but in 1896 he continued his prelections, taking up one after another of the Christian doctrines. He had in this way delivered eight lectures, when a paralytic stroke rendered it impossible for him to go on.

In the previous year he had had a good deal of harassing University business, and the additional effort of writing and delivering the lectures was too much for him; he had indeed complained once or twice before his seizure of increased difficulty in thinking and writing. The stroke mainly affected his left leg, and he gradually recovered sufficient strength to be able to walk about slowly; but he never completely got over the effects of it. In particular he was never able in any way to review or revise his Gifford Lectures, as up to the time of his death he hoped to do. They are now published as they came from his pen, with only a few necessary corrections. They have the defects of words written to be spoken and heard, rather than to be read. Some points of importance to the argument are left undeveloped, others are repeated more than once, and occasionally the rhetorical form prevails over the didactic. It is probable that, as in the case of the Croall Lectures, my brother, had he lived longer, would have rewritten them as chapters of a book, and greatly modified the form in which they were given as lectures. At the same time, they contain much that is fresh and valuable, especially on the ethical bearings of Christian doctrine; and they express so fully his leading thoughts, that I could have no hesitation in publishing them. What Green said of the *Introduction to the Philosophy of Religion* is true also of them. The line of argument followed is not, in the highest sense, original; it is in the main Hegelian, though not by any means following Hegel slavishly; the thought has been thoroughly assimilated and recast in the writer's mind, and is developed with the same lucidity and beauty of expression and fulness of illustration which are characteristic of his other writings. In a letter to a friend who had expressed some admiration of one of these lectures, he says :—" I have just got your kind note and can only thank you for your cheering and encouraging words very heartily. It is very little, I am profoundly sensible, that my poor talk can do ; but I shall be satisfied, if it leads some few who are in doubt on the highest matters, to see that Christianity and Christian ideas are not contrary to reason, but rather in deepest accordance with both the intellectual and moral needs of man."

In the Summer vacation that followed his paralytic seizure, my brother thought seriously of resigning the office of Principal, but the improvement of his health was such, that he finally resolved to delay his retirement a little longer. During the whole of next session he was able to attend the meetings of the University Court and the Senate, and generally to discharge almost all his official duties ; and at its close he gave his usual address[1] with all his former fire and energy. These, however, were the last words he spoke in public. Throughout the summer he seemed to retain all the strength he had gained, but he did not make decided progress. His weakness in walking remained, and he did not feel able for any consecutive intellectual work ; and, in the beginning of next

[1] The last Address in the volume of *University Addresses.*

session, 1897-98, he made up his mind to resign, unless some definite improvement should take place. In February, 1898, he had an attack of dangerous illness of an inflammatory kind which, however, proved to be connected with some more deeply seated evil. His vigorous constitution so strongly resisted the progress of the disease that, after being twice at the point of death, he revived, and seemed on the way to recovery. In July he had rallied so far that he could be removed to Greenock, where he intended to settle; but the effort proved too great, and he sank under a recurrence of illness on the morning of July 30th, within a week after his arrival at Dungourney, the residence of his brother Colin. He had some time previously sent in to the University Court his resignation of the office of Principal, but the date fixed for his demission of office was July 31st, so that in effect he died still Principal of the University of Glasgow. He is buried in the Greenock Cemetery.

In the summer of 1897 he had written to a friend who made some inquiries about his illness : " It does not interest me much to write of myself or my ailments ; but I may say that I had last winter a paralytic affection of the left side, which arrested my power of walking, but did not affect my power of speaking, nor, so far as I can judge, of thinking. I am slowly recovering the former power, but as yet can only walk with the aid of a friendly arm, and even then in a limping fashion. Take it any way, this is the first distant note for me of the *ringing-in bell*; and though I cling to the thought of going on with my familiar and much loved work for a little longer, I am aware that it can be but for a little, and I am trying to meet the inevitable issue, if not with anything of the feeling you quote from Archer Butler, yet without perturbation or dread. I have felt, not only during my illness, when thinking was impossible, but often even when the mind was free from all physical disability, the necessity which you express of falling back on the simplest and most practical religious thoughts; and one of such thoughts I have tried to express in one of the undelivered Gifford Lectures. Perhaps, though, it is too long for a letter. You will forgive my quoting it, as it is easier to quote than to express anew." My brother proceeds to quote the last paragraph of his Gifford Lectures, and then goes on as follows : " There are many simple ideas like this, which have the special value, I think, of implying no painful effort of memory to bring

them up when the mind is beclouded and the will
unnerved by illness.   But I must not run on longer
on such themes, lest the imperfect MS. should betray
the imperfect thinking, and show that my illness
has not been so purely physical as I above averred.
I am only too glad to think, though I can scarcely
understand it, that any poor words of mine should
have helped to comfort and strengthen you in times
of suffering."

Among the many tributes to his memory,
which were written at the time of his death, I
think the one which most nearly expresses the
truth is the following from his old colleague and
friend, Sir William Gairdner :

Of Principal Caird I may say that, notwithstanding his
great reputation as an orator, no man ever crossed my
path in life who impressed me more as a character of
great simplicity and, I would almost say, homeliness,
absolutely without affectation or parade, and, if not unconscious of his great gifts—which, indeed, he could not
possibly be—yet in all ordinary human intercourse behaving
as if he were unconscious of them—a common man among
common men : universally revered, and, by those who
knew him well, deeply loved, but never under any circumstances self-asserting or obtrusive.   He was, indeed,
by nature almost a shy man ; and in everything that he
did and said you came at once to feel that if anyone
else could have done it nearly as well he would at once
have gladly stood aside and yielded position as to an

equal or a superior. I have seen and heard his hand and voice tremble in the announcement of a common piece of University discipline; the most splendid orator of his day, afraid to use words lest they should be found not exactly fitted for their purpose.

Nothing was ever more clear to me, in almost forty years of close intimacy with him as professor and principal, than that John Caird used his great gifts (as Tennyson says of the linnet's singing) because he must; and that, not with a view to himself at all, but to much higher and nobler ends. It was, indeed, this entire absence of self-seeking—and by this I mean not only unselfishness in the ordinary sense of the word, but also great inborn modesty and unobtrusiveness in all the things for which men strive and assert themselves—that gave to his oratorical efforts their greatest charm to those who knew the man. He was conscious—as it appeared—only of the high matters with which he dealt, not of the person who was the instrument of dealing with them. In a very real sense of the words, you would have said that, as a preacher, his "life was hid with Christ in God."

And so, in more ordinary matters, down even to after-dinner speeches, it might be plainly perceived that the great orator had no sense of his own importance, but only aimed at discharging a duty—often a duty irksome to him, and which he would rather have avoided—so as to secure some higher—often the very highest—end. That, I think, is the key to Principal Caird's character and his life. All men know the outcome, whether in the pulpit, the professor's chair, or as the administrative head of the University. There may be differences of opinion as to the absolute value of that outcome. Some may think that his theology was too broad—others, that it was inadequate. Of that I am no judge. But of one thing I can speak with the most full assurance. In all that he said, or thought, or did, Principal Caird was manifestly under the guidance of a higher spirit than that of most of us. He preached, and prayed, and lectured, and went about his work of ruling and administration, alike under a very noble and exalted idea of duty. Thus he was able—nay, he felt obliged, at times—to do and to say things that traversed the cherished views of other men. Yet he made no enemies, because everyone was satisfied that he was doing his duty and no more.

Of my brother's character and predominant tendencies of mind, it is not easy for me to speak, and they are perhaps sufficiently indicated in the foregoing sketch of his life. He was a man of great simplicity and directness of nature, with a strong love for what is beautiful, and an equally strong aversion to what is artificial and conventional. He was an essentially pure-minded man, to whom no one could speak of anything doubtful or equivocal. He was reserved, and generally disinclined to any but indirect expressions of feeling; and one might say he had freer utterance of himself when he was addressing a general audience through the pulpit, than in his private intercourse with individuals. In consequence of his position as a clergyman, and afterwards as Principal, he had to live a good deal in general society; but he was never so happy as when he could get away from its demands, to enjoy the companionship of his brothers, or of a few intimate friends, such as Dr. Watson or Professor Weir. He had a keen enjoyment of natural beauty, and till he was disabled by illness, his greatest pleasure was to take long walks in the country, in the wild mountainous scenery of the Highlands, along the varied banks of the Clyde, or among the hills and valleys of the border country. He was, I think, the most modest man I ever knew in his estimate of his own abilities and acquirements; and his great power as a speaker never seemed to awake in him any feeling of self-satisfaction. It was, indeed, so habitual, and, I might say, natural to him to move men by his gift of speech, that he never seemed to attach any special importance to it. On the other hand, he was apt to idealize and overestimate the gifts of others, especially if they had any knowledge or ability which he did not himself possess. He was a very sensitive man, and towards the end of his life he was easily harassed and disturbed by anything that did not go to his mind; but he had so much self-control and power of keeping his own counsel, that few except his most intimate friends were aware of it.

In his intellectual life, what was perhaps most remarkable was his gradual but continuous progress from youth to age. Thrown early into the active work of a minister, which was made more trying and exacting by the great effect of his speaking, he was not, like many clergymen in similar cases, content to rest with the attainments he brought from the University. He was, on the contrary, almost contemptuous of his own acquirements, and possessed with an ideal which kept him continually reading and thinking up to the last. Hence it is not wonderful that he passed through many stages of growth. Beginning with a strong faith in the Christian creed in the form in which he had received it from his earliest teachers, he never ceased to hold by what he conceived to be essential to Christianity ; and his increasing knowledge of philosophy and theology did not undermine his first conclusions, though it awoke a desire for some *rationale* or explanation of them. And this again modified the original form of his beliefs ; among other things it rendered him increasingly indifferent to all but what he considered the vital issues of Christianity. He tended to concentrate his thoughts upon the leading aspects of truth, and to let secondary matters drop into the background. He could hardly understand, and had almost no sympathy for, those who attached great value to special religious practices, or questions of the government and the outward organization of the church. Controversies about ritual, about the theory of the Sacraments, even about the miraculous, seemed to him of secondary importance, and could not interest him deeply. This tendency to concentrate upon what seemed to him the great issues of the Christian faith—upon the love of God and the revelation of Him to, and in, man—was characteristic of his preaching even from the first, though it was modified by later studies of theology, which taught him to see meaning and value in doctrines which had at first seemed to him of less practical import.

With the increase of his knowledge and power of thinking, there came also a gradual advance in his powers of expression, both in writing, and, I think, also in speaking. For I do not agree with those who speak of my brother's earlier preaching as the best. Some of the fervour of youth had, indeed, evaporated, and the vehemence of utterance and gesture had abated ; but I think there was a gain in weight and in impressiveness which more than compensated the loss. In any case, there

can be no question as to the greater comprehen-
siveness of thought and literary beauty of expression
in his later sermons and lectures. I believe that
any one who compares the volume of *University
Sermons* with those published at an earlier time
will be sensible of this, though the full effect of
either could only be appreciated by those who heard
them.

He was essentially a speaker, and even when
he wrote, there was in the flow of the sentences
something that reminded one of spoken words.
His powers of thought and imagination seemed
always to be working towards such an arrangement
and exposition of his theme as would be effective
in addressing an audience. As a thinker, he had
not perhaps the highest kind of originality, but he
never simply repeated the ideas of others, or
uttered anything that he had not made his own.
The thoughts he assimilated from others were
those for which his own intellectual development
had prepared him, and which therefore he could
carry on to further issues. And—as I have already
said more than once—it was the ethical bearing
of his principles that his mind seemed to grasp
most firmly, and which he showed most resource
in evolving and illustrating.

Christianity and Idealism were the two poles of my brother's thinking, and the latter seemed to him the necessary means for interpreting the former. He had, therefore, the strongest repugnance for all theories that divorced faith and reason—equally for those which empty reason of its religious content, and for those which deny reason in the supposed interest of orthodox theology. In later years, he thought much on the question of immortality, as will be seen in the following lectures ; but the only evidence for it that seemed to him of any real value, was that derived from the spiritual view of the nature of reality and from the goodness that must belong to a God who is a Spirit. " He is not the God of the dead, but of the living ; for all live to Him."

There is something in the impression of a living man that no description can convey to those who have not seen and known him. But I hope that at least in the minds of his friends, this sketch may revive something of the power and presence whose passing away has taken so much from our lives.

In perpetuum frater, abe atque bale !

THE FUNDAMENTAL IDEAS OF CHRISTIANITY

THE FUNDAMENTAL IDEAS OF CHRISTIANITY.

INTRODUCTORY NOTE.

THIS course of lectures is published from my brother's manuscript with only a few, generally verbal, corrections. Owing to the last half of the lectures being delivered three years after the first half, he found it necessary to recapitulate what he had previously said ; and, even apart from this, repetition is often necessary in spoken lectures when it would be out of place in a book. I have not attempted entirely to remove such restatements ; indeed, it sometimes seemed impossible to do so without disturbing the connection of the argument. I have no doubt that if my brother had lived to edit his own lectures, he would have corrected these defects, and would also have endeavoured to make his treatment of Christian doctrine more complete.

A

The lectures must, to a certain extent, be regarded as a *torso*, and not as a finished work. At the same time they fairly represent my brother's thought on the subjects of which they treat, and would not probably have been altered in substance by any revision he might have given them.

E. C.

LECTURE I.

NATURAL AND REVEALED RELIGION.

THE conditions prescribed by the founder of this Lectureship would seem at first sight to exclude Revealed Religion from the class of subjects with which it deals. The province to which it is limited is that of Natural Theology, defined as the science which treats of "the nature and attributes of God, the relations which man and the whole universe bear to Him, the nature and foundations of Ethics, and of all obligations and duties thence arising"; and the founder further expresses his desire that the subject shall "be treated as a strictly natural science like Astronomy or Chemistry."

Waiving the question whether it is possible to treat of the nature and relations of spiritual beings by the same method of investigation which we employ in dealing with inorganic substances, I think it may be shown that a Gifford Lecturer, whilst he may treat of the other historic religions of the world, need not feel himself precluded by any conscious unfaithfulness to the intentions of the founder from attempting a philosophic treatment of that religion which is the culmination of them all. If we ask on what grounds this seemingly arbitrary distinction between Christianity and the pre-Christian religions, or between the Christian religion and the subjects embraced under the phrase " Natural Theology " could be maintained, the answer which some would be disposed to give is that which is involved in the popular distinction which has come down to us as a legacy from the rationalistic theologians of last century—the distinction, I mean, between natural and revealed religion. But if we examine what that distinction means, I think we shall find that it is either wholly untenable, or that in the only sense in which any meaning can be attached to it, it lends no sanction to the proscription of Christianity as a subject of philosophical treatment.

The ordinary notion expressed by this distinction is that there are certain religious ideas, doctrines, principles, such as the idea of the Being and Attributes of God, the Moral Government of the world, and the Immortality of the soul, which are discoverable by "the Light of Nature," or lie within the province of human reason, and have actually been evolved by it; whilst there are other ideas or doctrines, such as the doctrines of the Trinity, the Incarnation, the Atonement, which lie beyond that province, which unaided reason could not have discovered, which have reached, and could only reach, the world by an external, authoritative, supernatural revelation. Philosophy is at home in dealing with the former class of ideas, but to deal with the latter, to examine into the rational grounds, the credibility and coherence of ideas or doctrines which, by hypothesis, transcend the grasp of reason, involves on the part of reason a self-contradictory attitude.

But when we examine more closely the precise import of this distinction, I think we shall see that it does not really involve the arbitrary fencing off of revealed religion from the critical or philosophical intelligence. The claim of philosophy turns, not on the source or origin, but on the contents or intrinsic nature of revelation. Whether thought can deal with Christian truth depends on what it is, not on whence it comes, or by what external mediation it has been communicated to us. The inherent nature and value of ideas which

have become a possession of the human mind is a
thing wholly independent of the question whether
they have been communicated to us in a miraculous
and supernatural, or in a purely natural way—on
the one hand, by a voice from heaven, from the
lips of an inspired prophet, by sacred tradition; or,
on the other hand, by the observation of nature,
by the study of history, by the teaching and influence of other minds, by the moral and spiritual
results of our own experience and reflection.

1. For, in the first place, it is to be considered
that much of the teaching of revelation consists of
the unveiling to us of the true meaning of nature
and human life. One function at least of the
inspired record is to help us to read the open
secret of the universe; to enable us, by the quickening of our spiritual discernment, to understand
the significance of the manifold expression of God
in the world and man, the phenomena of nature,
the changeful incidents of the individual life, the
conflict of man with himself and the world, the
mystery of good and evil, of freedom and necessity,
of life and death; to enable us to see the revelation
of God with which these things are fraught; and
again, to help us to discern, behind the veil of outward
contingency, that moral order which is involved in

the history of nations, the rise and fall of empires, the development of thought and civilization, the progressive life of the human race. In this respect at least, it is the office of revelation, not to instruct us as to some transcendental order of things, not to superadd to what comes from ordinary and human sources of knowledge, something that pertains to a superhuman, supernatural sphere; but rather to enable us to penetrate to the moral and spiritual meaning of the world in which we live, and the teaching which, could we only read it aright, it yields to our minds. And obviously, when revelation fulfils this function, the essence of the teaching it gives is not, so to speak, in itself, but in that system of things whose meaning it unfolds. We cannot get at the religious ideas it contains by reading the words of an inspired book, and constructing out of them correct theological propositions, but only by looking at that other book of nature and life whose pages it illumines and verifies, and letting our souls be penetrated by the light that is ever streaming from it.

Let me offer one or two illustrations of this point. When we find a sacred writer speaking thus: "When I consider thy heavens, the work of thy fingers, the moon and the stars which thou hast ordained," and going on to deduce from a contemplation of the material world spiritual lessons as to man and his relations to God and nature, the teaching may, indeed, be contained in an inspired Scripture; but the real revelation is that to which the words refer, which they call attention to and point out. No man who had never looked on the nightly heavens, or who was incapable of seeing in them the manifestation of an invisible thought and will, could get at the revelation of the mind of God which this passage contains. And the question whether in this and similar cases the revelation is true, what it amounts to, its rational and spiritual content, its relations to other ideas in the system of human thought—this is a question which is not placed beyond the province of rational investigation because the matter with which it deals is included in what is regarded as a supernatural revelation. Again, when the Bible records for our instruction the life, action, and experience of individuals, or the history of nations, the principle is the same. When, for instance, we read the words of an inspired Psalmist: "Against thee, thee only have I sinned and done this evil in thy sight." "Cast me not away from thy presence and take not thy holy Spirit from me"; or these of an inspired Prophet, " Oh that my head were waters and mine eyes a fountain of tears, that I might weep day and night for the slain of the daughter of my people " ; or these of an inspired Apostle, " The good that I would, I do not, but the evil which I would not, that I do." " I see another law in my members, warring against the law of my mind." " Oh wretched man that I am! who shall deliver me from the body of this death ? "—the words, in all these cases, do indeed convey to us a revelation of divine truth ; we learn from them inspired lessons as to sin and repentance, as to the conflict between man's higher and lower nature and the longing of the soul for spiritual deliverance and freedom ; but we do so just because they bring before us with marvellous vividness the revelation of sin and sorrow which is uttering itself in the experience of a thousand human hearts. Here, too, the distinction as to its matter between revealed religion and natural religion vanishes.

The same is true when we turn from the history and experience of individuals to that of nations. The historic books of the Old Testament are part of revealed religion ; but they are so because and in so far as they are the record of that revelation of the mind and will of God, of that moral order

which is unfolded to us in the life of nations and
the course of history. The element of fact which
they contain is not invented by them, and it no
more withdraws itself from examination and criticism than when it supplies materials for ordinary
historical investigation. Nor is the moral and
spiritual element of sacred history an independent
supernatural communication, to be apprehended
simply by listening to the voice of an inspired
teacher, or construing the words and sentences of
a book. The Spirit of God in the sacred narrative is instructing us concerning the principles
of the divine government—the inherent might of
right, the irresistible prevalence in the long run of
good over evil, the tendency of selfishness and
wrong to sap the vitality and undermine the fair
prosperity of nations. But these are principles
which are not simply authoritatively announced in
the pages of that narrative, but are woven into the
life of humanity. They are at work around us,
hedging in our course of action, rewarding duty,
executing vengeance on unrighteousness, causing
peace, health, wealth, to follow on the steps of
national virtue and integrity, and decay and ruin
to track, silent and sure, the path of licentiousness
and wrong. They are written, not merely in words

and sentences, but—as we contemplate the rise and fall of states and empires—now in the living language of greatness, power, world-wide fame and influence, crowning national purity and integrity, and now in the flaring characters of the disaster and ruin that are the providential retribution of national corruption.

And not only is this revelation of history that on which the book-revelation is based, but it far transcends the special examples of its operation which any book, inspired or uninspired, can contain. The everlasting law of righteousness is reflected in the destinies of modern Europe as really as in those of ancient Asia, in the history of England or France or Germany, as in the history of Israel or Egypt or Assyria. The providential order of the world did not hold itself aloof from the fortunes of all but one race or people, nor has it stopped when the period to which the Canonical Scriptures relate came to an end. Those great silent forces which are the expression of the eternal will cease not, and never can cease, to sway the destinies of nations, and in their slow and cyclical movement, to bend all things to that infinite end and purpose to which the whole creation moves. If, then, these eternal

laws and principles relate to things earthly and
human, if they manifest themselves in the successions of events in the past and present life of
humanity, it is the special function of the philosophy of history to elicit and verify them ; nor
does the fact that specimens of them are recorded
in a sacred book, ear-mark them as outside the
sphere with which the philosophic historian is per-
mitted to deal.

It may be said, however, that, even admitting
that much of the content of the verbal revelation
is, in one sense, a reproduction of the real revelation of nature and human life, and can be comprehended only by reference to the latter, this
principle does not apply to what may be termed
the distinctively supernatural element of revealed
religion.   If philosophy can claim to deal with
nature and history, are not miracles and acts of
interposition with natural and historical law, by
their very definition, placed beyond the scope of
human reason ?   With respect to such doctrines
as the Existence and Attributes of God, and the
Moral Government of the world, intellectual satisfaction may not be beyond our reach ; for they
relate to things of which the proof and verification
are to be found in the phenomena of nature, the

events of history, and the moral consciousness of man. But can we venture to say as much of such doctrines as the Trinity, the Divinity of Christ, the Atonement, Regeneration, the whole revealed economy of Redemption? Can we maintain that in announcing these doctrines, revelation is, in any sense, simply unveiling to us the meaning of nature and life? Do they not belong to a transcendental sphere, altogether above and beyond the natural order of things of which reason can take cognizance, and which nothing in that order could enable us to know and verify?

Now, without discussing here the general question as to those doctrines of revelation which, as is sometimes said, though not contrary to reason are yet above reason,[1] I think it may be shown that, in one aspect of them at least, these doctrines form no exception to the principle that the distinction between natural and revealed religion is an arbitrary and misleading distinction, and that it is the highest function of revelation to enable us with quickened spiritual discernment to understand the true significance of nature and man and human life. I will take, for example,

[1] See the discussion of this distinction in the *Introduction to the Philosophy of Religion*, chap. III., p. 71.

the one cardinal doctrine of Christianity, the Divinity of Christ, and I confidently maintain that, so far from carrying us into a region foreign to human experience and human consciousness, so far from being a mere oracle in a book, it points to something in fact and life that is most profoundly true and real—to ideas and principles that interpenetrate the very being and essence of humanity ; to hopes, aspirations, ideals, which are the very web and woof of the drama of human history. For I ask you, for one thing, to re- member that the Divinity of Christ, however we conceive of it, was a Divinity that was capable of being expressed ∧ in a human life and through the words and acts of a human personality. Say that his was a perfect life, that it touched the supreme height of what is possible for a being made in God's image, yet whatever lay absolutely beyond the range of human nature, whatever of Divinity could not organically unite itself with and breathe through a human spirit, was not and could not be present in one who, whatever else he was, was really and truly human. The Divinity of Christ was not that of a divine nature in local or mechanical juxtaposition with a human, but of a divine nature that suffused, blended, ?

[margin note:] sufficiently but not fully.

[margin note:] Kenoticism of a priori type.

? identified itself with the thoughts, feelings, volitions of a human individuality. If it had consisted of a merely quantitative infinitude, a spatial
omnipresence, a physical omnipotence, it would
have been something foreign to human nature and
human sympathy. But the very end and purpose
of the Incarnation, we are expressly told, was to
make us " partakers of a divine nature," to call us
to rise above the narrow limits of time and sense
and to become sharers of that eternal life which
was manifested in the life of Christ; so that what
the Son of God was, we too may hope to become
—sons of God, one with Him as He is with
the Father, heirs of God and joint heirs with
Christ. If this be so, revelation, in this highest
mystery of the supernatural, is still intensely
natural. So far from dealing with matter transcending human thought, it is just that which
throws light on the profoundest experiences of our
spiritual nature and life, unveils to us the secret
of our boundless capacities of good and evil, of
our deepest sorrows and divinest joys, of the
hopes and endeavours after an excellence and
blessedness which no finite attainment can satisfy.
A philosophy, therefore, which pretended to deal
with man in his spiritual nature and relations

without taking cognizance of the person and life
of Christ, would be leaving out of sight the one
all-important element of its investigations, neglect-
ing the key to its deepest problems.

2. Another consideration which seems fatal to
the arbitrary distinction between the provinces of
natural and revealed religion, and therefore to the
exclusion of philosophy from the latter, is that, by
universal admission, the teaching of revelation finds
its best and only sufficient evidence in the consciousness of the believer. If this be conceded, it
matters not what theory we hold as to the outward
origin of revelation—whether, in other words, like
great discoveries in science, or original ideas in
philosophy, or immortal productions of art, new
ideas in religion owe their origin to minds endowed
with a special religious genius and attaining in
moments of spiritual elevation a height of spiritual
discernment transcending that of ordinary men ; or
whether, on the other hand, the original depositaries
of these ideas received them by a process as independent of the activity of their own intelligence
as that by which the mirror reflects objects presented to it.

It might, indeed, be said that the latter method
of revelation would imply a superfluous step in

the communication of divine truth to the world, inasmuch as, to be of use to mankind, it must, sooner or later, be apprehended not mechanically but spiritually. The outward revelation would still need to be inwardly appropriated by the spiritual intelligence. Neither moral nor religious ideas can be simply transferred to the human spirit in the form of fact. They cannot be made intelligible to the mere logical understanding, nor verified by any evidence outside of, or lower than, themselves. Their rich content can only pass into and become nutriment to the soul that by its own spiritual energy appropriates and assimilates them. Even if the first prophet had been a mere infallible conductor of words, yet the witness of the spirit, the inspiration of the religious intelligence, must be present in the minds that truly apprehend them.

But if this be so, revealed truth cannot belong to a different order from all other truth that appeals to the human consciousness and with which it is the province of philosophy to deal. Even conceding the barest notion of external infallibility in the original communication, this must be so. For, however inferior the faculty of recognizing and verifying may be to that of discovering or excogitating, recognition and verification would be

impossible if the truth recognized did not belong
to the same order with all other truth, or if the
mind that receives and authenticates were not
essentially akin to the mind that communicates.
It is no doubt true that the measure of intelligence
which qualifies a man to receive and appreciate
thought falls short of that which qualifies him to
create or excogitate it. Creative, originative minds
belong to a class or order distinctively superior to
that of those who are merely or mainly receptive.
Nevertheless, widely as they may differ in the
measure and range of their intellectual power,
the apprehending mind proves, by the very fact
that it can apprehend and appreciate the products
of the inventive or creative mind, that it is of
the same essence, kindred in nature and faculty
with it. Unless there were in my mind something essentially one with that of the greatest
scientific or philosophic thinker, no bridge could
be built over which thought could pass from
mind to mind. Is it not a common-place that
the power to charm and thrill men's minds,
the secret of the spell which the great poet
wields over multitudes of other minds is this, that
he is giving voice to the dumb, inarticulate poetry
within their own breasts—to thoughts and feelings

which, though his alone is the capacity to give utterance to them, the common heart and spirit of humanity recognizes as its own? The teaching, in short, of great and original minds may be a communication of new ideas to us, but it is so, because it interprets us to ourselves.

And the same principle applies to the case before us. The power to apprehend and verify the truths which inspired writers have taught us proves, not indeed that by any *a priori* process of thought the individual mind could have excogitated them, but that in the deepest sense they are congenial to man's nature, and that no hard and fast line can be drawn between them and those religious ideas which, it is alleged, have been the fruit of unaided inquiry and reflection. Nay, if we were to compare the teaching of revelation with that of the so-called natural religion in point of accordance with reason and conscience, I unhesitatingly affirm that the former is more profoundly rational, more deeply true to our spiritual intelligence, than the latter. The idea of God as Father of spirits, essentially one with humanity, having His highest manifestation in a human person and life, and dwelling in us by His spirit, is not less but more satisfactory to reason than

But the lack of power to excogitate them in the first instance aside from reveln. vindicates the distinc'n. he is criticising.

the conception of God as a "First Cause" or a "Creator and Moral Ruler of the world," which is the doctrine of natural religion. The perfect moral ideal which broke upon the world in the person and life of Christ contains in it elements of moral truth and beauty not less but more accordant with our capacity of knowing and appreciating what is good and fair, than the ethical ideas which moralists have struck out apart from it and by what is called the light of nature. The "eternal life" which Christianity reveals—a life of union and communion with God, in which the finite spirit rises above the power of change and decay into participation in the very life of the Eternal—this is a doctrine more true to man's being and its infinite capabilities, not less but immeasurably more accordant with thought and reason than that notion of a mere survival after death, or of an "immortality of the soul," based on vague speculations and imperfect analogies, which the light of nature is supposed to yield.

3. And this leads me to remark further, that the impossibility of marking off certain religious ideas as due to natural reason, from certain other ideas as pertaining to the province of revelation, is shown by this, that Christianity or Christian

thought annuls and transcends the religious ideas
of natural religion. The notion that there is one
set of truths, such as the existence and providence
of God, the principles of morality, and the natural
immortality of the soul, which we can accept on
the testimony of reason, and another set of truths,
the peculiar doctrines of the Gospel, which we
must accept, if at all, on the testimony of revelation, is for Christian thought futile and
impossible. The truths of natural religion, in
so far as they are contained in Christianity,
are not contained therein simply by addition or
accretion, but rather by absorption and trans-
mutation. You cannot as a Christian simply
hold in common with Deists or Jews or Moham-
medans, the doctrines of natural religion, while
you add to them certain other doctrines which are
peculiar to Christianity. The new element which
Christianity has introduced into the thought of
the world transforms, elevates, works a fundamental change in all the previous materials of
religious knowledge. It takes up these materials
into itself, but it takes them up as the plant takes
up air and earth and moisture and light, or as the
living body takes up the matter which constitutes
its food—not transferring them wholesale, but by its

The idea wh.
underlies this
whole arg.

True tho' pushed
too far.

inward organic chemistry, subduing, disintegrating, reconstructing all that it receives into similitude with its own higher nature. There is not a single doctrine of natural religion which, when it enters into the content of the Christian faith, remains what it was outside of Christianity. The God of natural religion is not the same with the God of Christianity. Christianity knows no such being as a "First Cause" or "an Almighty Creator and Governor of the world"——a being framed at best after the image of man, an anthropomorphic potentate seated on a celestial throne, publishing laws and dispensing rewards and punishments after the manner of an earthly sovereign or magistrate. By its cardinal doctrine of the unity of God and Man, Christianity has dissolved the dualism which such notions involved, bridged the gulf between the finite and infinite which, apart from Christianity, was never spanned, and by its conception of the self-realization of God in humanity, solved the problem which baffled the greatest minds of ancient times.

Christian morality, again, is not the same with natural morality; it has had an infinite element infused into it. Virtue has been transformed into holiness, obedience to an outward

law or even to the imperative of conscience,
into participation in a divine spirit and the
realization in all social relations of a divine
organic life ; and on the other hand, vice has
become sin, disobedience to law has deepened into
selfish alienation from God and the arresting or
abandonment of an infinite destiny. Our ideas, to
name no others, of human freedom, of repentance
and reformation, of the dignity and value of the
soul, of the equality and brotherhood of men, of the
future destiny of the race, are not mere comple-
ments of the ideas of natural religion. They are,
as I have said, profoundly rational, but if there are
ideas analogous to them in extra-Christian thought,
these have so felt the leavening touch of Christianity
as to be, in their independent existence, annulled
and superseded. They no more continue to exist
side by side in the same system of thought with
Christian ideas, than the dawn continues to exist
side by side with the light of noonday, or the
blossom, fruit and flower side by side with the
seed or germ. There is therefore, we repeat, no
such thing as a natural religion or religion of
reason distinct from revealed religion. Christianity
is more profoundly, more comprehensively rational,
more accordant with the deepest principles of

*True, if we speak
in the concrete.
is no relig (true)
in real comⁿ w.
and only reveln.
brings this.*

human nature and human thought than natural religion; or, as we may put it, Christianity is natural religion elevated and transmuted into revealed.

4. Philosophy then cannot limit its province to natural religion to the exclusion of Christianity, for this, if for no other reason, that Christianity interprets natural religion to itself. And for the same reason, let me add finally, philosophy claims to deal with Christianity as the key to the other religions of the world. The study of the other historic or pre-Christian religions is unquestionably of deep interest and importance for the inquirer into the nature of religion in general; but its importance has often been made to rest on false grounds. Writers on what is called "the Science of Religions" have sometimes argued for that science either on the ground, that the true idea or essence of religion is to be reached inductively, by comparing all the religions of the world and discovering what is the common element in them; or, on the ground that these religions rise out of each other by a process of development, and that by going back to the earliest origin of religion and following the steps of the process upwards, we shall be able to account for Christianity on purely natural grounds, or as

the natural product of causes at work in the pre-Christian religions. Such writers, I cannot help thinking, misunderstand the relation of Christianity to the other religions ; and they do so because they fail to see what is really involved in their own idea of a process of development. For, if there be such a process in religion, it implies, first, that you can never get at the true idea or essence of religion merely by trying to find out something that is common to all religions, and, second, that it is not the lower religions that explain the higher, but conversely, the higher religion that is the explanation of all the lower religions.

As to the former of these points, the essential element of religion is not to be reached by leaving out from the various positive religions the special characteristics which distinguish them from each other, and retaining only those ideas or beliefs which are found to be common to all. For it is obvious that wherever in the phenomena we observe we are obliged to introduce the notion of growth or development, wherever, in other words, that which we contemplate is a thing that reaches its perfection not by accretion or accumulation of like materials, but by gradual evolution from the germ to the perfect organism, there the true idea of the thing is not what is common to the lowest and highest and every intermediate stage of its existence. To have regard only to what is common to the fruit or flower with the seed and stalk and stem, would not help us to the essential idea of the plant. It is not that which is the same in the embryo and the full-grown body, but rather that differentiation of organs and functions in which the latter rises above and differs from the former, that gives us the true conception of the organism. Nor is the nature of man as an intelligent being to be discovered by the application of a common measure, which would embrace only what pertains alike to the highly developed intellect in the maturity of its powers and to the rude gropings after knowledge of the world and of itself, which mark the dawn of intelligence in the infant. On the contrary, in all organic development, the perfect organism, whilst it comprehends, at the same time transcends and transmutes all that pertained to the earlier stages of its life ; and that which is really common to all these stages is something that cannot be reached inductively, but only by grasping the idea which is present only potentially in the lower, and is never fully realized till the organism has reached its highest stage. In like manner, a merely empirical consideration or comparative view of the various religions of the world, however important it may be, as supplying the material for a Science of Religions, does not in itself constitute such a science. If in the religious history of mankind we can discover indications of a progressive development, it is not by leaving out of view what is peculiar to Christianity, those ideas which constitute its special glory and excellence, and taking account only of that which we see or suppose to be common to it with the earliest and rudest nature worship, that we can discover the real meaning of that history : for it is just that in which Christianity differs from all the pre-Christian religions which realizes, for the first time, the true idea of religion. As the absolute and only perfect form of that idea, Christianity, whilst it explains the latent significance of all that was true in the imperfect religions, at the same time transcends, and in transcending, transmutes and annuls or supersedes them.

Moreover, it follows from this that those writers are on an altogether false quest whose aim, covertly or avowedly, in tracing the history of religions, is to reduce Christianity and its doctrines to a purely natural product. The underlying principle of their speculations seems to be, that if

they can discover the earliest form of religion—
ghost-worship, ancestor-worship, nature-worship or
what not ; or the tendency or sentiment in human
nature—wonder, awe, abject dependence, craven
fear of the supernatural—which is expressed in
these forms, they will have possessed themselves
of the key to the whole subsequent religious history of mankind.   By the ordinary law of cause
and effect they can trace from this source the rise
of the various forms of religion, polytheistic, pantheistic, or monotheistic.   In these they find merely
the complex result, under various conditions and
circumstances, of an intelligible and purely natural
process, and in Christianity itself only at most the
culmination of that process.

But the fallacy which underlies any such theory
of man's religious history is that of confusing the
final with the efficient cause of the phenomena to
be explained; in other words, of overlooking the
distinction between the historical beginning of a
thing and its essential principle or end.   Even if,
for argument's sake, we concede the unconditional
application of the principle of development to
religion, it is not in the beginning but in the end,
not in the first but in the last manifestation of
the principle of religion, that the true explanation

of the process is to be sought. By an analogous application of the idea of evolution, there are, as we know, certain scientific thinkers in our day, who have persuaded themselves that mind is only a function of matter, that the organic world is only a complex result of mechanical and chemical forces, that biological phenomena are resolvable into physical, and psychological into physiological, and that thought, sensation, feeling, and intelligence in general, are only a product of nervous action, a function of material organization. As these thinkers find the key to the phenomena of the universe in the mechanical laws that govern the movements of an atom, so the writers on religion of whom I speak find the ultimate explanation of all religious phenomena in the primitive religious sentiment modified by the action and reaction of outward environment. But, as I have said, if we are to seek anywhere for the true cause or origin of an organic process, the true explanation of all the phenomena of growth, it is not in the factual commencement, but in the final result, or rather in that ideal end which silently dominates the beginning and every successive step of its outward history. The true origin of the plant is not the first stirring of vital activity in the seed or germ, it is that ideal principle or plan of its existence which dominates and determines the outward phenomenal beginning, and silently directs its whole subsequent history. So, it is only because, and in so far as, the power of the highest or absolute religion is already working in the earliest and all subsequent forms of man's spiritual life, dominating, shaping, transmuting, elevating them, that these religious phenomena have any meaning or reality. If, therefore, as we have seen, philosophy cannot deal with natural religion to the exclusion of Christianity, because it finds in Christianity that which explains natural religion to itself; by parity of reasoning, philosophy must refuse to treat only of the pre-Christian religions. For it is Christianity, as the highest and only perfect realization of the idea of religion, that explains all the imperfect expressions of that idea; in other words, it is Christianity that throws light on the " unconscious prophecies of heathendom," those fore-shadowings of moral and spiritual ideas, those partial anticipations of Christian thought which the pre-Christian religions contain.

LECTURE II.

FAITH AND REASON.

In my first lecture I attempted to show that the distinction between natural and revealed religion cannot be held to be an absolute distinction. Neither moral nor religious ideas can be simply transferred to the human spirit in a form of fact, nor can they be verified by any evidence outside of or lower than themselves. They can pass into and become nutriment only to the soul that by its own spiritual intelligence appropriates and assimilates them. And if this be so, revealed truth cannot belong to a different order from all other truth that appeals to the human consciousness, and with which therefore philosophy can claim to deal.

But though it may be granted that spiritual truth must be spiritually discerned, it may be maintained that this by no means implies the competency of reason to deal with the content of revelation. That there must needs be a response in the human consciousness to the truth it receives, does not necessarily mean that the response must be that of the reason or understanding. Spiritual knowledge, it may be held, is not speculative or ratiocinative knowledge; and there are many religious thinkers who altogether repudiate the claims of philosophy in the sphere of religion, on the ground that whilst finite truth can be apprehended by the understanding, it is by a different, and in one sense higher organ, that we hold communication with God and divine things. The appeal of religious truth, it is said, is not to the head but to the heart, not to reason but to faith. Belief in it is not of the nature of a conclusion from logical premises, but of an immediate, intuitive recognition, arising in the devout mind on the presentation to it of spiritual truth. Such a mind does not attain, *e.g.*, to a knowledge of the existence and nature of God by following the steps of a metaphysical proof. Religion is the immediate communion of the soul with God, and the Spirit of God is to the devout and believing mind its own witness. And the same principle applies to all the essential truths of our Christian faith. Our belief in the divinity of Christ is not the result of any elaborate theory as to the

Incarnation or the co-existence of two substances, a divine and human, in one person ; the personality and life which the Gospel narrative brings before us awakens in us the sense of an infinite presence, an immediate recognition of the glory of God in the face of Jesus Christ. What constitutes belief in the Scripture doctrines of redemption, of the forgiveness of sin, of the reality and efficacy of the atoning sacrifice of Christ, is not intellectual assent to any theory of atonement or of imputed righteousness or of justification by faith. The awakened soul, as it listens to the Gospel message of pardon through Him who bore its sins and carried the burden of its sorrows, responds to it with a simple unhesitating assurance that is beyond the reach of doubt, and rests on no process of theoretical argument.

From its very nature, therefore, according to this view, religion belongs to a sphere which lies beyond the jurisdiction of reason. If there be any kind of knowledge that is analogous to it, it is to be found, not in the sphere of science, but in perceptions, such as the intuitive or instinctive perception of beauty in nature and art, which are independent of the logical or theoretical faculties, and which are often keenest and quickest in natures

c

whose reasoning powers are feeble or untrained.
The responsive sympathy with nature, the thrill of
admiration that fills the soul in the contemplation
of her glory, is indeed in one sense full of intelligence ; but it is a kind of intelligence altogether
different from that which takes cognizance of
scientific definition and demonstration, and which can
formulate its results in propositions and arguments.
And so, it is maintained, religious belief may be
implicitly rational, but the knowledge it contains
is not reached by any theoretical process, but comes
to the soul as an immediate vision of spiritual
realities, an intuitive perception of their divine grace
and truth.   It may even be maintained, not only
that religious knowledge is primarily intuitive, but
that it can never be anything else.   Intuitive conviction from its very nature cannot, it may be held,
render any account of itself.   A belief that proceeds
by process from one thing to another admits of
formal statement.   But how can we reproduce in
reasoned form a conviction that rests on no process
of reason ?   How can we re-cast in dialectic mould
that which in itself is beyond all dialectic ?   Such
a condition does not admit of any apologetic
buttress, for that would be to seek support for a
higher in a lower ground of certitude.   Its only

reply to rationalistic doubt or to reason's demand for systematic statement is the simple assertion, " I see it, I feel it to be true."

Now it must be conceded that there are many considerations which seem to favour this view of the nature of religious knowledge, carrying with it the exclusion of philosophy from the sphere of religion. Some of these considerations I shall now briefly examine. I have dealt with this subject elsewhere in a somewhat different form, but a re-statement of it is required for the methodical treatment of the subject of these lectures.[1]

It may be conceded, for one thing, in favour of the view just stated, that the organ of religious belief cannot be any faculty in the human spirit which is not universal. A religion which is for all must be intelligible to all. The recognition of its truth cannot depend on evidence which is beyond the range of a limited intelligence. If Christianity is to be a universal religion, constituting the principle of a new life for all mankind, a world-redeeming, regenerating power, its reception cannot turn either on the accurate knowledge of historic facts, the evidence for which it requires much research and critical acuteness to appreciate, or on the apprehen-

---

[1] Cf. *Introduction to the Philosophy of Religion*, chaps. II. and VI.

sion of ideas which only minds endowed with no
little dialectic skill or speculative insight can grasp.

Moreover, the reception of religious truth implies
a moral and religious, and not a merely intellectual attitude of mind.   It cannot be an act
equally possible to the irreligious or even immoral,
and to the pure and spiritually-minded.   Belief
in Christ cannot be as independent of any moral
element as belief in Socrates or Caesar or any
other historic personality ; or, again, as belief
in the Copernican system or in the Kantian or
Spencerian philosophy.   The faculty of historical
criticism by which the element of truth is ex-
tricated from any narrative of events in the past
may be possessed in fullest measure irrespectively
of the moral and spiritual character of the critic,
and the process of historical investigation may be
carried on successfully or unsuccessfully without the
investigator being either in the one case the better,
or in the other the worse.   The intellectual sub-
tilty and deftness which enables a man to grasp
the salient points of an argument, the speculative
insight in virtue of which he can appreciate a
philosophical theory, are qualities altogether apart
from the moral tone and temper of his spirit or
the purity and elevation of his life.

[margin note:] Are these beliefs independent of moral elements?

[margin note:] not wholly.   ?

[margin note:] too unreserved

On this ground therefore—that the organ of religious belief cannot be a faculty which is the special prerogative of a limited class, and which may be and often is developed in highest measure in the most unspiritual minds—it does not seem possible to evade the conclusion that, in the province of religion, the province of spiritual truth, on the knowledge of which turns the relation of the soul to God, the organ of knowledge cannot be any faculty whose end or aim is simply intellectual satisfaction.

Further, it is urged with no little force that the attempt to give rational or intellectual form to our spiritual intuitions deprives them of their spiritual vitality and power. The impatience with dogmas and theological systems to which many in our day have given forcible utterance, and the demand to go back to the simple and informal presentation of divine truth in the life and teaching of Christ, arises, it may be said, mainly from the felt inadequacy of theological dogmas to embody the vital experience of the Christian life. The knowledge which comes to us by faith contains in it infinitely more than the understanding by any intellectual process can reproduce. Philosophical and theological ratiocination is the attempt to bring into clear consciousness what is implicitly given in Christian experience; but at best the former must ever fall short of the latter. In the attitude of communion with God, intuition takes in at a glance what scientific definitions, however elaborate, can only imperfectly and partially evolve. As the initial act of self-surrender to Christ is the germ which contains in it the potentiality of the whole future spiritual life, so faith is the potentiality of all knowledge; and the devout soul, even if it were associated with the keenest intellectual power, would in vain attempt to give definite form and expression to what is contained in one act of genuine Christian experience. The religious life in general, the ever-growing sense of the beauty and glory of the things unseen and eternal, the emotions of love, aspiration, reverence, self-devotion, have in them an element of infinitude akin to the nature of their objects. But the categories of the understanding are narrow and finite, they can express only separate aspects of truth; what they can give us is only a number of intellectual abstractions standing in hard and fast distinction from each other, and the one thing they are incapable of reproducing is the living harmony and beauty of spiritual truth as it presents itself to the eye of faith.

The conclusion, then, to which, as it has often been held, these considerations seem to lead, is that faith or intuition, not reason, is the organ of religious knowledge, and that in the immediate response of the spirit to the teaching of revelation, we have an uncritical certitude, an implicit strength and fulness of conviction, to which by no exercise of the logical or reasoning faculty we can ever attain. The appeal from faith to reason is the appeal from a higher to a lower and less reliable authority ; and even if the formulating of the content of our spiritual experience in a reasoned system of doctrine be not an impossible achievement, the result would at best be the reproduction in an imperfect and inadequate form of what in the immediate consciousness of the spiritual life we already possess. Let us now briefly examine what force there is in these objections to the endeavour after a rational or philosophical knowledge of the content of our religious belief.

1. It is no valid objection to this endeavour to say that the primary organ of spiritual knowledge is not reason but faith. That we must *begin* with intuition or immediate knowledge is no reason why we should not go on to mediated or scientific knowledge. The practical

and the scientific, the spontaneous and the reflective tendencies, may co-exist, and there is no reason why the one should prove a hindrance and not a help to the other. The popular outcry against dogma is, in some measure at least, based on a misapprehension of the end aimed at by theology in dealing with religion and religious ideas. Neither theology nor philosophy proposes to substitute scientific for immediate or experimental knowledge; or if in any case they do, they lay themselves open to the objections above adduced. To insist on the acceptance of a theological proposition or theory as the test of a man's Christianity, to conceive it possible that the state of the soul before God should be determined by its capacity to apprehend a theory of the Atonement or of the Person of Christ, or that its salvation should turn on the ability accurately to discriminate between the many conflicting creeds and confessions, all alike claiming to be based on the same inspired authority, is a notion which, it is to be hoped, has almost entirely vanished from the world. In the recoil from any such notion, thoughtful men have sometimes set themselves to inquire how much theological error may be consistent with genuine religion and a right to the Christian name. But to my mind the right answer

This is crude tho plausible. A Creed is accepted because one must express his faith, + a true Creed does not trouble one whose implicit faith is true.

would be that, directly and in the first instance,
neither theological accuracy nor theological error,
neither orthodoxy nor heresy, has anything to do
with the matter. The response of the Christian
consciousness to the glad tidings of the Gospel,
the spiritual appropriation of the great ideas of the
Christian revelation, the Fatherhood of God, the
forgiveness of sin, the sinless perfection of the person
and life of Christ, the call to participation in a life
of Sonship and sacrifice akin to his own—the appeal
which these and kindred ideas present to the believing mind, and the act of spiritual apprehension
by which it responds to that appeal—are, in whatever way we describe them, wholly different from
intellectual assent to consciously and deliberately
reasoned opinions or to the articles of a theological
creed.

But this concession does not by any means
imply that no place or function is left for reason
or rational investigation in the province of religion.
Theology is not religion, but neither is ethical
science morality, nor aesthetical science the sense
and enjoyment of beauty, nor grammar and rhetoric
the gift of speech. The sciences of Optics and
Acoustics are not meaningless because we can see
and hear without a knowledge of them, nor the

sciences of Anatomy and Physiology, because the knowledge of them is not necessary for the performance of the bodily functions. " We act before we reflect and philosophize about our actions. We enter into social relations, we create institutions, silently and spontaneously the self-conscious nature that is in us gives birth and development to the organizations of the family, the tribe, the nation ; and only later do we reach the point of progress at which thought turns back to reflect on the significance and ground of its own creations and to discern the principles that have been at work in their formation and development."

In like manner, religion exists and must exist as a life and experience before it can be made the object of reflective thought ; but there is no more reason, in this than in other instances, why experimental knowledge should exclude scientific knowledge. There can be no question that piety may be genuine and fervent where there is little or no capacity for theological investigation ; but where the capacity exists, it is neither possible nor desirable that the intellectual impulse, the impulse after grounded, coherent, systematic thought, should be stifled. In religion as in other spheres of human activity—in morality, in art, in social and political life—there is present the underlying element of reason which is the distinctive characteristic of all the activities of a self-conscious intelligence ; and the endeavour, by reflection, to elicit and give objective clearness to that element— to know what our religious ideas mean, what conceptions of the object of worship and of our own spiritual nature are involved in them, on what grounds they rest and to what results they point, to trace their relations to each other and to other branches of knowledge ; to infuse, in short, into the spontaneous and unsifted conceptions of religious experience, the objective clearness, necessity, and organic unity of thought—this in religion as elsewhere is the aim of science. And it is no futile aim. To renounce it would be, for many at least, a kind of intellectual suicide ; to pursue it, with even partial and imperfect success, is the only rest for minds in which the intellectual instincts are strong and irrepressible.

Nor, again, does there seem to be any real ground for the charge of repulsive hardness and narrowness as the characteristic of scientific theology, in contrast with the intensive serenity and harmony of religious experience. It is true that, here as elsewhere, science does not present its objects clothed with the spontaneity and beauty of nature and life. Analysis, division, abstraction, are the instruments with which science works. It must needs break up the fair and rounded wholeness and harmony of immediate experience. It must deal with abstractions, and be content to give up for the moment that concrete harmony which the world possesses for ordinary observation. But it is only to the unreflecting mind that science has an aspect of hardness and crabbedness. The botanist's herbarium, the collection of classified specimens in a museum, have lost the spontaneous beauty of nature, the attractiveness of delicately-moulded form, the ever-varying loveliness of colour, of light and shade, of motion and life. But though the scientific collection has lost this kind of beauty, it has gained for the educated observer another kind of beauty—the beauty of order and law, of identity of principle under diversity of form, of relation of organ and function, of organic development towards an ideal end.

But, indeed, the loss which science involves is by no means so great as this illustration suggests. For it is to be considered that scientific knowledge does not destroy, but leaves wholly unimpaired the simpler charm which nature pos-

sesses for ordinary observation. The science that
unfolds the types and orders of plants, the organic
laws of vegetable life, does not obliterate to the
eye of the expert the inartificial beauty of form
and colour which nature scatters from her inexhaustible treasury over the world's face. The
knowledge of the principles of art does not suppress, but rather stimulates, the appreciation of the
works of the great masters in the mind of the
cultured observer.

But if this be so, may we not, on the same
principle, be prepared to admit the futility of the
contrast frequently drawn between religion or
religious experience and scientific theology? It
would be strange indeed if, in the highest of all
provinces of human experience, intelligence should
be compelled to renounce its birthright, and a
check be put on those intellectual instincts which
in every other province lead the human mind to
reflect, to analyze, to endeavour after the rational
grounding, harmonizing, systematizing of the materials
which experience supplies. Nor is there any in-
compatibility here, any more than elsewhere, between
the scientific and the intuitive life. There may
be a temptation in some cases to substitute a
scientific for an experimental interest in religion,

and it is possible that the zeal of speculative investigation may not be accompanied by a corresponding ardour of the religious affections. But it is not the legitimate effect of science to dull our religious any more than our domestic and social sensibilities; and a thousand examples go to prove that profound learning and fervent piety is no impossible combination.

2. That we must begin with faith then, is, we have seen, no reason why we should not advance to science. That the primary organ of religious knowledge is not reason but faith, leaves to reason still an important office to fulfil. What then, let us now go on to inquire more closely, is that office? What function or functions has reason to perform in order to the attainment of a scientific or systematic knowledge of the content of our intuitive religious belief? I answer that faith is but implicit reason, reason working intuitively and unconsciously, and therefore without reflection or criticism of its own operations. Hence one of the functions of conscious reason is to purify our intuitions from foreign or spurious admixture. The sanction of intuitive or immediate certitude may, experience shows, be claimed for much to which it really does not extend. Truth is indeed

its own witness to the spiritual mind, but not all
that *seems* to be true. Grant that the witness of
the spirit is the touchstone of truth, it is possible
for the individual mind to be mistaken as to that
to which it really does bear witness, and in different
minds it may seem, and has often seemed, to bear
witness, with the same irresistible sense of conviction, to the most diversified and discordant
beliefs. The response of the consciousness, which
is due only to the kernel of truth, may seem to
accredit what is but the accidental husk of form
or even the subtle admixture of error. The underlying element of truth, in other words, has come to
men under manifold forms and in combination
with much that is either irrelevant, or arbitrarily
connected with it, or even that tends to disguise
or corrupt it. A thousand influences of tradition,
education, early association, and so on, have
gathered round the arbitrary or accidental form a
reverence due only to the inner reality. It may
be that a particular theological formula or system
of doctrine or ritual or church order, has been to
many a good man, all his life long, the medium
of his religious experience, bound up with the
lessons of childhood and the teaching of revered
instructors. It has been the conventional form or

mould under which a sense of divine things has taken hold of his spirit; it has furnished the language in which he has prayed and worshipped and held communion with God. What wonder that religious feeling should blend inextricably the eternal reality with the transient form, and that faith should seem to lend the same sanction to the outward letter as to the divine spirit that operates beneath it? If therefore it cannot be assumed that our moral and spiritual intuitions, taken in the lump, are an absolute criterion of objective truth, and if the same sanction may be pleaded, and has been pleaded, for the most various and even antagonistic beliefs, it is no unimportant function that is left for reflective thought, when it claims to examine the content of the religious consciousness, to distinguish between the substance and the spurious adjuncts, between that which has a right to dominate the mind and that which derives its influence only from accident and external association.

And now, finally, what has just been said may enable us to perceive, in a general way, the function which reason and reflection have to perform in dealing with the materials supplied by religious experience. That function, in general

terms, may be said to be this—that reason trans-
lates the necessarily inadequate language in which
ordinary thought represents spiritual truth, into
that which is fitted to express its purely ideal reality.
We can see at a glance that the language in
which faith embodies its ideas of divine things,
though sufficient for its own practical needs, cannot be taken in its bare and literal form as true
or adequate to the realities it would represent.
When, for instance, the religious thought of a
primitive time applies to God anthropomorphical
or sensuous conceptions—when it speaks of Him
as having eyes to behold the righteous and ears
that are open to their cry, when it conceives of
Him as working for a certain period and then
resting from His labours, or again as enthroned
in some celestial locality or seat of power and
sending hither and thither emissaries to execute
His behests, or again as repenting of some past
action and only prevented by intercession from
destroying the work of His hand, or as being
roused to anger and wrath and appeased by gifts
and sacrifices,—we see at a glance, in these cases,
that the form is not strictly homogeneous with
the matter to be expressed, and that to get at
the truth, we must by reflection discount the

merely symbolical or analogical element in the
form in which it is expressed.

But even to the language of a purer and more
exalted spiritual experience, a measure of the same
inadequacy clings. When we apply to God and our
relations to Him the notion of human paternity, or
again when we think of Him as acting or operating
on our spirits from without, as one physical agent
on another, as exerting on them a mysterious
force, or pouring forth remedial influence into
them, or of His making them His temple or
dwelling place,—here again it needs little consideration to see that such conceptions, though
they may serve as the medium of devout thought
and feeling, yet cannot be regarded as literally
true, or adequately representative of the ideas
they seek to express. If we limit them to their
proper use—that of suggesting or calling up in
the mind spiritual ideas through pictorial, sensuous,
anthropomorphic forms, they suffice for the practical needs of the religious life. And though they
are not, and cannot be dealt with, as exact
equivalents for spiritual truth, yet in a certain
intuitive and unconscious way the spiritual mind
rises above the poverty and inadequacy of the
medium it employs, strips away from the finite

image the inapplicable and unspiritual element,—with the result, that language which, literally construed, would ascribe to God and divine things the conditions of space and time, the physical and mental limitations of human personality, becomes for the devout soul the suggestive symbol of spiritual thought and the food of the religious life.

But, on the other hand, when we attempt to identify the letter with the spirit, and to extract from these representative conceptions exact definitions and doctrines, to strain out of them every conclusion they will logically bear, they become the fertile source of misconception and error. How many, *e.g.*, of the controversies, divisions, heresies, that have marked the history of Christian thought have originated in the attempt to apply to things spiritual conceptions and categories that are applicable only to things physical? The apparently contradictory ideas and doctrines that gather round the problem of the relation between the human spirit and the divine, between grace and free will, between the all-embracing agency of God and the moral independence and activity of man, have seemed to be contradictory, just because men have tried to apply to inward and spiritual relations the categories that pertain only to material and sensible phenomena.

So long as we do so, the ideas of divine and human agency are absolutely irreconcilable, and there is no escape from contradiction save by abandoning or tampering with one or other of the elements of the problem, and landing ourselves either in a Pantheism which identifies the world with God, or in a Deistic conception of freedom which makes man independent of God. Apply the category of causality to God, and His Omnipotence becomes the Omnipotence of unlimited and irresistible force, in the presence of which all finite activity becomes an illusion and there remains no agency in the universe but one. Apply the same category to the nature and life of man, and he can be or become free only by the assertion of a force that can resist or overcome all other power, even the power of God, and secure for itself a life and activity apart from His.

It is true that the religious life is the practical solution of the problem. The experience of every devout mind is the tacit refutation of the seeming contradiction. For every such mind it is not one or other of the alternatives, " God is all in all," " Man is free and responsible," which consciousness asserts, but both. Wherever the spiritual life is deep and real, there is, on the one hand, the instinctive claim and assertion of moral freedom as a reality which no sophistry can explain away, the profound and inalienable conviction that our moral destiny is in our own hands, that there is for each of us a sphere of thought and action which no other human being, which not even Omnipotence can invade. And, on the other hand, there is the equally irresistible conviction that our spiritual life flows from a higher than finite source, rests on a thought and inspiration that transcends our own individuality. In my conscious weakness and dependence, beset by temptation, conscious of an infinite ideal which my utmost endeavours made in my own strength are baffled to reach, I can yet feel that that very ideal is the revelation in me of a power that is mightier than my own ; that the supreme command, " Thou oughtest," is the utterance, only different in form, of the same voice in my spirit which says, " Thou canst"; and that my highest spiritual attainments are achieved, not by self-assertion, but by self-renunciation and surrender to the infinite life of truth and righteousness that is living and reigning within me. It is this seeming paradox, this coincidence of the lowliest humility with the loftiest aspiration and endeavour, which is of the very essence of the spiritual life, and which finds expression in such language as this of St. Paul, "When I am weak, then am I strong," "Work out your own salvation, . . . for it is God that worketh in you," "I live, yet not I, but Christ liveth in me." He who so speaks has realized in his own experience that play and activity of seemingly conflicting tendencies by which the spiritual life maintains itself and which have found in the unity and harmony of that life their practical reconciliation.

And what faith and Christian experience thus intuitively assert, it is the highest task of philosophy to justify. Philosophy seeks to lead us to a higher point of view, from which the seeming contradictions vanish, from which reason, following in the wake of faith, grasps the great conception that the religious life is a life at once human and divine —the conception that God is a self-revealing God, that the Infinite does not annul, but realizes Himself in the finite, and that the highest revelation of God is the life of God in the soul of man ; and, on the other hand, that the finite rests on, and realizes itself in, the Infinite ; and that it is not the annihilation, but the realization of our highest freedom, in every movement of our thought, in every pulsation of our will, to be the organ and expression of the mind and will of God.

LECTURE III.

THE CHRISTIAN IDEA OF GOD.

IN the last lecture I endeavoured to point out in a general way what I conceive to be the function which reason and reflection have to perform in dealing with the materials supplied by religious experience. That function, as has been indicated, is to translate the necessarily inadequate language in which ordinary thought represents spiritual truth into that which is fitted to express its purely ideal reality. And the general reason for this inadequacy is that faith speaks, and necessarily speaks, in the language of one world, the world of sense and sight, concerning the things of another world, the world unseen and eternal. It presents the spiritual to us through images borrowed from the sensible and external, and it is only by rising above the symbolical or representative form that we can grasp the reality which they " half reveal and half conceal."

It is impossible within the limits of these lectures to prosecute further the inquiry into the relation of faith to reason, or into the proper function of philosophy in dealing with Christian truth. The principles I have imperfectly suggested will, I think, be better understood by tracing their actual application to Christian thought. I propose, therefore, in this and the following lectures to consider, from the point of view I have indicated, the leading ideas or doctrines of Christianity; and I begin to-day with the most fundamental of all these ideas, the Christian idea of God.

So far from bringing God nearer to Christian thought, the doctrine of the Trinity has very generally, even by those who accept it as an article of the orthodox faith, been relegated to the region of the mysterious or unintelligible; and there are probably few who even attempt to construe to their own minds what it is they understand by this, the distinctively Christian idea of God. The conceptions of Natural Theology, the idea of God as the Creator, Preserver, Moral Governor of the world, and of the 'Attributes' of Power, Wisdom, Goodness, and so on, with which He is invested, do not seem foreign to our intelligence, for they are based on human analogies, and even where they transcend all finite parallels, they can be represented to our minds as only an indefinite extension of human qualities. Ordinary thought, in other words, finds no impossibility in representing to itself a personality who is simply a magnified man. But whilst a God who is a being like ourselves, only indefinitely larger and greater, is not beyond our apprehension, our ordinary notions of individuality, of personal existence and identity, are altogether baffled by the idea of a Being who includes in Himself a three-fold Personality, into whose single self-consciousness is introduced a division or distinction that seems absolutely irreconcilable with individual unity. If by some easy intellectual device we contrive to think of the doctrine as not involving a direct contradiction in terms, yet the result for many minds, it is to be apprehended, is, that it is regarded as a metaphysical or theological enigma, and that, in their thought of God and their practical religious life, a deistic or unitarian conception of the object of worship is tacitly substituted for that in which they profess to believe.

Yet the attitude I have thus indicated is surely not one in which any thoughtful Christian mind should be content to rest. The doctrine of the

Trinity is undoubtedly mysterious, in the sense
that all things pertaining to the sphere of the
infinite are mysterious, and that the mind of man
can never exhaust the idea of God ; but it may
be questioned whether in treating it as an enigma
there is not, under the appearance of humility, a
culpable disregard of that light concerning the
nature of God which this doctrine contains.　The
Trinity is the distinctively Christian idea of God,
and it is scarcely conceivable that the new or
distinctively Christian element should be, not light,
but darkness, and that that by which Christian
theism is distinguished from the imperfect theistic
notions of the pre-Christian religions should be
itself only an unintelligible dogma, a burden, and
not a help to faith.

The obscurity or mysteriousness, which at first
sight is involved in the notion of a Being who
combines in His nature absolute unity with equally
essential differences or distinctions, may be shown
in a general way to arise from its very elevation
and grandeur.　Such a conception does not, as
has been supposed, imply any self-contradiction ;
on the contrary, in all but the very lowest order
of beings, and perhaps in them also, this union of
different and even opposed characteristics presents

itself to us, and it is just the highest natures in the world in which the departure from sameness or self-identity, and the combination of unity and diversity is the most strongly marked. The parts of a stone are all precisely alike, the parts of a piece of skilful mechanism are all different from each other. In which of the two cases is the unity more real?—in that in which there is an absence of distinction, or in that in which there is essential difference of form and function, each separate part having an individuality and activity of its own? In the one case the parts have no essential difference, and therefore no internal relation to each other, and their unity is merely that of juxtaposition or agglomeration; in the other case they are not merely stuck together, but they exist and act each for the rest; no one can fulfil the function of another, each is necessary to the others and to the whole which they constitute. In the former case the unity is that of blank identity or sameness; in the latter that of ideal design and end, of order, proportion, harmony, co-operation—the unity, not of dead matter, but of matter transfused and elevated by the presence of an ideal or rational element. In other words, we have here a unity which is higher and more profound, just because it is a unity which embraces, and which we are forced to think of as embracing many distinctions.

But there are higher unities than this. In the simplest form of animate life, and more palpably in a complex organism, such as the human body, there is brought before us a nature in which the unity is deeper and richer just because the difference is greater. That it is a higher and richer unity is obvious, in the first place, from this, that it is a unity which exists, not simply for you, the observer, but, in some measure at least, for the organism itself. The parts and members are not merely related to each other, but they *feel* that relation. The common life so suffuses them that each member suffers in the injury or suffering, is happy in the happiness and well-being of the rest. Moreover, they are not merely necessary to each other, but, though each has a distinctive character, they exist or maintain themselves, each by giving itself up or surrendering itself to the rest. Each member or organ maintains itself only by giving up any separate, self-identical being and life. It is for ever losing itself, only for ever to receive or find itself. Instead of ceasing to possess what it gives away, if it began to seclude itself or set up any independent identity, it would be marred or arrested. And on the other hand, the whole, the unity of the organism, has no life save in and through the life and activity of its organs; it maintains itself in communicating itself to them, and gathering back perpetually into itself the wealth of the life it gives. Finally, unlike the machine, the organism may be said to be, in a sense, its own creator. In the former, the end or purpose is in the mind of the contriver, and the unity of the mechanism is imposed on it from without, and is purely accidental to the materials of which it is composed. But in the organism there is a self-productive energy, a self-activity which works out diversities of member, form, function—differentiating itself by its own inherent spontaneity, and developing itself from the germ or embryo to the perfect, full-grown organic structure. It is not fashioned into completeness by any external force, but the idea or design, and the power to realize it, lie hid in itself from the first; it is the author, so to speak, of its own future, the potentiality of its own perfection is in it from the beginning, and it is the unity not only of all its parts and members, but of its own beginning and end, and of all the stages through which that end is reached.

And now, applying these considerations to the nature of mind or self-conscious intelligence, I think we shall find here the last and only perfect realization of the principle that the highest unity is that which combines in itself the elements of unity and difference. The principle, as we shall see, is one that is applicable to all intelligence, to mind as mind, but we may first view it as exemplified in its highest finite type, our own self-conscious being. In our earliest way of looking at things, every individual seems to be a separate, self-contained unit, having a being and life of his own, apart from all other beings, from all other individuals, and from the external world in which he lives. He may have manifold relations to his physical and social environment, but in the midst of all these he stands by himself, a separate, independent existence, a self distinct from all other selves, and which he could conceive to exist in all its reality though every other human being should cease to be.

Yet very little reflection is needed to see that mind or intelligence cannot be adequately described as a self-contained, self-complete unity. The pure abstract self-identity you ascribe to it is an illusion. The earliest dawn of conscious life, the first act by which mind or spirit becomes conscious of its

own existence is the breaking up of this trans-
parent, untroubled unity; and as it advances in
conscious experience, it becomes, so to speak, the
mirror in which the complexity and variety of the
world is reflected. Every change in its environment, every object and movement of outward
nature, every aspect and event of the social sphere
in which it lives, re-produces itself in the ever-
mobile susceptibility of mind. In its sensations,
feelings, ideas, its whole inner experience, it is
perpetually taking up into itself the play and
movement, the infinite diversity of the world.
Moreover, the seemingly indivisible self never remains for ever so brief a period the same. The
current of experience is continually changing it.
Every present affection of the self enters as a factor
into the future self; and sometimes in the course
of its history it undergoes changes which, it would
almost seem, could not be more radical if the
individual, instead of one permanent, self-identical
being, consisted of a series of beings, each at every
successive stage supplanting the former members
of the series, to be again supplanted in its turn.

It might be urged in reply to this that we can
conceive, or even that we are conscious of, a self
that runs through or underlies all change and

variety.   I can conceive of a soul, a spiritual nature, endowed with capacities of thinking, feeling, willing, prior to the *exercise* of such capacities, existing behind them all, and before the outward world has begun to disturb the pure unity of its essence ; or again, I can, nay must, conceive of my spiritual self as a substance that continues constant under all the changes of my outward or inward experience, a something I speak of as " I," " Me," which maintains itself through all the stages of life, and lies beneath or behind all passing ideas, feelings, volitions, present to them all, but identifiable with none of them.   But the answer is, that this abstract self, prior to and apart from all objective experience, is an illusion.   When you speak of mind as a unity endowed with capacities prior to and apart from the exercise of such capacities, what you are really thinking of here, is not mind or spirit, but the mere blank potentiality of mind, which slumbers in the unconsciousness of the embryo, the self which has not yet entered on the life of rationality or intelligence, and which, so far from being the essence of mind, is only that from which it must emerge in order to *be* mind. Or if you speak of the self as that absolute unity which runs through all outward and inward ex-

periences, linking them together, yet not capable
of being identified with any of them, it must be
remembered that this blank spiritual substance or
substratum of mind is a pure abstraction, a conception which, when we try to think it, slips from
our grasp, at best a half-thought which, divorced
from its complement, has no meaning or reality.
For the very essence of mind or spirit is intelligence
or self-consciousness, but self-consciousness is not
conceivable as a simple, abstract unity.   It includes
of necessity two inseparable elements, a self or
subject which thinks, and an object which is thought
of—not to speak of a third element, the unity or
oneness of these two.   You can no more conceive
of one of these elements apart from the other than
you can think of a positive without a negative,
an inside apart from an outside, a centre apart from
a circumference.   For mind or spirit to think
nothing is to *be* nothing.   When you have chased
it to its ultimate retreat, you find that it is not a
simple, self-identical unity, but that an element of
dualism or difference is involved in its very essence.

It is here, then, that we come upon that thought
of which we have been in quest—the organic unity
of spirit, mind, or intelligence, a unity which is
and realizes itself through difference.   There is a

E

sense in which it may be said of every living intelligence that it is not one but two, that there is another, a second self, in and through which alone it can know and be itself. Locked up in its abstract unity it is only a blank possibility of being ; it needs another, a world of externality, in relation to which it may find itself, realize its hidden wealth, become reclaimed from nonentity. For it is easy to see that as the whole outward world passes into knowledge, there is not only a discovery of that world to the observing mind, but a revelation of the mind to itself. Shut out from nature and man, without a world of objects in time and space, without other kindred intelligences, without society and history, without the ever-moving mirror of the objective universe, thought in us would slumber in unconsciousness. Of the ideas that are awakened in us through the media-tion of sense, of those conceptions of law, order, causation, system, which, as the revelation of reason in nature, are the realization of a kindred reason in ourselves, of those ideas of beauty which are brought to the birth in us by the objects and aspects of the material world, and of all that life of elevated thought and feeling in which imagination responds to the quickening touch of art, we should never, if isolated in our own individuality, become the conscious possessors.

And if we find ourselves in nature, still more profoundly do our social relations become to us a revelation of ourselves. Suppose a human being shut up from infancy in isolation from all other human beings, of how much would his nature be mutilated that is necessary to the very idea of humanity? One side of that nature would remain practically extinct. All that range of experiences which are possible only in the various social relations; all that is meant by such words as love, sympathy, admiration, reverence, self-devotion, patriotism, philanthropy; all that treasure of moral ideas of which we become conscious only through our relations to the family, the community, the state, would never emerge into being. To a human being thus isolated the creation of a brother spirit would be as the creation of a new soul within his breast : in the other's life his own would be reduplicated.

Finally, this principle is true, not only of the intellectual, but also of the moral life. It is only in relation to a world of external beings who are subjects like himself that a moral life becomes possible for man. For morality, or the moral life, may be described as the renunciation of the immediate, private, exclusive self, and the identification of my being with an ever-widening sphere of existence beyond me. The social environment in which I live, the corporate unity of the family, the civil and political organizations and institutions of the community or state, constitute a moral order external to me, but so related to me that apart from it my life as a moral being would be as impossible as the independent life of a severed branch or an amputated limb. What love, friendship, paternal, filial, fraternal affection mean, is that I have emerged from the void and narrow life of immediate, self-centred individuality, that my latent, sympathetic capacities have been liberated, and that another and larger life has begun to flow into mine. There is here a giving up or surrender of self which is yet, not the impoverishment, but the enriching of self. So, again, what benevolence, justice, patriotism, courage, self-devotion mean is simply this, that the private, personal self has expanded into a still wider and larger personality, that the pulse of its life has begun to beat with the play and movement of a richer, subtler organic life, and that the spiritual self has reached a yet fuller and higher stage of its evolution. Lastly, the escape from the individual self, the capacity of a universal life, finds its highest realization when the life of the individual is identified with the progressive life of the race. In the few nobler spirits to whom the brotherhood of humanity is more than a barren sentiment, in whom the love of kindred and country has expanded into an affection yet more comprehensive, and who have found it possible to identify their happiness with the welfare, the progress, the higher destiny of mankind—in these the nature of man has touched the supreme height of moral elevation, a point that can only be transcended when self-surrender passes beyond all finite limits into identification with a life that is infinite and eternal.

And now it remains for us to apply the principle we have attempted to explain to the subject before us, the Christian idea of God. That principle obviously is one that is applicable not merely to human intelligence but to all intelligence. It enters into the very idea and essence of spirit as spirit, and therefore into the essence of the nature of God. To conceive of God as an abstract, self-identical infinite would be to make Him, not greater, but less than man—to leave out from His nature elements of spiritual perfection and blessedness which finite natures contain. If we are to ascribe to God an intellectual and moral nature, if we are to think of knowledge, goodness, holiness as essential elements of His being, if we are not to deny to Him the perfection and blessedness which are expressed by the words love, self-surrender, self-sacrifice—then can this result only be reached by that conception which is expressed in the Christian doctrine of the Logos or Son of God—the conception of a self-revealing principle or personality within the very essence of the Godhead.

The simplest way in which we can make this thought clear to ourselves is by considering that, regarded as a mere solitary, self-identical infinite, the nature of God would be a stranger to that which is the highest element of a spiritual nature—the element of Love. Without life in the life of others, as we have seen, a spiritual being would not be truly spirit. To go forth out of self, to have the hidden wealth of thought, feeling, action called forth in relation to other and kindred beings, and to receive that wealth back again redoubled in reciprocated knowledge and affection—this is to live a spiritual life; not to do this is to take from our lives all that makes them spiritual.

But all this we leave out of our idea of God if we conceive of Him as an isolated, self-identical infinite, complete and self-contained in the abstract unity of His own being.

It is true, as I have already said with reference to our own nature, that we can separate in thought the *capacity* of love or of any other spiritual quality from the actual manifestation of it ; and as we can think of God as possessed of creative power anterior to the exercise of it, so we can think of Him prior to the existence of all other spiritual beings, as having in Himself infinite capacities of goodness, love, compassion, of all those elements of spiritual excellence which are only revealed or become actual in His relations to the world. But what has been said of the finite is equally true of the infinite nature, viz., that an unrealized capacity is something different from, and less than, one which has become an actual, conscious, manifested reality. All the future plant is, in a sense, present in the germ, all the rich content of the cultured intelligence slumbers in the nature of the infant or the embryo ; but the full-grown plant is something more and higher than the seed or germ, and the mind that has awakened to self-consciousness through the mediation of nature and human life, is something more and higher than the same mind whilst it is as yet only the blank possibility of intelligence. Nay, we may go further and say that, inasmuch as it is of the very essence of intelligence to be conscious of itself, and as that which has not entered into my thought is that which for me does not as yet really exist, so it is only that in me which has passed out of possibility into actual self-conscious thought that can be said to be reclaimed from nothingness. And this is a principle which holds good of all intelligence, divine as well as human. If therefore we say that in the self-contained solitude of the divine nature, apart from any actual relation to what is in a manner other than Himself, we can still think of all the treasures of wisdom and goodness as hid from all eternity in the secrecy of His being, the answer is that this solitary, self-sufficient God would be only a potential God. To *be* God, His knowledge must be eternally adequate to His being, He must for ever realize Himself in all the infinite riches of His nature. And this implies that there must be something to call forth that wealth, something to be known and loved by God, in order that knowledge and love may truly exist in God.

Can we think, then, of this finite world as constituting for infinite as for finite intelligence the medium of its self-realization? Have we here that second self of infinitude, in the knowledge and love of which the riches of the divine nature, its boundless capacities, are unfolded? There is a sense in which this is true—God reveals Himself to Himself in nature and in the finite spirits He has made in His own image. The capacity of love in the heart of God may be said to find a new channel for its outflow in every human soul; and in the responsive love which that love awakens there is something which we can think of as adding a new sweetness and joy to the very blessedness of the Infinite. Nay, seeing that love reaches, and can only reach, its highest expression, in suffering and sacrifice, and that the richest purest blessedness is that which comes through pain and sorrow, can it be wrong to ascribe to God a capacity of self-sacrifice, a giving up of Himself, a going forth of His own being for the redemption of the world from sin and sorrow?

Yet, apart from other considerations into which I cannot here enter, we cannot conceive of nature and man, of the finite world, as the adequate medium for the self-consciousness, the self-revealing

knowledge and love of God. That which is finite
can never exhaustively express or reveal that which
is infinite ; that which exists in time can by no
indefinite prolongation of its life represent or reflect that which is not in time but is eternally
perfect and complete. Even an original finite
intelligence, a great human author or artist, is
ever greater than his works ; and to the end, the
noblest productions of his genius leave within him,
a world of ideas unexpressed, a fountain of thought
unexhausted and inexhaustible. So, even the
glory and splendour of nature is but the limited
manifestation in space and time of an infinite
beauty " which eye hath not seen nor ear heard,
neither hath it entered into the heart of man to
conceive," and which can never fully reveal itself in
the mirror of the material creation. And though it
is true that there is what may be termed an
infinite element in the nature of man, the infinitude
of human intelligence is that, not of a nature that is
without limit, but of a nature that is ever finding
itself in that which limits it, ever advancing towards
an ideal which it can never exhaustively realize.
All of knowledge and goodness therefore, that has
ever been attained, or that is attainable, by the
individual or by the race can be only a partial

and imperfect mirror of an intelligence and goodness which are limited only by themselves.

Moreover, if the finite world were the only
medium of the divine self-revelation, it would follow
that the nature of God is a progressive one, and
that we can think of a past time when He was less,
of a future when He will be more and greater than
now. Not only must we think of a time anterior
to the existence of the world when God was a
solitary God, a being existing in the isolation of
a still unmediated self-identity, and when therefore
He was less perfect, less blessed than now ; but
seeing that the world has a history, that its intellectual and moral life is a progressive one, and
that to the end of time there will be ever new
objects calling forth new manifestations of the self-
communicating love and grace of God—from all
this it seems to follow that the nature and life of
God must be an ever-growing one, and that, as
for the finite, so also for the infinite nature, absolute
perfection is a goal that can never be reached.

It is this difficulty which finds its solution in
the Christian idea of God. If God be not merely
the Spirit of the World, growing with its growth
and partaking of its incompleteness, we must think
of all that unfolds itself progressively in the history

of the world, of all possibilities of truth, goodness, beauty, which are disclosed in time, as already comprehended in the eternal self-revelation of God. In the New Testament Scriptures there are several remarkable passages which bring before us the idea of an anticipation of the history of the world, " as it were under the form of eternity " ; or, in other words, which represent the course of the actual world as only the temporal manifestation of what has existed ideally and eternally in the mind and purpose of God. St. Paul speaks of the spiritual destinies of the Church, not as the accidents of time, but as the revelation of a " purpose and grace which was given as in Christ Jesus before the world began." Moreover, according to his view, the Christian redemption is not a device struck out to meet the spiritual exigencies of a fallen world, nor is the life of Christ a wholly new and unanticipated revelation of God. In his later Epistles and in the Logos doctrine of the fourth Gospel, the idea is brought before us of a Being or Personality transcending the limits of time, in immanent, indivisible relation to the very being of God, the mirror or image of the invisible thought and life of the Infinite. The language of religion indeed, and of the New Testament, as of other religious writings, is not that of scientific or speculative thought, but of ideas couched in analogical or figurative form. But when they speak of a Being who is " the image of the invisible God," of an eternal Logos or Word who was " in the beginning with God," and who " was God"; of a Divine " head of the body, the Church," " in whom dwelleth all the fulness of the Godhead bodily," in whom " are hid all the treasures of wisdom and knowledge"; of an " only-begotten Son," who was before all worlds " in the bosom of the Father"—our foregoing reflections may perhaps enable us to apprehend the principle which underlies these and other representations of things divine under forms and figures derived from things earthly and finite. We have spoken, for instance, of the world as the objective medium of self-consciousness, in and through which we become aware of the hidden wealth of our own thought and life. In the process of knowledge, slowly and gradually the world, so to speak, passes over into thought, and we spell out from step to step at once *its* meaning and the meaning of ourselves. But could we conceive of the whole realm of intelligence as gathered up or condensed into a single personality, and of a mind so enlarged or expanded as to be capable of grasping its significance, we should have before us perhaps what the New Testament writer seeks to express by the conception of an "image of the invisible God," the living mirror "of all things created, that are in heaven and that are in earth, visible and invisible."

In the purest and most elevated earthly natures, again, that suppression of a mere abstract individuality, that identification of two personalities in a deeper, richer unity, which is the true interpretation of love, is an ideal at best only imperfectly realized by us.   Self-surrender, self-sacrifice, even in the noblest natures, never achieves an absolute victory over self-regarding impulse.   But when the sacred writer speaks of an Eternal Son, "only begotten of the Father," who loved him "before the foundation of the world," who participated in the glory of the Father "before the world was"—they lead us, under the form of human relationships, to rise in thought to relations that are beyond the limits of time.   They suggest to us the thought of an eternal past as the scene of the movements of an ineffable and boundless love, of an absolute reciprocity of thought and feeling in the life of the Eternal, of Infinitude yielding itself to Infinitude, of God as knowing and being known, loving and being loved by God.   And perhaps in these images of things divine, we may discern the expression, under human analogies, of that principle of unity in difference, of that oneness of elements, distinguishable but indivisible, which we have seen to be the very essence of all intelligence, human or divine.

We cannot, however, fully develop the meaning of the Christian idea of God, as a self-revealing Spirit, until we have considered, as we shall proceed to do in the next lecture, the relation of God to the world.

LECTURE IV.

THE RELATION OF GOD TO THE WORLD.

1. THE PANTHEISTIC VIEW.

WE have seen that the highest unities are not simple but complex, that is, unities in which an element of difference is contained, and that the unity of God does not exclude, but necessarily involves, the existence of distinctions within the very essence of the divine nature. But the problem would seem to be a more difficult, if not insoluble one, when we are called to reconcile in thought the idea of an infinite, all-comprehending Being with that of a finite world outside of Him to which any real existence can be ascribed. Can we think of God as infinite and absolute without swamping the reality of nature and the individuality and independence of man; or of nature and man as possessing any reality and independence without tampering with the absoluteness and infinitude of God? Do we not seem to be driven by an inevitable necessity of thought to reject one or other of the two alternatives, and to refuse our assent to any theory or doctrine which, whilst accepting both, leaves them in hard, unsolved opposition to each other? On the one hand, does not the very idea of God preclude the existence of any other being than His own—of any object in the universe that has a nature which is not one with the divine essence, of any event or action that is not the immediate expression of the divine will? If without a contradiction in terms we cannot conceive of an infinite will and power calling into existence a world that becomes a limit to its own infinitude, are we not forced to explain away the seeming reality we ascribe to nature, and the moral life and freedom of which we seem to be conscious in ourselves? If we think of God as the one originating source, the sustaining energy, the final cause or end of all things, must not the apparent individual existence of material things, each of which seems to the ordinary eye to have a nature of its own, and must not the play and movement of the vast material system in which every object, from the minutest atom to the mightiest orb in space, has its own place and function, and is the

F

centre of an activity and energy that belongs
to no other,—must not this aspect which the
world presents to our ordinary apprehension be
regarded as an illusion which deeper reflection
would dissipate? And for the same reason, must
not that consciousness of an individual intellectual
and moral life, that sense of freedom and self-
identity which sets each human spirit apart from
every other being in the universe, be after all only
a dream of our imagination? And if we could penetrate to the true source of human action, would
we not be compelled to regard ourselves, with all
our fancied freedom, as only puppets of an infinite
will, and our very existence as the insubstantial
evanescent accident of the one infinite substance?

On the other hand, if we fall back on our own
immediate consciousness, on that conviction of the
reality of ourselves and the world in which we live,
which seems to be clearer and stronger for us than
any theory as to the origin of the universe, how shall
we retain without modification our faith in the
absolute and infinite nature of God? If, in other
words, we abide by what to the ordinary consciousness is the inalienable conviction of the reality of the
outward world, and by what to beings capable of
a moral life is the still more indestructible sense of

freedom, of being masters of themselves and makers of their own character and destiny, are we not constrained to have recourse to some conception of the relation of the infinite and finite, the divine and human, which, in claiming for man an independent spiritual nature and a sphere of moral activity that not even Omnipotence can invade, necessarily imposes a limit on the absoluteness and infinitude of God?

In the history of human thought we shall find that the alternatives I have thus stated are those to one or other of which the mind of man has often turned in its attempt to deal with the problem of the relation of God to the world. The first and simplest solution of that problem is *Pantheism*, the theory which so emphasizes the infinitude and absoluteness of the divine nature as to reduce the world to an illusory appearance or semblance of reality, and virtually to annul the freedom and moral life of man. Again, in the recoil from this pantheistic exaggeration of unity, human thought has often betaken itself to the opposite exaggeration of difference which is in-volved in the *Deistic* or dualistic attitude of mind, —a view which so emphasizes the reality and independence of the world as to reduce God to

an anthropomorphic personality, a Creator or Contriver conceived after the analogy of a human
artist, or a Moral Governor, after that of an earthly
ruler or law-giver.

Finally, there is yet one other conception in
which, as I believe, lies the only complete and
satisfactory solution of the problem. In *Christianity* and the Christian idea of God, we reach
a conception which embraces and does full justice
to the elements both of unity and difference, a
principle in the light of which the opposition of
Infinite and Finite is seen to be no longer an
absolute one. In the idea, in other words, of God
as infinite Self-consciousness or Self-revealing Spirit,
we attain to the conception of an Infinite Being
who neither limits nor is limited by the finite
world, but reveals or realizes Himself therein ; and,
on the other hand, of a finite world which is
neither absorbed in, nor irreconcilably opposed to,
the Infinite, but finds its reality and perfection
only in union with the being and life of God.
For, as I shall attempt to show, it is of the very
essence of mind or spirit that it contains in it the
necessity of self-manifestation in objective form, and
therefore that which we speak of as " the creation
of the world " must be conceived as the expression

not of arbitrary will, but of the very nature and being of God. Yet, on the other hand, whilst infinite mind or spirit implies a world of objects, in one sense external to and other than itself, it is also of its very nature that it should not be limited, but, so to speak, expanded and enriched by their existence. Finally, it is involved in the idea of Infinite Intelligence that whilst it comprehends and subordinates to itself all finite things and beings, it yet does not suppress or tamper with their individuality and independence, but is rather the very source and principle of it ; and therefore the infinitude of God, so conceived, is not only not inconsistent with, but is the very spring and secret of the life of nature, and of the moral and spiritual life of man.

Following out the train of thought I have thus indicated, I shall, in the present and following lectures, ask your attention to a brief examination (1) of the *Pantheistic*, (2) of the *Deistic* or *Dualistic* and (3) of the *Christian* view of the relation of God to the world.

"*Pantheism*" is one of those terms to which, though of familiar use, vague and often contradictory meanings are attached. Perhaps, what it generally stands for in popular thought is the notion or doctrine which identifies God with the world. According to this view, all things and beings are parts of the divine nature, all events and actions expressions of the divine activity. The forces of nature, the movements of the human spirit, the incidents of each individual life, the history of nations and of the human race, all thinking things, all objects of all thought, are immediate manifestations of the being and life of God. We do not need to rise above the finite world to find God, or to discern in nature and man proofs of the divine existence ; for nature and man are themselves divine. Pantheism, so understood, is simply the deification of the finite world. But it needs little reflection to see that this identification of the Infinite with the finite is an irrational and impossible notion, and that apart from the self-contradiction it involves, it is a notion devoid of any religious significance. It is of the very essence of religion, even in its most elementary form, that it involves the elevation of the human spirit above the world, an aspiration at least after something beyond the visible and temporal, deeper and higher than the immediate objects of sense and sight. Even the stock or stone before which the most ignorant idolater bows is to him something more than a stock or stone. There would arise in his breast no feeling of fear or awe or absolute dependence, if he saw in it nothing more than a piece of matter he can touch and handle, if it did not awaken in him some dim conception of that which the eye cannot see or the hand grasp,—an immaterial presence of which the material object is only the sign or symbol.

When we inquire into the real significance of Pantheism as a phase in the religious history of the world, we find that it is not only something different from, but the very opposite of, this deification of the world. It means, not the divinity, but rather the nothingness and insubstantiality of the things that are seen and temporal. One of the first manifestations of religious feeling, one of the earliest evidences of the religious consciousness in man is the awaking sense of the evanescence, the mutability, the lack of permanent reality, which seems to be the universal characteristic of earthly and finite things. It is a much later stage of thought when, in the manner of the modern natural theology argument, it attempts to rise from the existence of the world to the notion of a First Cause or of an all-wise and powerful Creator. It is not what the world is, but what it is not, that first sets the mind on feeling after, " if haply it may find," a reality above and beyond it. " The world passeth away and the lust thereof" ; "the things that are seen are temporal" ; "what is your life? it is even but a vapour that appeareth for a little and then vanisheth away": such words as these express a feeling coincident with the very dawn of reflection, the feeling which is called forth by the fleeting, shifting character of the scene on which we look, by the brevity and uncertainty of life, the unsatisfying and disappointing nature of its pleasures, the lack of any permanent object which our thought can grasp and on which our hearts can rest—the feeling, in short, which the insubstantiality of the world and the things of the world awakens in the mind. It is out of this sense of the vanity and unreality of finite things that a pantheistic conception of God naturally develops itself.

For it is not so much by the affirmation, but by the negation, of the finite that the idea of the infinite first reveals itself in the human spirit.[1] The so-called cosmological argument, to which I have referred, attempts to find in the existence of the finite world the proof of the existence of an

---

[1] Cf. *Introduction to the Philosophy of Religion*, chap. v.

infinite being as its cause. But neither as a logical demonstration nor as an account of human experience is this argument tenable. It starts from the assumed reality of the finite world as finite, and infers from it the reality of an infinite cause or creator. But an infinite confronted by a finite to which equal reality is ascribed—an infinite with a finite world outside of it—is a contradiction in terms. On the other hand, it is not by starting from the finite as real, but rather by the undermining of its reality as finite, that the mind rises to the conception of an Infinite to which alone reality can be ascribed. And what this means is, not simply that in the consciousness of our weakness we feel the need of some higher power to support us,—the longing for some permanent object of trust, some "life continuous, being unexposed to the blind shock of mortal accident." It means rather that the sense of the unreality of the finite is itself the implicit recognition of the existence of such a Being. The knowledge of God as a conscious object of thought may be a later step in the spiritual experience, but what is second in time is really, though implicitly, first in thought. The discovery of a limit is the proof that the discoverer has already transcended it. The mind's discernment of the finite as finite is due to the presence of the Infinite within it ; the power of the eternal betrays itself in the very capacity to recognize the evanescence of the things seen and temporal ; it is the rock on which, though we know it not, our feet are resting, that enables us to perceive the flux of the rushing stream which is bearing all finite things away. The idea of God as the only reality is thus the *prius* or presupposition that expresses itself in the sense of the transiency and unreality of the world. The impression that comes first in time may be that the world is nothing, but that impression would have no existence or meaning if really, though latently, the first principle of Pantheism were not this, ' God is all.'

The conception of the relation of God to the world which I have thus endeavoured to trace is (1) that which finds its practical expression in pantheistic religions such as Brahmanism and, in one point of view, Buddhism ; and (2) that to which pantheistic systems of philosophy seek to give speculative justification. Of the latter, it is in the philosophy of Spinoza that Pantheism may be said to have found its most developed and systematic speculative expression.

With respect to the former, the practical expression of Pantheism in religion, and especially in the religions of India—it would detain us too long from the general argument to attempt anything of the nature of a detailed examination of these religions. I will offer only a few brief remarks in so far as they illustrate the foregoing view of the essential nature of Pantheism. Brahmanism was, from one point of view, a natural development of the primitive Indian religion which is represented by the sacred hymns of the Veda. At first sight this religion, so far from being pantheistic, seems to be simply a polytheistic nature-worship, the worship, that is, of a number of distinct divinities identified with various natural objects, such as the sun, the dawn, the daily and nightly firmament, the fertile earth, rivers and streams, winds and storms. The Rig-Veda is a collection of hymns, invocations, prayers, songs of praise, addressed to various individual devas or divinities—Indra, Mitra, Varuna, Agni, etc., who seem at first sight to be personifications or deifications of the phenomena and forces of nature. It would appear, therefore, that in so far as this religion represents the dawn of man's religious life, the origin of religion is to be found, not in Pantheism, but in a polytheistic nature-worship.

But when we look a little more closely into the matter, we find reason to regard the polytheism of the Veda as only the superficial aspect or veil of another and different conception of God —a conception which gradually revealed its real significance as it dropped more and more the polytheistic form and developed into the undisguised Pantheism of Brahmanism. Careful students of the Vedic hymns have found in them many indications that the various individual divinities are separated by no hard and fast distinctions from each other, and that they are in reality only different names for one indivisible whole, of which the particular divinity invoked at any one time is regarded as the type or representative. In the minds of the writers of these hymns we can detect the latent recognition of a unity beneath all the multiplicity of the objects of adoration—an invisible reality which is neither the heavens nor the earth, nor the sunshine, nor the storm, which cannot be fully represented by any one material object or aspect of nature, though each for the moment may serve as its symbol or exponent. In the Vedic divinities not only is the personal or anthropomorphic element never emphasized, as it is in Greek and Roman mythology, so that the personality ascribed to

Mitra, or Varuna, or Indra, or Agni, is scarcely more real than in the thinly veiled metaphors in which modern poetic language speaks of the smiling heavens, or the whispering breeze, or the sullen, moaning, restless sea ; but the language in which these various divinities are addressed shows that they flow into each other, and are only varied expressions, from different points of view, for the grander and wider presence of mighty nature—a presence which clothes itself in innumerable guises, but which, however varied, whether soft and gentle, or wild and wrathful, whether it delights or over-awes or terrifies, is still one and the same. Nay, we find, especially towards the close of the Vedic period, this instinctive sense of a unity that lies behind and comprehends all individual diversities, finding direct expression in various passages of the Veda. "There is but one," says one of the writers, "though the poets call him by many names." "They call him Indra, Mitra, Varuna, Agni ; then he is the beautiful winged Garutmut. That which is and is one, the wise name in diverse manners."

The pantheistic attitude of mind does not here fully formulate itself into a developed and conscious religious belief. The consciousness of weakness and evanescence, and the aspiration after some higher and abiding rest for the soul, in which we have said pantheistic religion takes its rise, betrays itself here only in a ruder and more elementary form. The mind of the worshipper indicates that which, in the consciousness of its weakness and dependence, it is groping after, by the deification of whatever objects in the outward world can become to it the types of stability and power. It fastens on anything in its surroundings by which it can represent to itself that abiding reality of which it is in quest. The sun that shines on in majestic strength and calmness, far above the capricious, changeful phenomena of the lower world, undimmed and undecaying through revolving years and ages ; the silent stars that pursue their mystic course, never hasting, never resting, shedding their pure light on the graves of a hundred generations; the solid and stable earth, the everlasting hills, the great rivers that flow on in seemingly exhaustless continuity while one generation after another comes and goes ; above all, that in nature which has for the simple observer the aspect of at least a relative infinitude, the all-embracing heaven which, go where he may, is ever above and around him, expanding as he advances, impenetrable in its liquid depths, and, amidst the instability and evanescence of human life, retaining the aspect of ever-during permanence, and pouring down, age after age, with no sign of impoverishment, its wealth and bounty on the world—in the half-conscious deification of these objects and of that mighty nature of which each of them for the moment is the vivid type and manifestation, the obscure and indeterminate longing for an infinite and eternal object of trust is expressed.

But the pantheistic element which was only implicit in the Vedic phase of Indian religion becomes explicit in Brahmanism, and in particular in the so-called Indian systems of philosophy and in the great Indian epic poems. The same inward movement which led to the breaking down of the limits of the particular divinities impelled the mind to a still further advance. The religious consciousness, dissatisfied with the effort to reach God by the mediation either of the grander objects of nature, or of nature in its totality, now attempts to pass beyond or beneath nature and all natural phenomena, and to grasp the idea of an invisible essence or substance of nature, lying beneath or behind all finite and sensible things. The conception of God which dominates the whole course of Brahmanic thought is that by which, at a certain stage of culture, the mind seeks to represent to itself the unity that underlies all the diversities of the world—the conception of a hidden substance beneath all the ever-changing appearances and accidents of things.

When we speak of any object, a plant, an animal, a human being, which has many different qualities or aspects, or which is undergoing perpetual phenomenal changes, as one identical thing or being, what is it that constitutes its oneness, its permanent reality? This flower or tree has a real existence, is one individual thing, though the qualities of form, colour, fragrance, and so on, by which I perceive it are many and various. It was the same plant yesterday as it is to-day, as it will be to-morrow and all its life long, though outwardly the matter that composes it and the appearances it assumes are never, two days or hours, precisely the same. When I say, *it* exists, *it* is one individual thing, *it* is the same plant which I saw a month ago, what is the "it" of which we speak? Not certainly what we perceive by the senses, for that is not one and the same, but many and various; not the outward material form, for that is perpetually changing, is not indeed for two successive moments the same. And the answer to which, at an early stage, thought, groping after the solution of the problem of the one in the many, half-consciously betakes itself, is that, beneath and behind all the varying qualities, forms, aspects of the plant, there is an unknown, invisible substance, a hidden something that remains constant amidst all changes, accidents, vanishing appearances, and that *that* is the true and permanent reality of the thing.

Now this, though only imperfectly formulated, is the conception in which Brahmanic thought seemed to itself to have found the key to the riddle of the universe. In the contemplation of the endlessly diversified, ever shifting forms of things, in the consciousness of the instability and evanescence of human life and of all its possessions and enjoyments, the Indian said : These are but the surface appearances, the insubstantial accidents ; beneath them all there is one and only one reality, one Being that is and never changes, and that is Brahma. These ancient thinkers did not reason, indeed, after the manner of the modern metaphysician. They were at the stage when the mind can only think in metaphors, and even in their so-called philosophical systems, their deepest reflections are embodied in sensuous figures and

images. But when they represent the supreme
God as declaring, " I am the light in the sun and
moon, I am the brilliancy in flame, the radiance in
all shining things, the light in all lights, the sound
in air, the fragrance in earth, the eternal seed of
all things that exist, the life in all ; I am the
goodness of the good, I am the beginning, middle,
end, the eternal in time, the birth and death
of all " ;—when, again, they represent the visible
material world and the life and actions of man as
the illusory phantoms and appearances which a
conjuror or magician calls up and the gaping
crowd mistake for realities, or as the personages,
scenes, events, of a troubled dream ;—when they
say that " our life is as a drop that trembles on
the lotos-leaf, fleeting and quickly gone," and that
such, so evanescent and unsubstantial are the
things that seem to be most real, " the eight great
mountains, the seven seas, the sun, the very gods who
are said to rule over them, thou too, I, the whole
universe which all conquering time shall dispel,"—
when, finally, they declare that, " A wise man must
annihilate all objects of sense and contemplate
continually only the One Existence, Brahma, that
is without dimensions, quality, character, distinction " ;—in these and many other modes of expres-

sion Indian thought is only ringing the changes on the one fundamental doctrine of its creed that God is the only reality, the substance of all things, the only Being who really is, and that the apparent reality of all other things and beings is only phantasmal and illusory.

And now let us turn for a moment to the philosophic justification of Pantheism, and especially to that modern system of philosophy in which Pantheism may be said to have found its most elaborate speculative expression—the philosophy of Spinoza.

It would be beside our purpose to attempt here anything of the nature of a critical exposition of the Spinozistic system, but a glance at its leading principles will, I think, serve to confirm the view I have given of the genesis and meaning of Pantheism. Spinoza's philosophy took its rise,[1] not primarily from the search for intellectual satisfaction, but from the endeavour to escape from the unrest and dissatisfaction which the ordinary desires and passions engender, and to find some object in union with which the soul would attain to a perfect and abiding rest—a rest such as could not be found in the ordinary objects of human desire. All such objects

[1] Cf. *Spinoza* (in Blackwood's " Philosophical Series "), p. 8.

as wealth, honour, the pleasures of appetite and sense, experience proved to be illusory and deceptive, filling the soul with vain hopes, and in the very moment of attainment vanishing from the hand that seemed to grasp them.

As he reflected on this universal experience, the great thought dawned on the mind of Spinoza that the secret of human unrest and unhappiness lies ultimately in this, that the whole point of view of ordinary intelligence is a false one, that it does not see things as they really are, and that looked at from a new and different point of view, the whole aspect of the world would be revolutionized. We are unhappy because the things on which we lavish our affections have literally no reality. The senses and the imagination practise upon us a fatal deception, under the influence of which we give a fictitious existence to nonentities, mistake fugitive forms and appearances for solid realities. The sure and only way to attain the end we seek is to expose and subvert the false view of the world, and to substitute for it the higher view of reason, which penetrates beneath the superficial shows of things to their real essence ; or, in his well-known phrase, to look at all things, no longer under the mask of time and sense, but "under the form of eternity." To this end he points out that the great and demonstrable defect of our ordinary view of the world is, that it gives to finite things and beings an individuality and independence which do not really belong to them. Common thought is the slave of imagination in this respect, that because it can *picture* to itself a world of separate individual existences, it supposes them to *be* really separate and individual. We can divide or set off by arbitrary lines bits of space from the rest, but the division is a purely fictitious one. No one part of space is an independent entity ; the periphery which carves out of space a square or circle is a thing of imagination, the portion within is not a really separate existence ; remove the imaginary boundary and it becomes one with the circumambient extension to which it really belongs. In like manner, looking on the innumerable and manifold objects in nature, we confound externality in space with independent existence, and represent to ourselves stones, plants, animals, etc., as possessed each of its own isolated, independent individuality.

But when we look at things with the eye of reason, the independent substantiality vanishes, and we begin to discover that each object is what it is only in virtue of its relations to other objects. Each object is only a link in an infinite series of causes

and effects ; its place, form, functions, activities, are
what they are, not merely through itself, but through
its connections with other objects and ultimately
with the whole universe of being.   Not an atom of
matter, not a single material substance can be
accounted for without taking into view, not only
its immediate environment, but the causes or conditions that have created that environment, and the
causes or conditions of these causes and conditions,
and so on *ad infinitum*.   And the same principle
applies to ideas as well as to corporeal substances,
to the world of mind as well as of matter.   By
a trick of the imagination we can look on ourselves as individual, self-determined beings, we
can ascribe to ourselves an imaginary freedom by
isolating our thoughts and actions from the motives
that create them, we can segregate in fancy our souls
as well as our bodies from other spiritual beings
and from the whole world of intelligence ; but,
apart from our relations to others, our individual
spiritual life is nothing but a mere blank potentiality.   Rightly viewed, each so-called individual,
with his whole life and the whole compass of its
thoughts and actions, is only a transition-point in a
process of thought which stretches back through
the interminable past, outward through the whole

totality of intelligent being, and onward through the illimitable future.

But if thus we cannot find reality, substantiality, self-determined, independent existence in individual things and beings, where is it to be found? The answer of Spinoza virtually is, that it is to be found only in God, that in all the universe there is no reality save in Him. Rise above the illusions of sense and imagination, sweep away the fictitious limitations which lend to finite things a semblance of reality, and you will discern beneath and beyond them the universal, unlimited reality in which their true essence lies. All determination is only negation; it indicates "nothing positive," not what things are, but what they are not, not real being, but privation or want of being. The real essence of every particular thing or thought is not in itself, viewed as a definite object in time and place. Nor is it even in its innumerable relations to other objects and to the whole collective totality of finite existences; but it is in the Infinite Extension or Infinite Thought from which it and they are only arbitrarily differentiated. Even this last and highest distinction of Thought and Extension, Mind and Matter, seems to be a distinction which exists only for finite intelligence ; it rests upon and presupposes a unity which lies beyond all difference, which is the *prius* and presupposition of all thoughts and things, the unity of that Infinite Substance which we designate God. In this lies the true essence of all things. " Every idea of every particular thing necessarily involves the eternal and infinite essence of God," of which all particular things are only vanishing modes or modifications. To reach the last secret of the universe, the true nature and essence of all beings, material and spiritual, we must cease to look on them from the point of view of time, we must rise to the point of view from which all temporal and special limits have vanished away, and in which all things are contemplated " under the form of eternity."[1]

From what has now been said we may perhaps be able to understand at once the strength and the weakness of Pantheism, the intellectual and moral aspirations from which it derives its plausibility and attractiveness, and its failure to fulfil them.

The great and fundamental defect of Pantheism is, that in the effort after unity it expunges

----

[1] In Principal Caird's book on *Spinoza* there is a fuller and more adequate account of the Spinozistic argument, and also of other elements in Spinoza's philosophy which modify its pantheistic results.

instead of explaining the existence of the finite world ; in other words, that it gives us an Infinite which obliterates, instead of comprehending and accounting for, the finite. It is true that in one sense all philosophy is pantheistic. It rests on the presupposition that there is in the universe no absolute or irreconcilable division, no breach of continuity, no element which, in its hard, irredeemable independence, is incapable of being embraced in the intelligible system of things. Every philosophic system that is not dualistic, and for which the terms Infinite and Finite have any real meaning, is pantheistic in this sense, that the ultimate explanation of all things is to be found in God, and that there is nothing in all the universe which has any independence or individuality that cannot be brought back into harmony with His being. Without rending the universe and placing beside or outside of God a finite world which limits Him, whatever reality or independence we ascribe to nature and man, it must not be pressed beyond the point at which it is consistent with their essential relation to God.

But, on the other hand, a philosophy which extinguishes the finite or merges it in God is

equally defective with a philosophy which gives it
an exaggerated independence. Even if we say
with Spinoza that it is only imagination which
lends to the things seen and temporal a semblance
of reality, that the existence of finite things is an
illusion, we must still seek in the idea of God a
reason at least for their illusory existence. To
say that the finite is the negation of the infinite
implies that there is in the infinite at least a
negative relation to the finite. Though we have
reduced the world to a mere appearance or accident, yet as appearance or accident it still needs
to be accounted for. If we are such stuff as
dreams are made of, yet our dreams presuppose
a wakeful world, and their fleeting vagaries have
their explanation in it. But more than that, what
is to be accounted for is, not merely the illusion,
but the mind that discerns or takes cognizance
of it. The mind which perceives and pronounces
on the nothingness of the finite world cannot
itself be wholly identified with that world. In
ascribing to human intelligence the function of
abolishing the false reality, we virtually exempt
intelligence itself from the process of abolition.

It is obvious, however, that the God of Pantheism is a conception from which no explanation

of the existence of the finite world, even as finite and contingent, can be derived. The Infinite Substance of Spinoza is a gulf into which all things are absorbed and from which nothing returns. The regressive movement, as we have seen, by which he reaches it, is simply the removal of the limits by which sense and imagination give a fictitious reality to finite things. To get at the reality, what we have to do is simply to withdraw these limits, and then the arbitrary creations fall back into the Infinite. But the Infinite we thus reach by the annulling of all determinate thought and being, is simply the absolutely indeterminate, the logical abstraction of the unconditioned. It is not the reason of the diversified existences of the world, but the unity that is got by abstracting from them. And as all differences vanish in it, so none can proceed from or be predicated of it. As there is no reason in the conception of pure space why any figures or forms, lines, surfaces, solids, should arise in it, so there is no reason in the pure colourless abstraction of Infinite Substance why any world of finite things and beings should ever come into existence. It is the grave of all things, the productive source of nothing. When we have arrived at it what we reach is not the living, creative origin of all thought and life, but the unfathomable gulf where all is still.

From this point of view we can see what it is in Pantheism that belies the hopes and aspirations which, at first sight, it seems to meet. The motive of Spinoza's speculations was, as we have seen, the aspiration after an infinite and eternal object, in self-surrender to which his spirit could find a rest which no finite object could give, in union with which, so to speak, it could unclothe itself of its own weakness, and be clothed upon with the absolute strength ; and undoubtedly this is an element which enters into the very essence of the spiritual life. But whilst Pantheism seems to meet the inextinguishable longing of the human spirit for emancipation from the narrow, bounded life of selfish desires and pleasures, and for participation in that infinite life to which, in the deepest basis of its nature, it is allied, what it really attains is not union with the Infinite, but only a pallid and unreal mimicry of that union. For the Infinite to which it would unite us is not an Infinite of larger, fuller life, but, as we have seen, an Infinite in which all thought and life are lost. Its last result is, not the conscious surrender of finite desire and will, in order to conscious participation in the thought and will of God ; but it is the passing away, as if by a suicidal act, of all consciousness, all activity, all individuality, into the moveless abyss of the unconditioned.

Finally, if we ask what is the ethical bearing of Pantheism, the answer must be that a thorough-going Pantheism knows nothing of moral distinctions. With the ideas of freedom and individuality, the ideas of responsibility and of moral good and evil disappear. If in the universe there be no being, no life but one, a finite moral agent becomes a contradiction in terms. The individual has here no life of his own to live, no ideal to fulfil or frustrate, no destiny to accomplish. Freedom is part of the illusion that gives a semblance of reality to finite beings. We dream that we are free, as we dream that we *are*. We are simply the sport of imagination when we regard our self-consciousness, our spiritual life, as anything else than a fragment of the Infinite, a transition point in the illimitable All. Nay, so far from regarding our consciousness of independence as the basis of morality, inasmuch as it is that which alone separates us from God, it must be regarded as in itself evil, and its extinction as the highest good.

If, again, we ask whether Pantheism does not

imply that God is the author of evil, the answer can only be that for God evil has no positive reality. Like everything else in the finite world, it exists only for an intelligence that gives a false substantiation to the finite.   For an intelligence that sees things as they really are, from the point of view of the whole, evil is only a shadow cast by a shadow on an imaginary or shadowy world.

It is true, indeed, that if we reflect on its practical results, there is a kind of morality to which, on a superficial view, the hidden logic of Pantheism seems to lead, and to which in point of fact it has led.   Regarded from opposite points of view, it may be said to lead, on the one hand, to asceticism and the suppression of the natural desires and passions ; on the other, even to the consecration of these desires.   If the finite world be nothing but illusion, the only way, it would seem, in which we can rise above the illusion is by detachment from its interests, by aiming at a more and more complete emancipation from desires and impulses that have their root only in vanity and falsehood. So, again, if the only reality be that which lies beyond the finite, beyond all we can see and name and know—the infinite void into which no pulsation of determinate thought and life can enter—is not

the only possible way to union with it, to quell
within us every movement of conscious life, to kill
out every human affection and emotion, nay, even
all personal consciousness, and so to approximate
more and more to that vacuity in which the divine
essence is supposed to dwell?

On the other hand, a religion in which God is
the Infinite that lies beyond the finite, can take
no account of any distinctions within the finite.
He is at once equally remote from, and equally
near to, the highest and lowest of finite beings, and
to that which is highest and basest in each. The
distance between infinitude and an atom is not
ater than between infinitude and a world. As
substance of a plant is as much in the un-
root or rugged stem as in the flower or
Being who is thought of as the sub-
ll things is equally related to all—to
things lofty, to gross matter as
the vilest and impurest as
exalted natures. It is
ght there is a sense in
ings. There is no object,
meanest weed or wayside
it the revelation of a divine
the deeper insight which it brings

it is possible to discern a soul of goodness even in things evil, a divine purpose beneath the discord of human passions and the strife and sin of the world.

But the Christian deification of the world is not a deification of it, so to speak, in the rough, an apotheosis of all things alike and without distinction. It can see more of God, a richer revelation of the infinite mind, in organic life than in brute matter, in human intelligence than in animal instinct, in a spirit devoted to unselfish ends than in one that is the slave of its own appetites and impulses. In Christianity, moral aspiration and endeavour, the struggle with the lower self natural desires, is possible, consistently with recognition of these desires as of divine because these natural elements of our the basis on which the higher or spiri is reared, and through the transfo a divine or spiritual life is a distinctions disappear in a of God as no nearer to that which is the haunt of Here the lowest appetites aspirations, the grossest impu heroic virtues, are alike consecrate of God. Nay, there is a sense in which the baser side of man's nature receives here a readier consecration than the higher. For while all true morality implies a struggle with nature, an ideal aim which forbids acquiescence in that which by nature we are, it is of the very essence of a pantheistic religion to discountenance any such struggle, and to foster a fatalistic contentment with things as they are. In a religion which finds God in all things and events alike, in which whatever is, simply because it is, is right, all natural passions, simply as natural, carry with them their own sanction; for immersion in the natural is absorption in the divine, and even the wildest orgies of sensual excess may be part of the homage rendered to the object of worship, seeing that in yielding ourselves up to nature we are yielding ourselves to God.

LECTURE V.

THE RELATION OF GOD TO THE WORLD.

2. THE DEISTIC VIEW.

THE great problem, as we have seen, which all monotheistic systems have to encounter is, so to conceive of the relation of the Infinite to the finite, of God to the world, as not to tamper with either of the two elements involved in it, *i.e.* either with the infinitude of God, or with the reality and independent existence of the world. Can we include in one system of the universe a God who is infinite and absolute, and a world in which reality is ascribed to nature, and freedom and individuality to man? Pantheism solves the problem, but solves it only too easily. It reaches the unity we are in quest of by the simple expedient of annulling the element of difference, or reducing it to a phantom of the imagination. If nature and man have no more substantial reality than the baseless fabric of a vision, and their seeming reality dissolves away at the touch of rational or philosophic thought, the religious idea of a system in which God is all in all, is reached at a single stroke. But this, as we have seen, is a solution which cuts the knot instead of untying it, or which attains the required result only by ignoring or making light of one of the conditions of the problem. As in philosophy it is only a spurious solution of the problem of the relation of mind to the world which subjective idealism achieves, by reducing the element of objectivity to a creation of the individual mind, so, in theology, or the philosophy of religion, the reduction of the world to a mere subjective illusion is an expedient which evades rather than meets the difficulty it pretends to remove. If there were no other objection to it, there is still this, that, even *as* an illusion, the existence of the finite remains still to be accounted for ; and further, that the intelligence which discerns and rises above the illusion cannot itself be comprehended in it, and leaves therefore the God of Pantheism with an element of difference still opposed to him in undissolved reality.

The natural reaction from a unity which rules out the element of difference is a view of things which, by exaggerating it, becomes virtually dualistic. In the recoil from a theory which swamps the finite in the infinite, the tendency arises to an excessive emphasizing of the independence of the finite world. In the endeavour to maintain the infinitude of the divine nature consistently with the ascription of any measure of reality to nature and man, Deism betakes itself to anthropomorphic analogies derived from the relations of man to the outward world—such as that of a human contriver or artist to the work of his hands, or that of a human potentate to his subjects. The artist is not identified with the materials with which he deals, or the result which he educes from them ; yet, on the other hand, by manipulating brute matter into the expression of preconceived designs or purposes, by transforming its merely outward and accidental relations into ingenious adaptations of means to ends, by infusing into it order, symmetry, beauty, utility, he produces wonderful manifestations of power, wisdom, genius, which we might also call creative. So again, in the command of a human potentate over the wills and actions of his subjects—whether it be by outward force or by the domination of a great intelligence over other minds—we have manifestations of a kind of power, which we have only to conceive of as heightened to infinitude, to supply us with the conception of that relation of God to the world of which we are in quest. Instead of an Infinite who is merely the negation of the finite, an Absolute that is merely the negation of the contingent, we have here the idea of an omnipotent and all-wise Creator and Governor of the world. In other words, we have the idea of a Being who is not merely the blank correlate of an unreal and evanescent world, but who of His own will and pleasure creates a world in which His infinite wisdom and power are manifested. And, on the other hand, we have the conception of a world which, instead of being absorbed in the Infinite, has a reality as distinct from God as that of a human machine or work of art from its contriver, a freedom and independence as real as that of an earthly kingdom in relation to its sovereign.

There is much in this view of the nature of God, and of His relation to the world, which recommends it to popular thought; and so long as it is regarded simply as a figurative, analogical, or pictorial representation of spiritual things, it is of no little practical use as an incentive to religious feeling. But when closely examined, it is inadequate as a rational solution of the great problem we are considering ; and it falls short of that deeper conception of the unity of the infinite and finite which, as we shall see, is the essential idea of Christianity.

1. It may be pointed out that there are obvious imperfections in the anthropomorphic analogies on which Deism is based. In the first place, an *external* contriver or ruler, even though indefinitely magnified, is not God, but only a bigger or colossal man ; and there are elements in nature and man for which such a conception does not account. Even in the material world there are things which we cannot conceive of as made from without ; and a *made mind*, a spiritual nature created by an external omnipotence, is an impossible and self-contradictory notion. A human contriver or artist deals with materials prepared to his hand. There are qualities in these materials, relations and laws which constitute their inner essence, of which he can only take advantage in shaping, moulding, fitting, constructing them into the piece of mechanism or work of art which he desires to produce ; and when he has completed his machine, his power as an external worker is at an end. He must needs

commit it to the custody of laws of nature, of natural forces and energies which are altogether foreign to the power that was at work in its construction—which live and operate *within* the thing, and without whose inner activity it would have no continuous existence. He may, it is true, at any subsequent time interfere from without with his own handiwork—touch it up where it seems defective, or modify or reconstruct it. But even here, his power, as external power, is limited. There is that in it which he can neither make nor unmake ; there are in it qualities of extension, weight, solidity, relations of attraction and repulsion, and so on, which are not, and cannot be, either communicated or altered or subverted by any external power. It may be said, of course, that these are limitations which apply only to a human or finite designer, and which vanish when the designer is conceived of as the creator not only of the thing, but also of the materials out of which it is made and of the laws and relations on which its existence depends. But the answer is, that the corrective or supplementary idea by which we thus distinguish the omnipotent and the human designer, is an idea which cannot be reached by the enlargement of an external agent even to omnipotence. It is, in

The inner working principle remains unaccted for, except by dualism, wh has insup'ble difficulties other words, when we examine what is implied in it, an idea which carries us wholly beyond the Deistic conception of God, and forces us to bring in an element altogether foreign to it—that, namely, of a God who is not an outside creator or designer, but an immanent spiritual presence, the inner life and thought of the world.

If we examine what we mean by the phrase, "creation of the world," I think we shall see that even in the realm of inorganic matter there is something which it baffles us to conceive of as produced merely by an external creator. Power, however magnified, presupposes an object on which it is exerted, and without which it passes off meaningless and unthinkable as a blow aimed at empty space. You may have recourse, indeed, to the notion of the mysterious and inexplicable, and endow the Author of the universe with the power of "creating out of nothing." But this is merely to solve our difficulties with a phrase. The gap between external power and material things, even of the lowest order, that have a nature of their own, cannot be bridged over by an arbitrary and inexplicable creative act. Even a stone has a distinctive character, is a centre of relations, a unity of manifold differences, the existence of which cannot be embraced under the notion of almighty power, or conceived as imparted to it by an external agent. The relations that constitute the existence and nature of a stone imply, with reverence be it said, a God who from the first moment of its existence is *in* the stone and constitutes the inner essence of its being.

ground

Now, if this be so even when we are dealing with inorganic matter, still more obvious is the limitation of the idea of external power when we try to make it account for organization and life. A plant or animal is *causa sui* in a sense in which a stone or a material construction, even though it be vast and complex as a planetary system, is not. Whatever the originating source of the existence and life of an organism may be, whatever the energy which correlates its members and gives rise to its growth and evolution, it cannot be apprehended as creating them or acting upon them from without. We are compelled in conceiving it to pass from external causation to the idea of self-causation or inner self-development. We must have recourse to something more than an external agent shaping and adjusting according to a plan or design in his own head, but foreign to the object on which he operates. We must conceive of an inner, formative energy which passes into, lives and breathes in the thing, inspiring the first minute germ or cell with the idea of the perfect whole, resisting, triumphing over, transforming all external influences into the means of its self-development. In other words, we are carried here beyond the Deistic Creator, dwelling in some celestial sphere and operating from above, to the conception of an immanent God, manifesting Himself in, and in a sense identifying Himself with, the inner life and being of the world.

Lastly, if we rise from nature to man, we are confronted with the conditions which the Deistic conception of God is wholly inadequate to meet. If a *made* matter or a *made* organism is an inconceivable notion, still more palpably unthinkable is that of a *made mind*, of a moral and spiritual nature created or constructed by an external agent. In thought, intelligence, self-consciousness, in moral activity and attainment, you come upon an order of things in which the very notion of an external relation vanishes, and the hard and fast division between the Creator and the created ceases to be any longer tenable. It is of the very essence of a spiritual nature that it cannot be originated or determined from without. Knowledge, morality,

goodness, are not manufactured articles. Spiritual
qualities are not things that can be rained into the
soul or deposited in it ready-made. Ideas cannot
be injected by a higher into a lower mind, or
appropriated by the latter, save by an internal
activity that is akin to, and in a sense one with,
that from which they proceed. Moral character,
again, is a thing which cannot be created or imparted. Not what I am, or find myself to be by
nature, or am made or moulded into by any external
power, constitutes my spiritual life, but what by
conscious activity and self-determination I make
myself to be. There are, indeed, certain elements
which constitute the basis or materials of our moral
life—a physical nature, appetites, desires, impulses,
passions—and in a sense we can think of these as
given or imparted ; but if these in their immediate
instinctive form constituted the sole spring of a
man's activity, he would be little more than an
animal. These tendencies, as they exist in man
even at the lowest, are transmuted by his spiritual
nature ; and even so, it is by a struggle with them,
by the awakened aspiration after an ideal end to
which they are opposed, by the continuous transformation of natural desires through the energy
of the higher self, that character is formed, and

[margin note: i.e. innate mind has an internal source but is not a self.]

morality is developed.   Now this process by which we rise out of nature into spirit, is one of which the essential condition is that it is free and unforced, that the activity by which it is produced is mine and not another's.   The sphere of the spiritual life is one which no external power, not even a power conceived of as infinite, can invade.   The power that could invade it would destroy it in the act.   It is obvious, therefore, that we have here, in the very nature of spirit and the spiritual life, conditions which the Deistic analogy fails to satisfy.   If God is to be conceived of as the author and sustainer of the life of the spirit, it must be in such a way that that life can be thought of as our own as well as His, as at once His and our own.   His action must be not simply action *on* us, but action *in* us, losing the character of externality and becoming in a sense identified with us—the action not of an external creator or ruler, but of an inward inspirer, whose thought becomes our thought, whose will passes into our will, the light of all our seeing, the inspiration of all our doing.

2. Another aspect of the Deistic relation of God to the world, in which it may be shown to be inadequate, is its *arbitrariness*.   To find in the idea of God the explanation of the existence of

the finite world implies that that existence must be traceable to something in the *nature* of God and not simply to His arbitrary will. At first sight it seems to lend exaltation to our thought of God that we ascribe all things to His absolute will and power. It furnishes food for humility and reverence to think of Him simply as a Being who "doeth according to his own will in the army of heaven and among the inhabitants of the earth." We shrink from anything that has the appearance of imposing necessity on the divine action, or of a higher law or principle to which the divine agency must conform itself. Constitutional monarchy subjects the mere will and power of an earthly ruler to checks and limitations ; but this arises, besides other reasons, from the weakness and imperfection of human agents, and from the inexpediency of making the welfare of a nation dependent on the caprice of an individual. If we could eliminate human imperfection and conceive a human potentate possessed of perfect and unerring wisdom, the need to canvass his procedure or to inquire into the reasons of his behests would cease. *Sic volo, sic jubeo* would in his case be reason enough. It would be the highest tribute to his greatness that we set no limit to his absolute power, but rather enlarge to the utmost the sphere of action in which his mere will and pleasure would be the ground of our obedience. In like manner, would it not lower our conception of God to think of His will and power as other than absolute? There may be much in His plans and operations that calls forth our intelligent admiration, but our highest tribute would seem to be rendered to Him when His works and ways pass beyond our intelligence, and are regarded simply as the expression of His infinite will. Is it not then a kind of impiety to ask for any reason for the existence of nature and man other than the will and pleasure of the Almighty, or to entertain any such notion as that God was under a necessity to create the world?

And yet when we reflect a little more closely on the attitude of mind which I have depicted, perhaps we may find reason to doubt whether it is one in which thought can rest, as an account of the relation of God to the world. In the first place, there is a sense in which it is no irreverence to set limits to the divine will and power, and to hold that there are eternal principles and laws to which even Omnipotence must submit. It is no more a limit to divine than to human power to say that there are things which are impossible to it—that,

[margin, handwritten] Only these laws must be in God Himself - in His nature.

for instance, it cannot make $2 + 2 = 6$, or transform a circle into a square. Neither in God nor man, again, is freedom a thing which excludes necessity. It is the lowest, not the highest nature, of whose actions no other account can be given than simply that it wills so to act. When you say of a human being that he does anything simply because he wills to do it, you degrade his action below the movements of a weather-vane or the vagaries of a straw tossed by the winds; for the latter are movements subject to conditions that admit of intelligent calculation. On the other hand, the more a human will is subjected to law, the less of caprice and the more of reason we find in its action, the higher and nearer perfection does that action become. And if we could conceive of a human spirit whose actions were necessitated by itself in so uniform and invariable a way that mere will as a principle of action was absolutely excluded, and its movements and activities had become as fixed and certain as the motion of a planet in its orbit, we should recognize it as having reached the highest ideal of spiritual excellence. The illustration here, indeed, falls short of the thing to be illustrated; for the conditions or laws to which a material object is subjected are some-

i.e. if the necessity was moral based on character ∴ consistent with true freedom.

thing external and foreign to the thing itself, whereas the laws and principles that determine a wise and good man's conduct are part and parcel of his own true nature, in being determined by which he yields to no alien power, but is self-conditioned, self-determined. And it is just because the human will, even in the best of men, is not thus absolutely determined, because there is still some part of its activity which is unreclaimed from arbitrary caprice and is due only to lawless impulse, that the agent falls short of the ideal perfection of a spiritual nature. But when we turn to the contemplation of the divine nature and divine operations, it is just because we are here in a region where mere will and power account for nothing, are absolutely eliminated; and, further, because we can think of the conditions by which the divine will is determined as not external to but entering into the very essence of God's own nature, that we can ascribe to Him alone the character of absolute spiritual perfection.

Now the Deistic conception of the relation of God to the world, whether as Creator or as Ruler and Governor, is one which rests essentially on the notion of arbitrary will and power. It traces the existence of the world, not to anything in the nature of God, but only to an arbitrary inexplicable act, by which of His mere will and pleasure He calls a world into being. In the system of the universe there is an unbridged gap, a dualistic breach of unity, so long as there is nothing to connect the essential nature of God with the world He creates. To make the system one and unbroken, what thought demands is a relation between the infinite and finite, such that in the very idea and essence of the infinite there is that which requires and implies the existence of the finite, *permits and justifies* and in the very essence of the finite that which finds its explanation in the nature of the infinite. In other words, there must be in the very being and life of God that which calls for the existence *accounts* of a finite world, and in the finite world that which has its explanation and origin, not in the mere will and pleasure, but in the inner being and life of God. When we ask why this world, with all its various orders of being, exists, it is only an explanation to the ear to say " God made it." The true and sufficient explanation can only be that there is in the very nature of God a reason why He should reveal Himself in, and communicate *can and did* Himself to, a world of finite existences, or fulfil and realize Himself in the being and life of nature

I

and man.　To discern this is to perceive, so to
speak, that His nature would not be what it is if
such a world did not exist, that something would
be lacking to the completeness of the Divine Being
apart from it—that, with reverence be it said, God
would not be God without it.　But the Deistic
God, complete in His absolute infinitude, choosing
to create a world which might as well not be as
be, leaves the existence of the world an unsolved
enigma, or explains it by a reason which would
equally well explain the existence of any world.
It leaves in absolute darkness the question why
the infinite, self-complete, self-sufficient Personality
should break through His eternal isolation, or by the
creation of finite beings seek to add to an existence
already infinite.　It gives no reason why, if a world
is to exist, it should be a world such as this—a world
of order and beauty rather than of darkness and
disorder ; or why inorganic nature should not be its
sole content ; why life, with its infinite varieties of
form and function and its boundless susceptibilities
of pleasure and pain, should be crowned by intelligence with its capacities of knowledge, its moral
aspirations, its possibilities of good and evil, its
conflicts with self and the world, its insatiable desires
and endeavours after perfection and happiness.

To say that God must have made the world is not necessary to the principle of non-arbitrariness & is unscriptl. Rather the will wherewith He made it was one wh. His nature made room for & justified. God's determination to holiness does not require creation but makes creation holy. So as to other prins. of determination in God. They determine character rather than particular actions, like creation.

Equally obvious is the inadequacy of the Deistic conception when it represents the relation of God to the world under the analogy of the relation of a human ruler or potentate to his subjects. When we so conceive of Him, we are precluded from the idea of any other basis of authority than arbitrary will and power. For the ultimate ground of external rule is not reason or the intelligent recognition of the principles on which its commands are based, but simply the will of the ruler, exerted either directly in the form of physical force, or indirectly by rewards and punishments. A benignant despotism may condescend to explain the reasons of its behests, but in so far as obedience springs, not from submission to outward power, but from discernment of the reasons and sympathy with the spirit of them, the fundamental principle of personal rule is departed from. What the subject acknowledges and obeys is no longer an outward ruler, but a power or principle that is common to, and supreme over, both ruler and subject—the power of truth, goodness, righteousness, dominating the intelligence and actions of a moral and spiritual nature.

And the same is true of the relation of God to man. Even when we magnify the external

potentate till he becomes the almighty ruler of
the world, his rule is still an arbitrary one.   If
Deism permits us to see marks of intelligence in
nature or in the providential order of the world,
if it allows an appeal to conscience or the inner
sense of what is good and holy and fair, it is
indeed meeting an essential want of the nature
which God has made in His own image ; but in
so doing it passes away from its fundamental idea
of external and personal rule, and sets us on the
search for a deeper conception of God and of our
relation to Him—the conception of a Being whose
nature and authority is one with the eternal
principles of truth and righteousness, and of an
obedience which is the intelligent submission to
these principles, the recognition of their rational
and moral authority, which is of the very essence
of all spiritual natures.   It is true, we do not need
here, as in the case of intelligent obedience to an
earthly potentate, to have recourse to the idea of
an authority common to and above both ruler and
subject, of a law of truth and righteousness to
which God as well as man must submit.   For, as
I have already said, this law is not something
foreign to, or outside of, the nature it controls.   A
nature absolutely controlled by it is, at the same

time, a nature absolutely identified with it. God *is* truth, God *is* righteousness, God *is* love : they constitute His very essence ; in being determined by them, He is self-determined, in acting out or revealing them, He is revealing Himself. And we too, in so far as we are emancipating ourselves from the control of impulse and appetite and entering into the life of truth and goodness, are determined by that which is not an alien authority but our own truest nature. In being determined by God, we are self-determined. The universal life lives in us. The eternal consciousness becomes our own ; for " he that dwelleth in love dwelleth in God, and God in him." But in so conceiving of our spiritual life and its relation to the divine, we have passed beyond the Deistic notion of an external, personal God, to that idea of God and of His relation to the world which, as I shall attempt to show in the sequel, is the fundamental principle of Christianity.

Meantime let me only remark, in conclusion, that the Deistic attitude of mind is so akin to our ordinary habits of thought that we find it surviving and betraying its influence even under a religion with whose fundamental principle it is radically inconsistent. We seem to get nearer to

God, when we can give no other account of any natural or spiritual phenomenon than that it is due to direct supernatural agency. A human contriver or artist is absolutely powerless to alter or modify the conditions and laws of nature under which his work is produced ; and we seem to discern in the suspension or alteration of physical laws a power transcending all finite agency. We have a more vivid impression of the presence of a divine agent when we think of Him as not limited by any fixed and invariable conditions, as no longer "imprisoned in natural laws," but as bringing about results of which we can only say, " The finger of God is here."

And the same tendency is manifested in the view we often entertain of the relation of divine agency to the moral and spiritual life of man. There are certain universal laws by which the thought and will of man are conditioned, certain processes by which slowly and gradually the individual passes from infancy to maturity, grows in the knowledge of himself and the world, and is disciplined into virtue and goodness. And on the larger field of history there is a certain providential order, according to which communities and nations slowly emerge from barbarism into

civilization, by which each successive age becomes
the inheritor of the intellectual and moral wealth
of the past, the peculiar genius and character
of a people is developed, and its advancement in
law, government, social order, in science, art,
morality, religion, is determined. But there is an
invincible tendency in many minds to regard all
this as the result of what is called natural law,
and to look above and beyond it for the most
signal and striking manifestations of divine agency.
When we can trace the growth of a human spirit,
its intellectual and moral development, to the
influence of education or example, the force of
circumstances, the teaching of experience, and the
like appreciable causes, we seem to see in all this
only the action of a natural and normal process,
and there is nothing in it to awaken in us the
sense of a supernatural presence and power. But
when we are forced to brush all natural agencies
aside, to rise, as we say, above " second causes,"—
when we can think, *e.g.* of knowledge as flashed
into the mind by an immediate communication
from above, or of a transformation of character as
effected at a stroke by an instantaneous, irresistible,
and inexplicable influence,—then we are impressed
with an overwhelming sense of supernatural agency,

and we see in the event the irrefragable proof of the presence and power of God. And the same principle, as I need not stay to show, governs our recognition of the presence of God in history.

Now, without entering here on any general discussion of the idea of the supernatural, and even without questioning the historical truth of events ascribed to supernatural agency, it may, I think, be shown that such events are lower and not higher manifestations of divine agency than the order of things we commonly refer to natural causes; and that the disproportionate value attached to them is due in a great measure to the survival, even in Christian minds, of the Deistic idea of God and of His relation to the world. It is because, consciously or unconsciously, we cling to the notion of an anthropomorphic God, a celestial mechanist or potentate, constructing and controlling from without the machinery of the world, that we receive such a comparatively vivid impression from supernatural acts and events. Even from the Deistic point of view, there would be some ground for the assertion that the suspension or alteration of physical laws is a feebler and not a fuller manifestation of divine power than their normal and constant action. The occasion for exceptional interposition with the mechanism of the world can arise only because something is to be accomplished which <u>could</u> not be embraced in the original plan, and which its designer can only achieve by special immediate acts. More ingenuity and power would be evinced in the construction of a self-rectifying, self-adjusting machine, capable, that is, of adapting itself to all possible circumstances and exigencies, than of a machine which served for ordinary purposes, but needed touching up and readjustment by the contriver on special occasions.

perhaps was wiser not thus to be included.

But the main source of the exaggerated importance attributed to what are called supernatural acts, lies in the Deistic notion itself . If the world had an existence absolutely independent of God, or if it were the product of another and independent author, then the suspension of its laws would manifest a power greater than that which dwells in these laws, interference with its order a power greater than that which creates and sustains that order. The arbitrary external agent would show himself more potent than the agent who carries on the ordinary course of nature. But if both have the same author, the exceptional interferences, as being by supposition not only few and rare but arbitrary and inexplicable, are inferior as manifestations of creative wisdom and power to the vast and coherent order, the uniform, constant, harmonious system of the universe. Nay, more than that, if, as we have seen, the idea of an external, anthropomorphic creator altogether breaks down as an explanation of God's relation to the world, if there is a sense in which we must conceive of God, not as acting on, but as immanent in, the world, as the inner principle of nature, the indwelling thought and life of man, then not only would the notion of special outward interferences involve the impossible thought of an external God acting on an internal God, or of God interfering with Himself, but it is a notion which drops away and disappears with the whole attitude of mind to which it belongs.

The immanent action of God in the existing order is of course supernatural, considered as God's action instead of in the phenomenal or secondary causation, and as mighty as any miracle. The signif. of the miraculous is that a step onward & beyond the previous cycle has taken place & this is the reason for the wonder — that nature can advance under God & is not confined to a cycle.

LECTURE VI.

THE RELATION OF GOD TO THE WORLD.

3. THE CHRISTIAN VIEW.

I HAVE attempted to show that neither in Pantheism nor in Deism do we find a true or adequate conception of the relation of God to the world. That conception must be one which, without throwing doubt upon the absoluteness and infinitude of the divine nature, must yet be consistent with the reality of the outward world and the freedom and individuality of man. This condition is one which pantheistic and deistic systems, in opposite ways, fail to fulfil—Pantheism by the annulling of the finite world or its absorption in the Infinite, Deism by reducing God to a finite anthropomorphic personality. But though imperfect and untenable in themselves, these systems may be regarded as steps by which the mind rises to the true or Christian idea of God and of His relation to the world. All thought of God must be pantheistic in this sense, that it starts from the presupposition that God is all. Without breaking up the unity of the universe and falling into dualism, whatever reality or independence we ascribe to nature and man must be consistent with the subordination of both to the all-embracing being and power of the Infinite. The manifold differences of the finite world must be capable of being gathered up into unity, and its seeming anomalies and discordances in some way be reducible to the eternal harmony. All the higher forms of religion begin with the negation of the finite and with the idea of God as the Being who alone is—with the idea, in other words, that the world is nothing and God is all.

But the implicit logic of religion will not suffer thought to rest in the idea of a God who is all only by the obliteration of the finite world. The impulse that forces us to rise above the finite refuses to be satisfied with a merely negative Infinite. The pantheistic notion of the unreality and illusoriness of the finite world involves a self-contradiction. For, as already said, even *as* a mere semblance or illusion it needs to be accounted for ; and that it is more than an illusion the capacity to detect its illusoriness is the unconscious wit-

[Margin notes: "wh. is the very gist of Pantheism."]

[Margin notes: "but not absorption. Nature is other than God, nor fills out his being."]

ness.   The mind that can look on the world from
the point of view of the Infinite virtually asserts
for itself something more than a negative relation
to the Infinite.   The contradiction thus involved
in its thought forces it onwards in quest of an
Infinite which <u>contains</u> and accounts for the finite
instead of annulling it—an idea of God which, though
in one sense the negation, is also the explanation,
of ourselves and the world.

The deistic idea of God may be regarded as
the first form in which this movement of thought
expresses itself.   In the notion of a personal
Creator or Contriver, a self-determined, self-conscious
Agent of infinite power and wisdom, who of His
own will and pleasure calls into existence a world
of order and beauty, we seem to have attained a
conception freed from the inadequacy and self-
contradictoriness of the pantheistic idea of God—
a conception which seems to preserve at once the
infinitude of the divine nature and the reality and
independence of the finite world.   Yet this view,
when closely examined, is one, as we have seen, in
which it is impossible for the human spirit to
rest.   It leaves religious feeling with aspirations
and longings which are unfulfilled, and it creates
for thought a breach between the Infinite and

finite, which in vain it attempts to remove by an arbitrary and inexplicable act. The religious consciousness is not satisfied by a freedom which isolates it from the infinite object of its love and reverence. Alike in its conscious weakness and dependence, and in its boundless desires and aspirations, it craves for a closer union with God than that of the creature with an external creator, or of the subject with its distant and absolute ruler. Even Pantheism, in its absolute self-abnegation and its blending of the inmost being with its infinite object, brings a kind of satisfaction to the religious instincts which Deism fails to provide.

And it is not less impossible for thought than it is for feeling to rest in the deistic attitude of mind. In finding a place for the finite in the presence of the Infinite, Deism satisfies the consciousness of freedom, but it does so only by rending in twain the system of the universe. It lends a false elevation to its anthropomorphic God, by placing Him in hard, transcendent opposition to the world, and it leaves in nature, and still more in the finite spirit, elements which are in no inner and essential relation to Him. The gulf between the infinite and finite remains unbridged, till we can think of God as not merely above us but within us, as

not simply the Creator but the indwelling life of the soul. Moreover the relation of the world to God remains still an unsolved enigma, till we can trace its existence not simply to the will, but to the very nature of God; till we can see in nature and man not the result of an arbitrary creative act, but the revelation of the very being and essence of the Infinite.

And now let us proceed to ask whether it is possible for thought to compass an idea of God's relation to the world which fulfils the conditions which both Pantheism and Deism fail to satisfy. Can we form an intelligent conception of God as a Being who is all in all, without sacrificing or suppressing the reality and independence of the finite world; who is not simply the external Creator of the world, but the inward principle and ground of its being; and who, finally, is related to the world, not by the link of arbitrary will, but by the inward necessity of His own nature? In answer to this question I think we shall be able to see that in the idea of God as Infinite, Self-revealing Spirit or Mind, if we examine what it involves, there are contained all the elements of which we are in quest. We shall attempt to show:

1. That it is Infinite Mind or Intelligence which

Epit. of baird's position.

constitutes the reality of the world, not simply as its external Creator, but as the inward Spirit in and through which all things live and move and have their being;

2. That by its very nature, Infinite Mind or Spirit has in it a principle of self-revelation—a necessity of self-manifestation to and in a world of finite beings; and

3. That the infinitude of God, conceived of as Infinite Spirit, so far from involving the negation or suppression of the finite world, is rather the principle of the individuality and independence of nature and man.

1. That Infinite Spirit or Mind constitutes the reality of the finite world is a proposition which conveys little or no meaning to the ordinary ear. But that it is not meaningless or unintelligible we may perhaps enable ourselves to see by considering that there is a sense in which, even with respect to human thought or intelligence, it may be said that it is mind or spirit which creates the world. It is, in one point of view, *our* thought in which the nature we know lives and has its being, our thought which redeems our world from chaos or nonentity. It is not a ready-made world on which we look; in perceiving our world we make it. The ordinary unre-

flecting observer seems to himself to be confronted by a world of realities existing in themselves just as he perceives them, and of which he is simply the passive spectator. All he knows of these outward realities, their permanent identity, their position in space, their forms, weight, solidity, etc., seem to him to be there as independant facts. The hues and colours are spread over mountain and meadow and forest, the woods are ringing with song, and the multitudinous music of winds and waves, of brooks and streams, is ever sounding and reverberating as though there were no ear to listen to it, and no conscious intelligence to apprehend and respond to it. The more cultured observer has, of course, got beyond such crude realism, knowing as he does that something at least of what the other ascribes to nature, exists only relatively to his own sensibility— that, for instance, the vibrating ether, the light waves or sound waves, might be propagated for ever through space, but that, if there were no organs of sense to receive impressions and no conscious intelligence to apprehend them, these material motions would never be transformed into light and sound. Nature would remain dark and silent ; the radiant, vocal world of our sensible experience would have no existence.

K

But, having got so far, reflection cannot stop
here.   A   large   element   of   what   before   seemed
outward   fact   is   now   seen   to   be   contributed   by
the   observing   mind.   What   sense   gives   us   is   not
a   world   of   concrete,   individual   objects   existing   in
space,   but   only,   at   most,   the   raw   material   out   of
which   that   world   is   to   be   created.   It   is   one   of
the   elementary   lessons   of   psychology   that   the   process   of   perception   implies   the   active,   constitutive
power   of   intelligence,   without   which   even   particular
sensations   could   not   be   individualized ;   and   the   bare
data   of   sensation—visual,   tactual,   muscular,   etc.—
would   give   us   no   real   information   as   to   the   individual,   concrete   existence   of   external   objects.   Even
if   our   sensations   could   be   determined,   identified,   distinguished,   each   from   that   which   precedes   or   succeeds
it,   without   the   qualifying   power   of   thought,   these
isolated,   transient   sensations   would   never   constitute
for   us   an   ordered   world   of   objective   realities.   Our
consciousness   would   be   but   the   stage   athwart   which
flitted   an   endless   series   of   fugitive   impressions,
chasing   and   obliterating   each   other,   incapable   of
being   correlated   and   combined   into   the   smallest
object   of   real   knowledge,   much   less   of   being   built
up   into   the   solid   frame-work   of   the   world   as   it
exists   for   science.   To   attain   this   implies   the

presence of some permanent amidst the variable,
some unifying concentrating principle amidst the
flux of impressions, co-ordinating them into a
coherent system of realities. Without this co-
ordinating principle, we should be no nearer to
an ordered world than a loose heap of printer's
types is to a scientific treatise or an epic poem.
And this constant amidst the variable, not given
by them but above them, is something which sense
does not and cannot provide—is, and can only
be, the self-conscious, spiritual self, the unifying,
constitutive power of thought. So again, it might
be shown to be only a more comprehensive
manifestation of the same principle, when we connect things or facts or mere co-existences and
successions of events, in an ordered system of
causes and effects, of uniform and invariable relations. And when the cosmos, the fair and ordered
world, rises into existence before us, this is only
another and higher result of the same process by
which, at the very outset of experience, thought
determines and correlates the data of sense.

It may be urged as a fatal objection to the
view that has now been presented, that at the
utmost it refers, not to nature itself, but only to
our ideas about it. Even if it were conceded that

the fabric of our knowledge of nature is built up by the activity of thought out of the raw material which sense supplies, still the result is only a subjective one. All this wonderful system, whatever its value, is only *our* thought or conception of the world, not the world itself—ideas about things, not things in themselves. No philosophy can argue us out of the conviction that there is a real world which our thought neither makes nor unmakes, and which would exist in all its reality without our existing to think it. It seems the very extravagance of idealism to make this objective, solid world only the phantasmal creation of mind. Nay, does not the admission that it is from what we have called the raw material of sensation that this ideal fabric is built up—that what we begin with is impressions which come to us from without, and which we do not create and cannot resist—does not this tacitly imply that there is a real material world external to and independent of us and our thoughts, of which our sensitive impressions are only the effects or reflexions?

The answer to this is twofold. In the first place, even if there were a world external to and absolutely independent of our thought, it is a mere identical proposition to say that that is not

the world we know; the only world we can conceive is one the <u>existence</u> of which is not independent of the active power of thought. The existence
of a world external to thought seems to us a possible
conception, only because in our ordinary observation
of nature, and even in our scientific investigations,
we abstract for the moment from one factor of
the process, viz., the mind of the observer, and
deal with facts and relations of facts <u>as if</u> they
were purely objective realities. But the least and
lowest fact is not fact *minus* mind, fact stript of
all relation to thought ; it is fact observed, perceived, thought about—fact as it is in and for
thought. The barest atom of matter is only a
thinkable atom. The atom as it is in itself, or
as it really is, is in relation to a thinking intelligence. And so, all things and beings, and all
the relations which we discern as constituting the
totality of nature—nature in its existence and its
whole content—is not nature behind and apart
from thought, but nature, so to speak, suffused
with the element of thought. Nay, we can go
further and say that any other nature is an
impossible conception. To say that we can think
an existence behind our thought is a contradiction in
terms. Even if there were such a thing as a

[right margin handwritten annotations:]

Knowledge - not existence.

How "as if," if it is inconceivable?

i.e. only such an atom as comes within the sphere of thought. In itself what it is prior to our thought of it.

but existing whether thought or not.

of course we cannot think before we think - i.e. we cannot conceive of nature prior to our conception of it, but when we do conceive of it we can conceive that it exists prior to & inde-pendently of our thought.

[margin, handwritten:] He plays the trick of changing to that in general, whereas the arg. is to show that our that creates. Of course a world full of design can not be conceived apart from its designer. But designing + creating are distinct. An object is not intelligible until that on, except potentially, nor at all if there is no intelligence. But its intelligibility is not its existence, wh. may be quite independent of it.

[margin, handwritten:] Not at all. What has disappeared is the lack of intelligibility of the intelligible element. Unintelligible reality, conceived of as real, but not understood, remains.

world beyond thought, we at least could never know anything about it, not even the bare fact of its existence; for that would be equivalent to knowing what we do not know, or knowing and not knowing in one and the same mental act. Starting, therefore, with the presupposition of the independent existence of the world, and inquiring what contribution mind gives to the conception of it, we find mind claiming for itself successively one element after another, until at length the whole has been brought within its own province, and the last unresolved element, the ultimate residuum of a reality beyond thought has disappeared.

But, in the second place, the foregoing view implies no such absurdity as the denial of the existence and reality of an objective world, or the assertion that it is only the creation of the individual mind, coming into existence or vanishing when we begin or cease to think it. Philosophy does not evaporate the common-sense conviction that the world and all that is therein, the round ocean and the living air and the blue sky, the whole fair and wondrous order of nature, would be as real and fair though we, and myriads such as we, were not here to perceive and know it. In far-away solitudes which no foot has trodden,

nature is not less fair and glorious than when it
fills the eye and sense of man with its wonder
and beauty. There are untold secrets of nature
which as yet human science has not grasped, and
in the illimitable depths of space there may be
worlds and suns and systems which lie beyond
the utmost scope of human observation. But to
say this is by no means inconsistent with the
assertion that a world outside of thought is a
contradiction in terms. If, as we have shown,
mind be the constitutive principle of nature, and if
the only existence we can ascribe to nature is an
existence relative to thought, then what this does
imply is that something analogous to our intelligence, yet not subject to its transiency and imperfection—an infinite and eternal thought, in other
words—is that in and through which all nature—
the world of our experience, and all worlds in the
unfathomable past or in the boundless realms of
space, live and move and have their being.

Nor, it may be added, and as we shall see
more fully in the sequel, is this Infinite and
Eternal Mind the constitutive principle only of
outward nature; it is the principle also of all finite
minds, that on which all finite thought rests as
its presupposition and as the element of its activity.

[Handwritten marginal note: This has not been shown at all.]

[Handwritten marginal note: It is true that an intelligible world implies that—i.e. design back of it, but it implies also physical causation—that being the condn of creation but not the creation itself—i.e. not proved to be so by this arg.]

The uniformity of nature, we are accustomed to say, is the tacit presupposition of all scientific investigation. It is only on the presumption that there is an order of nature, a system of invariable relations, laws, sequences of causes and effects, that any attempt to know nature becomes possible. The rationality of nature, in other words, is the ground of any attempt to grasp it.

In like manner, and as a further extension of the same principle, all finite thought, every manifestation and movement of mind, implies and rests on the presupposition of an Absolute Intelligence. In all thought, even the most elementary, we tacitly appeal to an absolute criterion of thought, an objective truth or reality to which our thought must conform, and without which our mental activity would dissolve into chaos. When I pronounce anything to be true, I pronounce it to be relative to thought, but not necessarily to my thought, to my individual opinions or notions, or to those of any other individual mind. These constitute no absolute standard. From *their* very existence I can abstract, *their* thought I can think away. But that which I cannot think away, that to which in the diversity and conflict of ideas and opinions all minds must appeal as their standard

is an Absolute Thought or Self-consciousness. It *not the same in idea*
is, indeed, the highest prerogative of our spiritual
nature that, when we think best, it is not our
own thoughts we think—that it is possible to rise
above ourselves as individual minds and to yield
ourselves up to a Mind or Thought that is other
and larger than our own. All intellectual and
spiritual progress may be said to be measured by
the degree in which we cease to think our own
thoughts, abnegate all self-assertion, and let our
minds become the pure media of the universal
and absolute intelligence. Yet in such self-
abnegation there is no pantheistic annulling of
our own life as intelligent and rational beings.
For the life of absolute truth or reason is not a
life that is foreign to us. If it is above us, it is
also within us. In yielding to it we are not
quelling but realizing our own truest nature. For
it is the freedom and the fulfilment of our spiritual
being to breathe in the atmosphere of the universal life, to become the organ of the infinite
reason. And the goal and perfection of our spiritual
life would be reached, if every movement of our
mind, every pulsation of our intellectual and moral
life were identified with it, so that in isolation from
it we had no life we could call our own.

2. We have seen, then, that Infinite Mind or Intelligence is not simply the creative source, but the inward, constitutive principle of the world, the presupposition of the being and life of man. But we can go further than this. Not only is it true that the finite world can be understood only in the light of the idea of God, but there is a sense in which that idea involves the existence of a finite world. In the nature of God as, self-revealing Spirit, there is contained, so to speak, the necessity of His self-manifestation in and to a world of finite beings, and especially in and to a world of finite intelligences made in His own image. If it be true, on the one hand, that, without the idea of God, nature and man would be unintelligible, there is a sense in which it is also true, on the other hand, that without nature and man God would be unintelligible. When, in the language of Christian thought, we say that all things exist "for the glory of God," that " of him and through him and to him are all things," that " the invisible things of him, from the creation of the world, are clearly seen, being understood by the things that are made, even his eternal power and Godhead," that finite spirits in their ideal perfection " are chosen in him," *i.e.* in Christ, "before the foundation of the world,"—what

This needs proof.

such expressions imply is not merely that all things
owe their existence to God's creative will and power,
or even that the divine thought is the constitutive
principle of all finite things and beings; but further,
that God fulfils Himself, realizes His own nature,
in the existence of the world, and above all in the
spiritual nature and life and destiny of man; that,
with reverence be it said, the very being and
blessedness of God are implicated in the existence,
the perfection, the salvation, of finite souls. Beyond
the relation of the creature to the Creator is the
relation of the spirit of man to Him in whose
infinite life we participate, and whose infinite love
finds in us its fulfilment and satisfaction.

That the existence of the world is involved in
the very nature of God is, from one point of view,
only the converse of what has been said above.
If nature and man have the principle of their
being in God, there must be something in God
which implies the existence of nature and man,
and which, without nature and man, would remain
unrevealed and unrealized. When we say that the
plant is related to the root or germ, not arbitrarily,
but by an inward and essential necessity of nature,
so that the former could not be what it is without
the latter, we imply conversely that the root or

[marginal annotations in handwriting:]
Hegelian.

*Then He is not
infinite in eter-
nity.*

non sequitur.

Because it was made for the purpose of producing the plant. God is not made for an end, but is his own end & self-sufficing.

germ has in it something which seeks its realization in the plant, and without the latter would remain unfulfilled and incomplete. So, when we say that, in its whole spiritual nature—its intelligence, its moral and religious life, the finite spirit rests on and is rooted in the Infinite, what we imply is that in the Infinite there is that which involves the existence of the finite spirit. If there be a divine element in man, there must be, so to speak, a human element in God, of which the whole spiritual life and history of the world is the manifestation. And that there is such a divine element in man we have already attempted to show. Our whole experience rests on the presupposition of an infinite ideal in us yet above us, of which science, art, morality, religion, are only the gradual and more or less imperfect realization. Our whole intellectual life, as I have above said, implies it. All knowledge involves a tacit appeal to an absolute criterion of thought an eternal truth or reality without which our whole mental activity would be baseless and illusory. All art, again, implies an absolute criterion of beauty, an ideal which does not come or go with the vision of the poet or artist, and of which his highest moments of inspiration are only partial revelations, and which, in the noblest products of his genius, he is struggling to realize. Above all, the moral and religious life presupposes an infinite ideal in us and yet above us. In our moral endeavours, in our religious aspirations, we have the consciousness of aiming at an end that is not of our own creating; we are claiming affinity with an object which, though we only dimly and imperfectly apprehend it, though it surpasses our highest attainments, is that in which we truly find ourselves and our true vocation, as spiritual beings—the mark of the prize of our high calling.

But, if this be so, if man cannot be explained without ascribing to his nature a divine element, it follows that the divine nature cannot be understood without ascribing to it a human element. A relation cannot be essential on the one side and only accidental or arbitrary on the other. If my whole nature rests on something in the very essence of the divine nature, if my life as a moral and spiritual being is not something in the air, an abstraction of my own understanding, a dream of my imagination, but the realization of an ideal which has its seat in the bosom of God, then without the existence of a world of finite spirits that ideal would be only an unrealized possibility in God. If we can claim affinity with God, if we are not merely His creatures but His children, then the filial relation on our part implies as its correlate the paternal on God's part, something in His very nature in virtue of which He is " Father of Spirits."

But, that the existence of the world is involved in the very nature of God may be shown not merely indirectly, or by inference from the nature of man ; it is implied directly in the very idea of God as self-revealing Spirit. In a former lecture I have shown it to be a principle of all intelligence, an essential characteristic of a spiritual nature, to be, not a mere abstract, self-identical unity, but a living process, a unity which realizes, and can only realize, itself by going forth from itself and returning upon itself. It includes in it of necessity two inseparable elements, a self or subject which thinks and an object which is thought of. Apart from a world of objects in and through which its hidden capacities of thought, feeling, action could reveal and realize themselves, a spiritual being would not be truly spirit, but only the blank potentiality of spirit. It is through the material and spiritual world around us that the latent wealth of the mind within us, its possibilities of knowing, loving, willing, are unfolded. A human being shut up from the birth in isolation from nature and society would never attain to self-consciousness. All that rich treasure of ideals, emotions, volitions, moral and spiritual energies and attainments, that wake to life at the touch of nature and kindred spirits, would slumber in unconsciousness. Especially do our social relations become to us a revelation of ourselves. Our social environment is not arbitrarily related to us, so that, so far as our own existence is concerned, society might as well not be as be. It is so necessarily related to us that we should never come to ourselves, our nature would be mutilated and suppressed, without it. All that range of qualities which are possible only through the existence of other and kindred natures, all that is meant by such words as love, sympathy, admiration, self-devotion, patriotism, philanthropy, would never emerge into reality. Apart from our relations to the family, the community, the state and its various institutions, no moral life would be possible for man, any more than physical life to a severed branch or an amputated limb. And with the highest moral life is connected the highest happiness possible for a human spirit. For the deepest and purest happiness is not that of a nature that is wrapt up in its own isolated individuality, self-absorbed, self-satisfied, self-sufficing.   To go forth out of self, to yield up ourselves and receive ourselves back again redoubled in reciprocated affection, to live in the life of others and so to enlarge and expand our own, this is the true secret of spiritual perfection and blessedness. Nay, seeing that love can only reach its highest expression in suffering and sacrifice, the richest, purest blessedness is that which comes through pain and sorrow—the bitter sweet, the sweetness that contains yet annuls the bitterness of suffering gladly borne for the object of a deep, unselfish love.

Moreover, we have seen that this is a principle which applies not merely to finite intelligence, but to all intelligence.   It enters into the very idea and essence of a spiritual nature, and therefore, above all, into the nature of Him whom we con- ceive of as Infinite Spirit.   To conceive of God as an abstract, self-identical, self-sufficing Infinite, would be to make Him not greater but less than man ; for it would be not only to deny to Him that which makes intelligence and self-consciousness possible, but to make Him a stranger to that which, as I have just said, is the highest element of the life and blessedness of a spiritual nature, the element of love.   It is true indeed, as we formerly saw,

that the highest manifestation of this principle is
only to be found in that conception which is expressed in the Christian doctrine of the Logos or
Son of God—the conception of a self-revealing
principle or personality within the very essence of
the Godhead. But, as will be seen more fully in
the sequel, the idea of God as self-revealing includes
in it the conception of a revelation in and to the
finite spirit He has made in His own image. The
capacity of love, so to speak, in the heart of God
seeks a channel for its outflow in every human soul ;
and in the responsive love which that love awakens,
there is something which we can think of as adding
a new sweetness and joy to the very blessedness of
the Infinite. For there is a form of love which
implies finitude, imperfection, moral and spiritual
inferiority and want in the objects to which it goes
forth. In our human relations to each other there
is a kind of affection which involves, on the one
hand, condescension, tenderness, pity, compassion,
protecting and fostering care, on the other, dependence, submission, gratitude, reverence, trust. Nay,
it may be said that the deepest, intensest form of
love can only be reached and revealed not merely
by the imperfection, but by the sorrow and sin of
its object. We have not yet sounded the depths

L

of what we express by the word until we think of a love which no ingratitude can exhaust, no unworthiness can alienate, no measure of infamy and degradation render hopeless of its object, or place it beyond the range of reconciliation and forgiveness; nay, more than that, till we can think of a love which, undeterred by the unworthiness of its object, will bear any hardship with and for it, and for which there is no measure of pain and sorrow and sacrifice to which it will not submit for the restoration of that object to goodness and happiness.   So, in like manner, may we not say that there is something in the very nature of God which would remain unrevealed and unrealized, but for His relation to the world, and especially to the finite spirits He has made in His own image. The nearest human analogy by which Christian thought permits us to conceive of God's relation to us is that of a father to his children, and it is only in and through the existence of his children that the father's heart can be revealed.   And in the Christian doctrines of the Incarnation and Atonement, whatever else they mean, we find a sanction for the thought that in the nature of God there is a capacity of condescending love, of boundless pity and forgiveness, yea, with reverence be it said, of pain and sorrow and sacrifice for the salvation of finite souls, a capacity which has been, and could only be, revealed and realized through the sorrow and sin of the world.

LECTURE VII.

THE RELATION OF GOD TO THE WORLD.

THE CHRISTIAN VIEW (*Continued*).

THE formula by which, in the language of Scripture, the self-revelation of God in man is expressed, is that man is "made in the image of God." This formula seems to imply that, in the nature and life of man, the perfection and harmony of the divine nature is reflected. Human nature, though in one view of it only a finite existence in a finite world, is yet differentiated from all other existences in this respect that it is, in a peculiar sense, a manifestation of the Infinite. At first sight the conception which this formula expresses would seem to involve a self-contradiction. Can we conceive of a finite manifestation of that which is infinite; of a limited, conditioned, imperfect likeness of that which can only be thought of as unlimited, unconditioned, absolutely perfect? A larger nature may resemble a smaller : there may be identity of essence though the *scale* of existence be different. But can we say the same of natures that are essentially heterogeneous, the very definition of which can only be expressed by logical contradictories? A smaller circle may represent a larger in respect of its circularity, but a circle, small or large, cannot be the image of a square. A stone may be the image of a huger piece of inorganic matter, a geological specimen of the structure of a mountain, but dead matter can never portray the nature of a being in which is the essentially different element of organic life. But is it not of the very essence of the nature of God that it contains elements essentially heterogeneous to the nature of man? Do not the attributes we commonly ascribe to God, such as self-existence, eternity, omnipresence, immutability, omnipotence, express ideas that are essential to His nature, without which He would cease to be God? And how can we conceive of these as reflected or imaged in a being who is mortal and mutable, who exists in time and space, who begins to be and passes away, and who, as regards at least one side of his nature, is but a transient link in the vast system of material causes and effects in which he finds himself and by which his individuality is infinitely transcended?

If it be said that the likeness to God, which is expressed in the phrase "image of God," is that which pertains, not to man's outward and physical, but to his spiritual nature, that the principle or essence that is common to the two natures is spirit—the principle of intellectual and moral life—is not this interpretation encountered by equally obvious difficulties?   Can we separate the material and spiritual elements in man's nature, so as to conceive of a life pertaining to the one in which the other has no part? Could the soul be what it is apart from the body, or the body apart from the soul?   Man is not a mere combination of two essentially different substances, so that what is denied of the one can be affirmed of the other.   Soul and body, the immaterial and the material, are not to be thought of as existing side by side, or for a time artificially connected, so that you could conceive of man as if, in virtue of the former, he were a pure unembodied spirit, and attribute to him, in this point of view, a resemblance to God which is foreign to his corporeal or animal nature.   The spiritual and corporeal are rather inwardly related moments or elements reciprocally implicated with each other in the unity of man's nature and life ; you cannot divide or abstract his intellectual and moral life from his sensitive and corporeal, or from the impulses, desires,

passions that spring out of the latter, and yet leave
to the former all that it essentially is. Without the
materials supplied through sense to spirit, human
intelligence would be reduced, at best, to a mere
blank or blind potentiality ; without the presence
of conscious intelligence, the body would be nothing
more than a mechanical or chemical combination of
material atoms and forces, or, at best, the organ of
appetites and impulses no higher than those of the
lower animals. Our moral life takes its special
complexion from the inseparable relation between
what we term our higher and our lower natures ; our
impulses, desires, passions, are what they are because
the conscious self is present to and in them ; and
whether it yields itself up to them or rises above
them, the result is one which is in some way conditioned by them. Moral action is not the pursuit by
a purely spiritual nature of an abstract moral ideal.
Without the materials which the impulses and
passions supply, the moral ideal, if it could
be conceived to exist, would exist in a vacuum.
Even in so far as virtue consists in the denial
or subjugation of the lower impulses, they must
be there to be denied. The attempt to reach a
moral perfection by holding ourselves aloof from
the natural desires is the vain endeavour to

attain a perfect moral life, in abstraction from that without which no moral life, good or bad, is possible.

How then, it may be asked, can a Being of whom we can only think as an Infinite Spirit, " without parts or passions," be the prototype of one in whose nature and life the sensuous or corporeal element is inextricably involved ? If, on the one hand, we cannot think of the divine nature as subject to the limitations and conditions of sense, or connect with our idea of it the impulses and passions that have their origin in the animal nature, or the moral conflicts to which these give rise ; and if, on the other hand, we cannot think of man's nature without these conditions, is not the proposition that man is made in the image of God reduced to a contradiction in terms ?

Finally, if we may not say that man's nature involves the necessity, it at least involves the possibility, of sin. Whatever may be said for the notion of the actual existence of evil as implied in the moral development of a finite nature, every step in that process implies a conscious self-determination to one of many possible objects or ends, a conscious identification of our will with one object or end which we conceive of as our good, and therefore the possibility

of an opposite alternative. Moral freedom does not
mean an unmotived will, but a will which has in it
the power of self-determination and therefore of
wrong determination. Goodness, in short, would lose
its essential character if our nature were incapable of
evil. How then can a nature of which this is an
essential characteristic be said to be the image of a
nature absolutely good and to which not only evil,
but the capability of evil, must be thought of as
impossible?

Such are some of the difficulties involved in the
Biblical idea of man as made in the image of God.
That they are not insuperable, that the idea, on
the contrary, is one which a philosophy of religion
must regard as profoundly true, there are, I think,
certain considerations which may lead us to see.

1. In the first place, it is to be considered that
what this idea points to is not the *initial* or
original, but the *ideal* perfection of man's nature.
It is human nature interpreted, not by what it immediately or actually is, but by what it is capable
of becoming. Theologians have often indulged in
imaginary pictures of an original perfection of
man. Either from a misinterpretation of the
Biblical account of the paradisaical state, or from
the popular notion that only what is perfect can

have proceeded from the hand of God, and
that evil therefore can only be conceived of as
the corruption of a nature originally good and
pure, they have represented the human race as
degenerating from a primeval state of perfection
and blessedness, and have endowed its pro-
genitors, as they came from the Creator's hand,
with all conceivable attributes of physical and
moral excellence.   To render man adequate to
the idea of a being made in the image of God,
they must needs ascribe to him a perfect soul
with a perfect body as its organ.   He must from
the beginning have been the happy possessor
of a physical frame of flawless beauty, symmetry,
and strength, of an intelligence of commanding
ability, miraculously gifted with knowledge independently of the later processes of observation
and experience, and of a will in perfect command
of the passions and in absolute harmony with the
will of the Creator.   Anticipating, in short, the
slow results of individual effort, and of the
laws that condition the progressive development
of the race, in this fancy picture the first repre-
sentatives of mankind are supposed to emerge
into existence full-fledged specimens of humanity,
equipped with the wisdom of the sage, the exalted

The Oath views speaks of innocence rather than of an anticipatory state of civilization.

virtue of the hero, the piety and holiness of the saint.

It needs little reflection to see that this day-dream of primitive perfection is devoid alike of historical and of rational authority. In the first place, it has no basis in the inspired record on which it professes to rest. It is not to man as originally created that likeness to God is exclusively ascribed in the Old and New Testament Scriptures. However we are to conceive of the paradisaical state, it is represented as prior to that " knowledge of good and evil," without which moral action cannot really exist, and goodness can, at most, be only the unconscious innocence of childhood. Though, again, the act of disobedience by which this knowledge comes is depicted as a retrogression, it is, on the other hand, described as an advance; though it loses one kind of likeness to God, it marks the rise of another : " Ye *shall be as gods*, knowing good and evil." And finally, the highest form of Godlikeness, according to the Scripture representation, is neither man's primitive state nor the restoration of that state. A return to forfeited innocence, a recovery of the unconscious harmony of nature which sin has broken up, is impossible. The angel with the flaming sword guards inexorably

the gates of the lost Eden. But the discord which
sin has introduced is but the transition step to a
more glorious harmony. Out of the death of nature
rises a higher and nobler life. On the soul that
has passed through the terrible experience of evil,
and, through the redemptive power of the Christian
faith, has triumphed over it, there begins to be
impressed a likeness to God, far surpassing in
spiritual beauty the lost image of Paradise. "Ye
have put on," writes the Christian apostle, "the
new man, which is renewed in knowledge after the
image of Him that created him." And this image,
never more to be obliterated, transcends the first,
as reason and consciousness transcend the unconscious innocence of nature; for "the first man Adam
was made a living soul, the last Adam was made a
quickening spirit; howbeit that was not first which
is spiritual, but that which is natural."

But not only is the notion of an original or
pristine perfection based on a misinterpretation
of the Scripture record; it is in itself irrational
and untenable. It is of the very essence of a
spiritual nature that its ideal perfection cannot
be an immediate gift of nature, but must be
wrought out by its own conscious activity. Not
what I am by nature constitutes my true spiritual

the Cath. view
makes it a super-
natural gift.

life, but what, in the exercise of my own thought
and will, I have made myself to be. For, as I
have suggested in a former lecture, neither knowledge nor goodness can be produced ready-made
or created at a stroke. A mind starting into
existence fully developed and furnished with knowledge is a self-contradictory notion; for we
cannot conceive of mind as a passive receptacle in which ideas are deposited. Ideas can
become the possession of the mind only by a
process in which a subjective activity is involved.
A higher mind cannot simply make over its
intellectual wealth to another, apart from an
apprehensive or appropriating activity akin to its
own. And the same may be said, not only of
the mind's content, but of the mind itself. What
we mean by such terms as ability, talent, intellectual
power, cannot from the nature of the thing be
conceived of simply as an original gift or endow-
ment. Intelligence that has not yet exerted itself
on the external materials of knowledge or begun
to realize itself through converse with an objective
world, is, at the utmost, only the abstract potentiality of intelligence; and though we may speak
of an individual mind as of 'great natural
capacity,' as 'dowered with the gifts of genius,'

But a mind
may be so perfects
by grace as to
be capable of
avoiding all
error or mistaken
argument, prior
to its acquisition
empirical knowl-
edge. Cf. the
human mind of
Xt.

Diff's of mental capacity argue the possibility of transcendent capacity. Then ampl gifts have to be allowed for & the absence of sin.

what we speak of can exist at first only as a latent possibility, hidden from itself and the world, which can become a reality only by action and reaction with its environment in nature and human society.

And the same principle holds good of man's moral nature. Moral character is not a thing which can be created wholesale or independently of the self-determination of the subject. That which is natural, instinctive, spontaneous, possesses no moral worth. Moral beauty cannot, like physical, be a gift of nature. A beautiful soul is a work of art, but in this case the work and the artist are one. At most, nature can only supply the materials, the natural desires and impulses on which the artist works, and which are to be transformed into spiritual beauty. Even when these desires and impulses have an outward semblance of what is good and fair, that which we call 'natural amiability,' in so far as it is instinctive, has no more moral value, no nearer approximation to moral beauty, than the loveliness of a flower or the gentleness and playfulness of an animal. To acquire that value, thought must put itself into these natural tendencies, reason and will must mould and transform them. Nature, indeed, may

i.e. if necessary But cf. God Who is perfectly holy by nature. See p. 128.

?

be said in one sense to have her own works of art. As every plant and flower, every living organism gathers up into itself the germinating influences of earth and air and moisture and light and heat, and slowly elaborates from the matter of the inorganic world the membered and fully developed totality which constitutes its ideal perfection—in producing this result, nature may be said to be anticipating in her own domain that self-creating power which is the prerogative of spirit. But the distinction is that nature here, if an artist, is a blind unconscious artist. Neither the idea at which she aims, nor the process by which it is achieved, exists for herself, but only for an intelligence that observes her operations. The seed or germ is not conscious of itself or of its own future, nor does it by any conscious effort seek to realize it. And though there is in the work of nature a mimicry of the higher work of spirit, there is yet an utter absence of that which gives to the spiritual creation its distinctive character and worth. For of the latter this is the essential characteristic, that it rises above that which it immediately is, to apprehend more or less clearly the idea of what it ought to be—above the narrow, bounded, finite sphere in which it exists as a thing of nature, to lay hold by the spiritual imagination of that image of God, that infinite perfection which it is destined to share—and that every actual approximation to that ideal is gained as the result of conscious aspiration and endeavour.

2. But whilst thus the ideal perfection of man's nature, which is expressed in the phrase, " image of God," is to be looked for, not at the outset, but at the final stage of the spiritual life, there is a sense in which it belongs to the original constitution of man's nature.   Last in time, it is first in thought.   The principle, the self-realizing idea out of which all the phenomena of man's historical life flows, is present in it from the beginning. And though we reject the notion of a primitive state of perfection, yet, even at the earliest stage of his life as a spiritual being we must conceive of that idea as manifesting its presence and power. In a great work of art there is a sense in which the idea of the perfect whole is present and operative from the beginning—in the first prelusive note of the great symphony, in the first line of the great epic or dramatic poem, in the first touch of the master's hand impressed on the canvas or the marble.   The idea of the future plant, again, or of the perfect organism, is present in the

germ or seemingly structureless cell, not indeed as a miniature or microscopic copy of it, but as the productive principle, the prophetic anticipation of its future. So, again, we say that the child is father to the man ; that the power that makes the philosopher, the poet, the hero, lies latent in him from the dawn of his conscious life, ere education and the discipline of life have begun to elicit it ; nay, that though, for lack of such external influences, it may never come to the birth, yet there, in the hidden spirit and being of the man, the un-realized ideal of human greatness is present. In like manner, whatever be the actual or immediate phenomena of man's empirical life, it is the presence and power of the idea of his nature, as made in the image of God, that gives to his whole life and history its distinctive character and significance. What, then, let us now briefly ask, are we to understand by that idea ? In what does man's likeness to God consist ?

It consists, I answer, in general in this, that as God is the Infinite Self-revealing Spirit, so in the very essence of man's nature as spirit there is a reflexion of the spirituality, and, in one sense, of the infinitude of God. At first sight it seems extravagant and self-contradictory to speak of

M

man's nature as infinite or as containing an infinite element. Outwardly regarded, man is but a part of nature, subject to its conditions, sharing in its limitations. He is but an atom in a boundless world, occupying but a limited portion of space and a brief section of time ; changeful, transient, mortal, determined physically in all his states and changes by relations that are independent of his will—by laws that are common to him with material nature, and by appetites, wants, impulses, passions, which he shares with the lower animals. Even with respect to his spiritual nature, his intelligence, affections, will, can we speak of him as other than finite ? His consciousness seems to be determined through and through by its relation to his bodily organization. The thoughts, emotions, volitions, which form the content of his conscious life are correlated to physical changes or motions in the brain and nervous system, and the healthy or morbid action of the mind seems to depend on the normal or abnormal state of a purely material substance. Moreover, it is, as we have seen, of the very essence of human knowledge and goodness that it should be, not an immediate possession, but the result of a process of effort and growth. Even at the best, therefore, intellectual and moral attainment can only in man be imperfect. We never are that which we may or ought to be. The sense of our finitude is forced on us anew at each step of our progress, as the intellectual and moral horizon expands before us ; and from the nature of the thing, it is deepest in the highest and noblest minds.

Yet, on the other hand, in whatever way we may explain its relation to our finite and temporal nature, there is another element or aspect of our being, to which in the truest sense of the word the predicate ' infinite' may be applied—that element which constitutes the principle of our whole spiritual life, the source of all knowledge, morality, religion. There is that in us as spiritual beings which rises above the limits of time and space ; which, as the *presupposition* of our knowledge of nature, is not subject to the conditions of nature and of our own natural experience ; which is, in one sense, uncaused, uncreated, unconditioned, having no temporal beginning or end, and of which we can think, not as that which is created by God regarded as an outward omnipotent power, but as the reproduction or reflexion of His own eternal consciousness and life.

The existence of this infinite element in man's nature may be established on various grounds.

1. It is implied in that very sense of finitude, limitation, imperfection, of which I have just spoken. It is only through the infinite in man that he can become aware of his finitude. It is the ideal in us that reveals the imperfection of the actual. If man were wholly finite, he would not know his finitude. Knowledge by the finite of its finitude is, indeed, a self-contradictory notion. Finitude means limitation by that which is outside of or beyond the finite object. A prisoner, who knew nothing of a world beyond his cell, would be unconscious of his confinement and incapable of the sense of bondage. So, if man's consciousness fell wholly within himself, the narrowness or limitation of his actual existence would be unfelt and unknown ; and, on the other hand, the fact that he knows and feels his finitude is itself the proof that he is not wholly finite. In all spheres of human attainment, in knowledge and action, in science, art, morality, the sense of inadequacy and imperfection betrays the presence in us of an ideal element, a standard of perfection with which our empirical life is contrasted. In the very beginning of knowledge, there is a sense in which the mind has already grasped the goal or end of perfect science and is conscious of its own essential

relation to it ; and it is this that is the secret of
the unrest and dissatisfaction to which error and
imperfect knowledge give rise.

It would, indeed, be absurd to say that there is
a conscious recognition of this idea in every mind
from the outset of its intellectual life, or that the
pain of ignorance and error is due to the conscious
falling short of an infinite standard. But unconscious or vaguely cognizant as the mind may
be of the ultimate basis of its own activity, it is
nevertheless true that in all thought, even the most
elementary, we presuppose an absolute criterion of
thought, an ideal of knowledge, to which our
individual thoughts and opinions must conform
themselves ; and that all our knowledge is only the
gradual realization of that self-consistent whole of
truth which, from the first movement of intelligence,
it presupposes. But for this ideal, the dissatisfaction
with all past attainments, the perpetual endeavour to
advance beyond our limits, would have no meaning ;
and it is to this infinite ideal ever hovering before
us, and implicated with the very essence of our
intelligence, that the unquenched and unquenchable
thirst for knowledge is to be traced.

And the same principle applies to our moral
endeavours and attainments. The whole meaning

of our moral life, and especially of the sense of imperfection and sin—our inward conflicts, our penitence, remorse, self-condemnation—lies in this, that there is in us, part and parcel of our spiritual nature, an ideal of excellence whose infinite claims we are in our actual life falling short of or denying. If we were wholly finite, creatures of finite desires, capable only of finite satisfactions, there would be no such experience as that of moral unrest and self-reproach. In the merely animal life there *is* no such experience. The animal is wholly identical with its impulses and satisfied in their satisfaction. In yielding itself to them it has no sense of bondage, no consciousness of a higher life unfulfilled. If man were wholly finite, if finite desires and appetites were the beginning and end of his being, these being satisfied, *he* would be satisfied. There would be for him no fretting against the limitations of life, no horror of the death that ends it. But it is of the very essence of a spiritual nature that it is capable of a life that transcends all finite desires, and which manifests itself, if not otherwise, at least in the disquietude, the unhappiness, the self-contempt of a life of merely animal and sensuous indulgence.

2. But it is not merely negatively, or by the consciousness of limitation, that the infinite element

in man's spiritual nature betrays its presence. As spiritual, self-conscious beings, we are not merely conscious of our limits, but conscious also of the power to transcend them; we are capable of identifying ourselves with an end which is essentially infinite. There are two aspects in which man's nature can be contemplated, in one of which he is like, in the other unlike, all other finite existences. In the former aspect, he can view himself as simply one amongst the innumerable objects to which his observation is directed. As he can observe and examine the other existences in the external world, classify them, discern the laws which regulate their changes and relations, so he can regard himself as a single object amidst other objects, observe the facts and phenomena of his individual nature, physical and mental, his bodily organization, his sensitive and intellectual capacities ; and out of the materials thus collected he can create sciences of anatomy, physiology, and psychology. But in so dealing with himself and other objects, there is one essential distinction which, thus far, he has left out, namely, that he is *not* simply one object amidst a multiplicity of objects in the universe, but that he has in him the principle in and through which he himself and all other individual objects have any existence or meaning. He is not merely one amongst innumerable objects observed and thought of, but he has in him that principle of thought to which all objects are relative and which all objects and sciences of objects presuppose. The sciences of observation abstract, and for their purpose necessarily abstract, in dealing with the outward facts and phenomena of nature, from that principle which is yet implicit and active in all the processes and methods of science—relation to the observing, thinking intelligence. And even when it is man himself that is the object of observation, the whole materials of a science of body and mind exist only in relation to the principle of thought or self-consciousness, which transcends as well as apprehends them.

Now, if we reflect on what is involved in this distinction, we shall see, I think, that it implies in man, as intelligence, that which raises him above nature, above all other finite existences, in one sense, above himself, and renders him essentially akin to the infinite source of all finite being. For it is obvious that that which is presupposed in the knowledge and even in the existence of finite things, cannot itself be one of them and nothing more. When we create sciences of nature, observe facts

and events in space and time, apprehend their relations of co-existence and succession, the thought
or intelligence that performs this function must be
something which, as it is presupposed in all these
finite objects and relations, cannot be included
in them, but must needs itself rise above them.
That, for instance, which grasps and correlates
objects in space, cannot itself be one of the things
in space ; that which apprehends and connects
events as succeeding each other in time, must
itself stand above the succession or stream of
events. In being able to measure them it cannot
be flowing with them. There could not be for
self-consciousness any such thing as time, if it were
not, in one aspect of it, above time ; if it did not
belong to an order which is or has in it an element
that is eternal. Our knowledge is indeed a thing
of time in the sense that it is progressive, acquired
by successive steps—in the sense, in other words,
that it takes time to think. But, as taken up
into thought, succession is not itself successive ; the
successive events enter into a region in which they
are stript of the form of time, and are present simul-
taneously, in purely rational relations, to the mind
that thinks them.

So, again, when it is our own individual nature

and life that is the object of thought, the principle by which we know ourselves as individuals
cannot pertain to us *as* individuals.   We think,
not as merely individuals, but as standing above
our individuality, rising into a universal point of
view from which we can survey our own transient,
finite existence in common with that of all other
finite things and beings, and in virtue of which
we can pronounce it to be transitory and finite.
And, in general, of our relation to the realm of
truth or knowledge it may be said that it does
not pertain to us as individuals.   The truth I
apprehend is not true for me as this particular
being ; it is true for all intelligence, and for me
as entering into the universal life of intelligence.
It is true, not as my opinion, but as God's truth,
and for me as capable of participating in the
universal, eternal mind.

Moreover, though it is true that infinitude can
never pertain to man, in the sense in which it
pertains to the mind for which the ideal and actual
are one, in which the whole of truth is grasped
intuitively and as a completed reality, yet it does
pertain to him in the sense that that completed
whole of knowledge is for every intelligence a
virtual possession.

From one point of view, knowledge is a never-ending advance into a realm that stretches far and for ever beyond us; yet, from another point of view, we can claim that illimitable future of knowledge as not a foreign territory, but a realm that is our own. For, in every advancing step of knowledge we are not conquering what belongs to an alien power, but realizing ourselves, reclaiming an inheritance which from the first is not merely our own but part of our very selves. It is the prerogative of intelligence that it can realize itself in everything that seems to limit it and to lie beyond it. A purely finite nature cannot transcend the barrier which separates its individuality from that of all other individuals. But it is the characteristic of spirit or self-consciousness that there is no external barrier which it cannot surmount. The externality which nature seems to possess, dissolves away before the thought that grasps it. As part of an intelligible world, every object which intelligence contemplates is its own object ; and as it enters into knowledge and yields up its essence to the mind that lays hold of it, it becomes for that mind a revelation of its own latent wealth, or rather of its capacity for participating in the wealth of the Mind for and in which all things have their being.

And the same principle holds good of our moral nature. On the practical as well as the theoretical side, there is an aspect of our nature in which it is not merely one amongst the multiplicity of objects in the universe, but the subject which is presupposed in all objects, and which therefore is akin to the infinite source wherefrom they proceed. We may regard ourselves as capable of leading not merely an individual, but a universal and infinite life. It is possible, indeed, to lead a life having its beginning and end in motives, aims, satisfactions which belong to me only as this particular self; which take in no wider range of being than my own and are commensurate at most only with my own finite, transient existence. For of the appetites, impulses, desires which belong to our sensitive and animal nature this, *prima facie* at least, is the essential characteristic, that their satisfaction pertains to the individual as this particular self; and even as regards that, that they have no relation to anything beyond their immediate satisfaction. The joy of agreeable feeling is my own and not another's; it is self-centred, self-included, or if it has any reference to others, it is only in so far as they are instruments or means of my personal enjoyment. Moreover, even within the individual self, the pleasures of appetite and impulse have in them nothing permanent. Each particular gratification passes away with its immediate experience, is gone with the feeling of the moment; and a thousand such experiences render me no richer at the end than at the beginning.

But, on the other hand, it is possible for a man to lead a life that is not merely individual. Indeed, even the desires and impulses of the individual nature take their peculiar complexion in man from the fact that a universal nature is present to them. They are not in man what they are in the merely animal nature. His desires are never mere impulses, but impulses through which the permanent self is seeking its own satisfaction. But the self-consciousness which thus qualifies the desires, is also the principle in virtue of which it is possible to rise above them.

As, in knowledge, we rise above the sphere of individual opinion into the universal life of intelligence, so, in the moral or practical life, we rise out of the sphere of individual impulse, of self-indulgence and self-assertion, into a sphere in which we will no ends but those that are common to all spiritual beings and enter into a life that is one with the universal and infinite will. In will as well as in intelligence, man's spiritual nature is the form of an infinite content ; and there is nothing in the whole realm of being which it cannot claim as the means of its realization. Every object of moral effort, every thing and being in the universe by which our moral development is attained, is *our own* object. It is not other *than* ourselves, but the other *of* ourselves ; and however far we may conceive humanity to advance in goodness, it will not be appropriating what is foreign to it, but only finding itself—realizing its own latent possibilities, appropriating its own inherent wealth. Even within the course of man's temporal existence, every man who endeavours to lead a good or holy life finds that there is nothing in his experience that may not become the means of his moral and spiritual advancement. The incidents of the individual life, its relations to nature and man, its opportunities and exigencies, its temptations and trials, all that is pure and noble and good in the world, and even the darkness, disorder, and evil with which the good is ever in conflict— all this constitutes a vast material of moral discipline, an external environment so related to the spirit of man as to become the means of its self-realization. And if we regard the history of the world as a manifestation of a divine idea or purpose which is ever moving on to its fulfilment, it becomes in a deeper way a revelation of the infinite possibilities of our spiritual nature. For, so regarded, the life that underlies it is one with our own moral life. The whole history of the world, seen in the light of the divine ideal that inspires it, is only the objective, or *other*, of that ideal which is the essence of our moral consciousness ; and all that realizes the former realizes also the latter. Of the will that is in harmony with the will of God it may be said, " All things are yours, whether things present or things to come " ; for " all things work together for good to them that love God."

But even when we have reached this point, we seem still to fall short of that capacity of an infinite or eternal life which is implied in the phrase " made in the image of God." The moral life, at the very best and highest, is and ever must be imperfect, a life in which that which *is*, is distinguished from and falls short of, that which *ought to be*. The goal of moral perfection recedes as we advance ; and beyond the highest and best which has been attained either by the individual or the race, there are possibilities of excellence which neither society nor the individual who reflects its moral ideal has achieved. I may surrender and abnegate my will as that of this private particular self, and identify my life with the organic life of the world, but that organic life is itself a limited and imperfect one. The ideal of an infinite life would, therefore, seem to be an ideal to which we may endlessly approximate, but which we can never realize.

Now, from one point of view, it must be conceded that this objection is an insuperable one; for to overcome it would imply, not simply that man is capable of likeness to God, but that he can become God. Infinitude can never be predicated of the finite spirit in the sense in which it pertains to that Infinite Spirit, in whom the ideal and actual are one. In the life of God there are no unrealized possibilities. The presupposition of all our knowledge and activity is that absolute and eternal unity of knowing and being, which is only another expression for the nature of God. In one sense, He is all reality and the only reality, whilst all finite existence is but a *becoming*, which never *is*.

But whilst thus, from one point of view, the ideal of spiritual perfection is ever a future and distant goal, from another it is, or may be, a present reality. For just in this lies the distinction between the moral life and the religious life which explains and consummates it,—that whilst the former implies a yet unsolved division between our actual and our true or universal self, an 'ought to be' which never wholly 'is,' in religion this division passes away. Religion is the absolute self-surrender of the soul to God. It means the giving up or annulling of the private, particular self, of every interest or satisfaction that belongs to me as this particular individuality, and the blending or identification of my will, and potentially of my whole life and being, with the will of the Infinite. It is the response of the human spirit to the command, "Be ye therefore perfect, even as your Father which is in heaven is perfect." That response does not indeed imply that all imperfection has vanished, that all desires and volitions which belong to this particular self are obliterated; but it means that in responding to the divine command, we wholly renounce that former self as false and evil, die to it and its affections and lusts, and put our whole will into that higher, truer self which is one with the being and life of God. The residuum of selfishness that clings to us, we put away from us as foreign to our real self; we hate and condemn it as if it belonged not

N

to us, but to another whom we regard as an intruder and enemy.

Our response to the divine command, again, does not imply that the religious life is not a progressive one, a life of successive acts and experiences; or that it can ever become one with the life of God in the sense, already referred to, of the absolute unification of the ideal and real. But wherever it is genuine, the *principle* of that life is present in it, and we may say that, though not extensively and exhaustively, it is intensively one and the same with the life of God. Endless possibilities of activity and attainment may lie before it; but the principle that gives its meaning and value to all spiritual acts, and which is the inexhaustible source from whence they flow, is there from the beginning. The whole future is gathered up into it. Likeness to God is not a far off hope, a light that gleams upon us through the mists of time, a prize to be won only when revolving years have passed. It is a present and immediate experience, or rather it is a thing which does not belong to the sphere of time and cannot be spoken of in forms of expression that belong to it. In religion the spirit passes out of the realm of time, rises above the passing shows of things, the vain fears and vainer hopes that pertain to the things seen and temporal. The outward life may be still in some measure a life of effort, struggle, conflict; but in that inner sphere in which the true life lies, the strife is over, the victory already achieved ; hope has passed into fruition, struggle into conquest, restless effort and endeavour into perfect peace—" the peace of God which passeth all understanding."

LECTURE VIII.

THEORIES AS TO THE ORIGIN AND NATURE OF EVIL.

I. THE AUGUSTINIAN THEORY.

IS it possible to maintain that conception of man's nature which we have seen to be implied in its being made in the image of God, consistently with what experience teaches of the moral and spiritual history of the world? This question, as well as many other speculative difficulties, is pressed upon us in the problem as to the origin and nature of evil. For that problem has an obvious bearing on our belief in God and a moral order of the universe. It affects our view of human freedom and responsibility, of the relation of the individual to the race, of the future hopes and destinies of humanity. Can we hold together in our thought the notion of a world which is the manifestation of infinite goodness, and that of a world in which

sin and sorrow prevail ; or reconcile our belief in
an absolutely beneficent will as the origin and
end of all, with our experience of a state of
things in which that will seems to be everywhere
opposed and frustrated ? Must not our sense of
responsibility, again, be greatly affected by the
notion of an inborn, hereditary bias to evil as the
universal condition of our moral life ; and does not
our reception or rejection of this notion involve
all the difficult questions as to the measure in
which individual freedom and responsibility are
affected by the relation of the individual to his
social environment—to the past history of the
race and the present moral atmosphere in which
he lives ? Finally, as the diagnosis of a disease
must precede and determine our view of the
remedy, must not our conception of the work of
redemption be determined or modified by our idea
of the moral and spiritual exigency which it is
intended to meet ?

But, apart from these more general aspects of the
problem of evil, the primary difficulty with which,
at this stage of our inquiry, we have to do, is that
which is involved in the rise or emergence of sin
in a nature which is by its very essence a reflexion
of the nature of God. How can evil be conceived

to arise in a nature created good? Without modifying the idea of its being made in the image of God and presupposing a latent tendency to evil in its very structure, does it not seem impossible to account for the moral blight which has fallen upon it? Do not all the various theories that have been propounded as to the origin of sin virtually trace it to some original flaw or defect in man's nature; and do they not thus presuppose the thing they would account for, and necessarily ascribe this evil element to the immediate causation of Him from whom man's nature proceeds?

Shall we explain the existence of sin, for example, as due to some malign external influence acting on a nature originally pure and good, marring the beauty of God's fair handiwork and introducing into it disorder and defilement? Not only, however, does the existence of any such foreign evil influence simply reproduce the difficulty in question at an earlier stage, but its triumph over man would be inconceivable, apart from the existence of something in his own nature to which it could appeal, some predisposition or tendency to evil by means of which alone any external temptation could prove successful. In a nature absolutely pure the seed of evil would find no soil in which to germinate.

How about self-determination involving possibility of wrong determin.? See p. 169 top.

Or, again, shall we have recourse to the only too easy and plausible solution that moral action implies in the agent an absolute freedom of choice between good and evil—that to lend any moral value to his actions he must be not only " sufficient to have stood " but " free to fall"? The inadequacy of any such solution is at once obvious when we reflect that a moral nature cannot be conceived of as one which is possessed of an absolute "freedom of indifference" between good and evil, but one which must be thought of as having a predisposition towards good as the realization of its own essence. An absolute equilibrium between good and evil would itself be of the nature of evil. Further, even if any such original equilibrium could be conceived of, it would not, in any given instance, account for the adoption of either of the opposite alternatives, still less for the persistent swaying of the balance to one or other of the two sides. From the point of view of absolute or indeterminate freedom as the inherent prerogative of human nature, it would be plausible to say that at least one half of the human race, or each individual in one half of his actions, should have gone right instead of wrong ; but it would be *only* plausible, for, to account for the turn of the balance either way, some new motive power or deflecting influence other than the will itself is needed.

Once more, shall we, with many, seek the explanation of man's fall from original innocence and of the universal prevalence of evil, in the power of the flesh over the spirit ?   But here again the futility of the explanation seems to be obvious ; for either we must suppose the flesh, the carnal or sensuous side of man's nature, with its appetites and passions, to be in itself evil, in which case the evil element is presupposed in its original constitution and its existence can only be ascribed to the author of that constitution ; or, if we conceive the original evil to lie, not in the sensuous appetites and impulses—which are no more evil in man than in the lower animals—but in the preponderance of these over the spiritual nature, then, either that preponderance must be natural or inevitable, and the responsibility must pertain to Him who made the flesh strong and the spirit weak ; or, if it be not inevitable, but due to the voluntary succumbing of the higher nature to the lower, then we only recur to that solution of the problem in the idea of freedom, which we have already seen to be inadequate and illusory.

Or, finally, to name no other solution, shall we accept the view of those theorists who see in evil only a necessary step or stage in the development of a finite spirit, and regard the final perfection of a moral nature as attainable only under the condition of its passing through the experience of evil? Then, indeed, in so far as this explanation rests on the idea already adverted to, that the true "image of God" is that which pertains, not to the origin but to the end of man's career, and that the glorious future which is God's purpose for humanity, the perfect reconciliation of man with God which is to be brought about by redemption and grace, presupposes that division and discord which sin has introduced into the world—in so far as the theory in question finds its basis in this idea, it contains an element which is profoundly true. Yet, on the other hand, it would seem to involve a principle from which the unsophisticated moral consciousness shrinks. The necessity of *physical* evil it may be possible to justify. The purest happiness, the highest good may be that which is attainable only through suffering and sacrifice, but can we say also that it is that which is attainable only through sin? Is it not possible to conceive of a spiritual perfection which is the result of a continuous and uninterrupted development, or, at most, of the struggle with temptation by a nature that never yields to it? And even if it be not so, can we conceive of a moral perfection for which sin is the necessary price? Could we legitimately purchase any good however great for ourselves or others at the cost of an immoral act; and if not, can the system of the universe be based on a principle from which the healthy moral sense revolts? Moreover, is not the necessity of sin a self-contradictory notion, denying in the predicate what the subject affirms? Are not guilt, and liability to condemnation and punishment, essential elements in the notion of sin; and can we connect penal desert with that which, in the order of the world or the nature of things, is the necessary condition of moral attainment?

These considerations may serve to indicate some of the difficulties which beset the problem of evil. Are we, because of these difficulties, compelled to abandon it as insoluble? It is true, indeed, that no theoretical difficulties can quell or over-ride the practical instincts that are the springs of our moral life. That God is good and can never be the author of evil, that we are responsible for our actions and justly punishable for our misdeeds, that no speculative theorizing can explain away the terrible reality of moral evil, that the voice of conscience tells us that we ought to struggle with it and therefore may hope to overcome it, and that there is no moral disability in our nature which exempts us from the conflict—these and the like are convictions which no speculative difficulties can subvert. On the other hand, it is hard to suppose that there should be any such cleft between the intellectual and the moral life as would be implied in saying that convictions, which are imperative to the conscience, are contradictory or inexplicable to the reason. At any rate, it would be at least a partial reward of inquiry to discover, by a careful review of past attempts, what the point is at which light fails us, and from which all future endeavours must take their start.

In what follows, therefore, I shall examine the various attempts, to some of which I have above briefly adverted, to throw light on the question as to the nature and origin of moral evil, and endeavour to show how far on this, as on other religious doctrines, philosophy is in harmony with

Christian faith. In what remains of this lecture I shall deal with what may be called the ecclesiastical theory, that which since the time of Augustine has dominated the mind of the Christian Church, and which has found its formal expression, under various modifications, in the Catholic and Protestant confessions and creeds.

The Church doctrine as to the present moral condition of human nature has for its necessary presupposition its further doctrine as to the *status integritatis*, the original, unfallen condition of man. The present state of the world, morally and physically, implies a previous part of the drama of human life without which it would be inexplicable. The course of history begins at a point where it can become intelligible only as the sequel to a prehistoric stage. Now, and as far back as history and tradition extend, man is seen to be not only subjected to physical evils, which seem to be irreconcilable with a beneficent and righteous moral government save as the penalty of moral transgression, but he comes into the world with an evil moral bias, which can be accounted for only as the result of a past moral history. As in the individual life we connect a man's present character with his past actions, and find, for instance, the explanation of an enfeebled constitution in former vicious excess, of evil habits in the depraving influence of past vices and sins ; so, the disastrous physical and moral conditions, to which from the birth all mankind are subjected, seem to point backwards to a stage of human history of which the present is the natural and necessary sequel. The old doctrine of Metempsychosis attempted to explain these unfortunate conditions, by regarding them as the results of the doings of men in a previous state of existence. By an analogous device the Augustinian theory would account for the innate bias to evil which is the universal characteristic of human life, not indeed as the result of a pre-existent or pre-natal individual life, but by regarding the moral life of the race as one connected whole, and its present condition as the fatal result of a moral probation to which, in the person of its first progenitor, it was sub-jected. The apparent anomalies of human life cease to be anomalous when we rise to a more comprehensive point of view, and, contemplating the race as one collective personality, discern in these evils the natural consequences of its own voluntary aberration from a state of innocence. If the creation of a race of beings, with a nature morally tainted or having in it the seeds of moral pravity, makes God the author of evil, such an inference seems to be no longer necessary when we conceive of human nature, as it comes from the hand of God, as morally pure and good. If responsibility implies freedom, and if a moral depravity and guilt, not the result of the subject's own acts, seem to involve a contradiction in terms, this apparent contradiction is obviated by the conception of human nature as originally endowed with an absolute freedom of choice between good and evil, and of its present deterioration as the natural consequence of its own misuse of that freedom. The physical evils which are the universal lot of humanity lose the aspect of arbitrariness and injustice, when we see in them the penal inflictions of divine justice for the sin of the race.

According to this theory, then, the sin to which all other sins are traceable is the sin, not simply of an individual historic person, but of humanity as represented or embodied in him. The first transgression poisoned human nature at the root. The direful consequences which are ascribed to it,— moral guilt and condemnation, the loss of original righteousness, estrangement from God, the total depravation of man's inward nature, including a fatal proclivity to sin, together with all the outward and physical ills to which flesh is heir—toil and trouble, pain and sorrow, disease and death,—these fatal effects of the first lapse from goodness, are to be regarded as affecting not merely the first transgressor, but human nature, as subjected in his person to moral probation, and as having misused its original gift of freedom. The link, therefore, on which the whole theory turns is the universal or generic character which is ascribed to the progenitor of the race. He stands out, in distinction from all the other members of it, as a unique personality, a kind of universal man, the idealized symbol or embodiment of humanity ; and the incidents of his moral history are lifted out of the character that belongs to them as the events of an individual life, and become invested with a universal significance, as the first acts of the tragedy of which humanity itself, regarded as one collective personality, is the hero.

And if we ask how we are to conceive of this universal character as pertaining to the first man, and of the generic significance that is ascribed to his acts, the answer of the Augustinian theologians has taken various forms. In what may perhaps be termed the crudest and harshest form, the generic significance of the moral history of the first man is represented as due simply to an arbitrary juridical arrangement on God's part, according to which the first man became the moral representative of the race, and by a divine determination or decree, the fate of the whole human race was made to turn on the issue of his probation.   Various analogies—such as the act of attainder by which the descendants of a traitor are implicated in his treason, or a community or nation are held accountable for the acts of its head or representative—are appealed to as giving a colour of reasonableness to this supposed divine economy.   In what is called the "Federal Theology," the figure of a covenant or pact between God and man is employed, not as an illustration, but as the account of an actual transaction, in which Adam, as the "covenant head" of mankind, concluded in his state of innocence a treaty with the Creator, according to which his moral failure or success should count as that of his whole posterity.

Or, again, finding it impossible to meet the objection that it is only for the acts or intromissions of a representative whom they themselves have chosen that his constituents can be justly held accountable, the idea has been gravely propounded that Adam, though not actually the representative, was in the divine foreknowledge the type, of all other members of the race ; and that the Omniscient Being, who foresaw that in every other case the moral trial would issue in a like result, might fairly regard them as acting as the first probationer acted, and condemn and punish them accordingly. But the failure of these and similar theological devices to give a colour of rationality to the notion of imputed sin, led to a modification of the doctrine of the relation of the race to its first progenitor. If there was nothing in that relation which made men actually partakers of Adam's guilt, an arbitrary decree or determination to hold them guilty was obviously nothing more than a legal fiction. Accordingly the attempt was made by St. Augustine, in what may be termed the second or modified form of the doctrine of imputation, to conceive, though in a way scarcely less fictitious than in the doctrine of arbitrary or constructive imputa- tion, of an actual participation by the race in the sin of its prototype. "We were all," Augustine writes, "*in* that one man, when we *were* all that one man, who fell into sin. Not as yet was the particular form created and distributed to each of us in which we were individually to live, but already the seminal nature existed from which we were to be propagated ; and this being vitiated by sin was bound by the chain of death and justly condemned."[1]

The harshness, or rather irrationality of the notion of constructive guilt or of the transference of the demerit of one man, not merely to all other men, but to the myriads of the race who at the time of the transaction did not even exist, Augustine conceived it possible to obviate by the conception that the unborn generations were seminally present in the person of the first man. By means of this conception we do not create an impossible separation of guilt from sin, or make those to share in condemnation and punishment who were not sharers in the offence. As the whole plant is virtually present in the seed or germ, or as the embryo contains in it the whole future of the organism, so all the generations of men were virtually present in the individual man from whom they sprang, and became culpable

---

[1] *De civit. Dei*, xiii. 14. *Omnes enim fuimus in illo uno, quando omnes fuimus ille unus qui per feminam lapsus est in peccatum. . . Nondum erat nobis singillatim creata et distributa forma, in qua singuli viveremus ; sed jam erat natura seminalis, ex qua propagaremar ; qua scilicet propter peccatum vitiata et vinculo mortis obstricta justeque damnata, non alterius condicionis homo ex homine nasceretur.*

because in a sense co-operating or consenting parties to the act by which he fell. But rightly construed, the conception of seminal guilt, or of a sin which contains or involves all future sins, if any real meaning could be attached to it, would seem to imply that Adam was guilty of all the sins of his descendants, rather than they of his. On the other hand, the logical consequence of the idea of actual participation in the sin of one from whom we are lineally descended, would be that every successive generation is guilty of the sins of all preceding generations; that on every individual, irrespective of his personal character, rests the accumulated burden of all the sins and crimes of his ancestry, and that it is the last and not the first man on whom rests the guilt of the whole race. That such a doctrine should have been seriously propounded by Augustine, only serves to show the extravagance into which a great and subtle mind may be led by controversial exigencies.

The last and simplest form in which the doctrine of original sin, or of the implication of the race in the sin of its first parent, has been held, is that which makes that sin consist simply in an inherited or innate bias of our nature to evil. Not by any participation, constructive or actual, in the first sin,

but by the vitiating influence which it has wrought
on the minds and wills of the first sinner's descendants, can we be said to participate in his guilt.
We are guilty from the birth because we are
sinful from the birth. Universal experience seems
to corroborate in this respect the teaching of
Scripture. The doctrine which the Biblical narrative
of the Fall, interpreted in the light of St. Paul's
reproduction of it in the Epistle to the Romans,
seems to teach, is that the entail of moral, is as
universal as that of physical evil. As all men
are by nature liable to pain and sorrow and death,
and as these evils affect us independently of any
will or act of the individual, so all men are by
nature inheritors, independently of any individual
action, nay, prior to the dawn of self-consciousness,
of an inborn propensity or proclivity to sin ; and
this congenital evil bias can be traced back,
through the whole past history of the race, to the
progenitor in whose person the virus of moral
evil was first introduced into the originally pure
and perfect nature of man.

Nor is this notion inconsistent with the well-
known laws which determine the character and
complexion of our individual life. The principle of
heredity notoriously applies, not merely to our cor-

poreal, but also to our spiritual nature. None can doubt the transmissibility of physical disease, or of liability to special forms of such disease, from parent to child ; and not seldom a constitution congenitally weak and sickly can be traced back for generations to some remote ancestor of the subject of it. Equally undeniable are the facts which seem to sanction the idea of hereditary moral characteristics. Vicious and criminal propensities, tendencies to intemperance, sensuality, dishonesty, and other vices, seem not seldom to run in the blood. Nor, however much we may pity the victims of such tendencies, do we regard these as in any individual case suspending responsibility, or exempting the perpetrator of immoral or criminal acts from moral censure and punishment. The Church doctrine, therefore, of original sin as an inborn predisposition to evil prior to actual sin, in virtue of which the subject of it lies under the wrath and curse of God, whatever speculative difficulties it may involve, is, it has been maintained, consistent with the facts of human experience, and with the principles by which our moral judgments are determined.

The doctrine of original sin, as I have now explained it, is in many points open to objection, and in its bare and literal form is no longer accepted by modern thought as a true represent-ation of the spiritual life and history of mankind. Nevertheless, reflection, I think, will lead us to see that it contains, under a hard, and, in the view of many, even revolting form, a substantial basis of truth. It may be useful to notice briefly some of the objections which have been urged against it, and then to point out what we conceive to be the element of truth that underlies it.

1. It may be remarked at the outset that this explanation is not really relevant to our present inquiry. It is not a doctrine of the origin of evil. It records the fact, but it does not explain the process by which sin emerges in a nature originally innocent or good. It seems, indeed, to rest on the principle that moral guilt and penal desert are conditioned by the free will of the agent ; and this free will, which it nowhere finds in the present experience of a corrupt and guilty race, it supposes to have existed in a pristine or pre-historic stage of its moral life. But it does not attempt to define or give any speculative account of the nature of human freedom ; or, in so far as it does so, it seems to waver between the freedom which pertains to a perfect moral nature, the freedom of complete harmony with the will of God, and the

freedom which is termed the *liberum arbitrium*, that absolute indifference or equilibrium between good and evil to which I have already referred. If we take it in the former sense, it lay beyond the province of the Augustinian theologians to enter on the purely philosophical inquiry as to the nature and definition of freedom, and that task, as we shall see in the sequel, it has left to modern philosophy to undertake. If we take it in the latter sense, which is by no means that of the ablest exponents of the doctrine, the freedom of indifference or indetermination is a notion which would now be regarded as untenable or even meaningless. A will that is endowed with absolute freedom of choice is a will that swings free from all motives. It exists in a moral vacuum ; it is incapable of any positive action, and if it could be supposed to act at all, its manner of acting would be purely a matter of accident. Neither within nor without is there any reason why it should depart from its moveless equilibrium. Not within, for the slightest movement of the balance would imply the surrender of its prerogative of indifference. Not without, for whatever external motives, whatever appeals to reason or passion, to interest or affection, hope or fear, may be addressed to it, it still retains by supposition the capacity to set them at naught, to resist all external impulse and retain in its own hands that absolute liberty of choice, which yet by its very nature it can never exert. If the state of innocence be conceived of as that in which human nature was possessed of freedom in the sense now described, it was an innocence from which there could have been no departure; a fall or descent from this imaginary elevation would have been an impossibility. It is obvious, therefore, that from this point of view, the objection urged by the opponents of the Augustinian doctrine, namely, that it failed to account, not only for the first sin itself, but also for the disastrous effects ascribed to it, was a valid one. A freedom of indifference, once possessed, could never be lost by any act of our own. It is impossible that a faculty should be lost or destroyed by the fulfilment of its natural or normal functions. An evil choice, quite as much as a good choice, is within the proper province of a will whose very nature is absolute freedom of choice. The loss of freedom and subsequent moral bondage of the will which is ascribed to the first sin means simply the suspension of the power to choose by reason of choosing, the paralysis of the power of motion by reason of moving.

Is this so with God? Does character make a will less absolutely free?

2. But, again, apart from any definition of freedom, it has been urged that the effects ascribed to the first sin are altogether disproportionate to the cause. No human being is ever rendered totally corrupt by a single lapse from the path of virtue. Even when the conditions of a life are altogether hostile to goodness, when the moral atmosphere into which a human spirit is born is charged with the germs of vice, the transition from innocence to moral depravity is a gradual one; and the case before us is that of a human being subjected to no unfavourable conditions, under no contaminating influence of evil example, breathing the pure air of paradisaical innocence, if not of paradisaical perfection. Whether, therefore, we suppose the pristine state of man to have been one of childlike ignorance of good and evil, or of moral perfection, that he should have become totally corrupt by a leap, through a single lapse from rectitude, is inconsistent with the laws which determine the formation of character.

It is to be remarked, however, that this objection, though plausible, is less cogent than it seems, and that there is a basis of truth underlying the Augustinian theory which it overlooks. When we reflect on the moral significance of action, we find,

If Adam was a child in knowl. moral failure wd. rapidly run into savagery, unless some hindering cause prevailed. Not a leap but a quick degenn. It shd be remembered that one sin is rebellion agst God & this is a radical fall. Many sins follow w. time & interior degrad is not instant. But alienation is immediate.

it is true, that single acts do not often of themselves
exert a sudden or violent deteriorating influence on
the spiritual nature ; and that moral declension or
depravation is usually the result of a long series of
such acts accumulating their force in the blinding
and hardening influence of habit.   But it is also
true that human experience includes such a thing
as critical acts, events that constitute the crisis of
a lifetime, occasions when the whole forces of good
or evil are roused into unwonted and decisive
conflict, and when one fatal step may be said to
carry with it incalculable results, if not to determine the whole course of a man's moral history.
Moreover, it is also to be considered that if there
be such a thing as an initiative act of our moral
life, a significance belongs to it which attaches to
no other.   Even where it is not in itself of the
nature of those critical acts which bring into play
the deeper moral forces of our nature, even where,
isolated from all subsequent acts, its moral importance may be slight ; yet, taken in connection with
them, set before the imagination in its relation to
them, its importance may be incalculable.   If we
could in any case retrace the moral history of a
man back to the first sin of childhood, that sin
could not be other than of an order possible to

childhood—a trivial yielding to appetite, a slight act of insubordination or disobedience to a positive command or prohibition, or the like. But whatever its external form, a deep significance would attach to it: not, indeed, as the cause of all the other sins of a lifetime, but as the start on a new stage of a human spirit's history: as marking the waking up from the sleep of nature to self-consciousness and self-determination, and so, in a sense, as fraught with the moral interest of its whole subsequent career. And if we apply the same principle to the generic history of the race, perhaps we may find here the underlying meaning of the simple, naïve, Mosaic story of the fall, and of the seemingly trivial nature of the temptation to which consequences so momentous are ascribed. If the origin of generic character be traced back to the childhood of the race, it is not surprising to find in this simple, pictorial narrative the transgression which marked man's first deviation from innocence represented as a childish one, whilst at the same time, in its real and hidden meaning, it expressed a transition so tremendous as to be described in the words, " Ye shall be as gods, knowing good and evil." Whilst, therefore, in one point of view, the effects ascribed in the Augustinian doctrine to

the first transgression may be regarded as disproportionate and exaggerated ; yet if it is viewed in the
light of the analogy between the individual and
the generic life, as the initiative act that marked
a momentous transition in the moral history of
mankind, the doctrine in question is no longer
untenable, but may, rightly understood, be regarded
as the expression of a deep and far-reaching truth.

3. It remains to consider, lastly, the most for-
midable objection urged by Pelagius and others to
the Augustinian doctrine, namely, that which relates
to the notion of innate or inherited sin.   According
to this notion, as we have seen, men are not by
an impossible fiction made to participate in the
guilt of the first sin, but they are inheritors of a
sinful and guilty nature.   They enter on existence
with a bias or predisposition to sin, which not only
leads, with the development of consciousness, to
the commission of actual sins, but is in itself of
the nature of sin, and therefore amenable to the
divine condemnation and wrath, and to all the
penalties, temporal and eternal, to which sin is
justly liable.   But any such economy as this, it
was with great emphasis urged by the opponents
of Augustine, in so far as it is not self-contradictory
and unthinkable, is inconsistent with the funda-

mental principle of human responsibility. Sin and guilt, anterior to any moral act or the possibility of any such act, is an impossible notion. A being in whom reason and conscience are not yet actually present, is a being who does not yet exist as a moral agent, and who cannot therefore be the object of moral approval or condemnation. If what is condemned in him is not sin, but only a latent and inherited proclivity to sin; if, in other words, the alleged sinfulness is transferred from the actions to the nature of the being implicated, the objections to the doctrine are not obviated by any such device.

It is true that disposition or inward tendency to evil is, apart from positive overt acts, an object of moral censure. What we condemn, indeed, in a bad action is the bad motive from which it springs, and not the mere outward form in which it is express¹; and a bad character, even though the power of outward action be suspended, is in itself an object of moral condemnation. But the ground of our condemnation of character is, that the agent himself has created it, that it is the result of acts committed by him in the exercise of his own freedom, the concentrated form of innumerable bygone sins. But in an evil bias or propensity infused into the individual nature from the beginning, no such ground for disapproval is present. The supposed bias represents nothing in the past history of the agent, nothing in which his own will has played any part, or for which he is more responsible than for a physical mal-formation or congenital disease.

Moreover, if, as Augustine contended, we cannot separate in our thought the original evil bias from the actual sins of which it is the source, if in condemning the latter we must needs carry back our censure to that of which they are only the manifold outward expression, then the original evil tendency, instead of increasing or intensifying, actually extenuates, if it does not wholly remove, the culpability of the subsequent actual transgression. If the supposed tendency be irresistible, the agent is as little responsible for its results as for actions done under physical coercion. If the tendency be resistible, to mean anything it must be of the nature of a provocative or temptation to evil or of a hindrance to good ; in either case it handicaps the agent in his moral career, and must be discounted in our estimate of his moral failures or shortcomings.

Finally, it was urged that it is difficult, if not impossible, to compass the notion of inherited sin, that is, of the transmission of moral qualities, good or bad, from parent to child. That by physical generation physical qualities should be transmitted, that the child should resemble the parent in its bodily structure, and that beauty or deformity, health or disease, should, in man as in the animal creation generally, be propagated by lineal descent; or again, in so far as mental characteristics are conditioned by bodily organization, that indirectly the former should in many instances be traceable to the latter—all this is no more than may be capable of explanation by physiological laws. But the transmissibility of moral qualities by physical generation is, it was alleged, either a grossly materialistic notion, or a process inconsistent with the known laws on which moral agency depends. Nor, it was held, is any such arbitrary hypothesis necessary to account for the fact, in so far as it is a fact, of the moral resemblance often traceable between parent and child. There is nothing more here than can be explained on rational grounds by the potent influence, especially in the early and receptive period of life, of example, imitation, a neglected or bad education,—the manifold outward elements which constitute the moral atmosphere of a household.

It would appear, then, that the doctrine of original sin is open to grave and perhaps unanswerable objections. But some of these objections are applicable only to the form in which the doctrine has been presented in the writings of Augustine and other Church writers, and not to what may be regarded as its real and essential import. When we examine the foregoing criticism, I think we shall find that it is based on a purely individualistic view of the spiritual nature and life of man, and that much of its plausibility is due to the abstract and one-sided principle from which it starts. That principle is the apparently irrefragable one of the absolute and inalienable responsibility of each individual for his own character and conduct. In the moral and spiritual life "every man must bear his own burden." Before the law of right, each individual stands isolated and independent. No other can share his responsibility, nor he that of any other. And if no other can share the responsibility of a moral act, no other can share in its production. From beginning to end the agent must be author of his own actions and shaper of his own destiny. He must start from a position of innocence, with a nature free from all moral bias; and in the working out of his career he must be exempt from all

implication with the lives of other men, from all
social and other influences that operate behind the
will, or mould the moral character irrespective of
his own volition. Whatever his relation to the
outward world, whatever the influences of his social
environment, there must be a point where they are
arrested, a sphere of free self-determination into
which they cannot intrude. However closely he
may be connected with his fellowmen, by the tie
of a common nature, by intercommunication of
thought and feeling, by the links of kindred and
affection, there must be a moral boundary surround-
ing the innermost citadel of the spirit's life ; and
all external influences must be regarded at most
as furnishing only the materials of moral action,
which, to have any real moral bearing, must be
translated by his own volition into the hidden fibre
of his spiritual life.

Plausible, however, as this representation is, I
think it may be shown to owe much of its cogency
to the fact, that it leaves out of sight that aspect
of man's moral and spiritual nature on which the
Augustinian doctrine mainly rests. Results, which
are reached by regarding man simply as an abstract
or isolated individual and ignoring those influences
which are due to his social nature, cannot be other

than inadequate and erroneous. The moral history of the world is not that of an aggregate of separate individualities, each working out his own character and determining the course and issue of his own career in absolute independence of the rest. On the contrary, it would be nearer the truth to say that the individual life is meaningless apart from other lives, and from that universal life of which all alike are only constituent elements or factors; and that the drama of human history derives its profoundest significance from the fact that, for good or evil, the life and destiny of every member of the race is implicated in the life and destiny of the whole. There are many considerations which lead to the conclusion that the moral order under which we live is inexplicable, if it be regarded from a purely individualistic point of view; and that it can only be understood in the light of what has been termed the corporate or organic life of the race. The popular notion which claims, on the score of justice, for each human spirit an absolutely isolated sphere of action, is based on a superficial view of the relation between the individual and the social life.

At first sight, indeed, the conception of society into which we naturally fall is that simply of an aggregate or sum of separate individuals, a multiplicity of independent units, each endowed with a complete, self-contained personality, prior to and apart from the external relations into which he enters with other individuals. Society, from this point of view, has no existence other than that of the individuals who compose it. It is only a name for the combination of these individuals, and these are the only real or actually existing elements in the associations which we designate as the family, the nation, the race. Their combination does not add anything to their essential nature ; nor can it infringe or modify that self-conscious, self-determined individuality which is the inalienable characteristic of each member of the community. Thus it is the individuals who create society, and we could conceive of each individual as existing and continuing to exist as really as now, even if all the other members of society became extinct.

Yet it needs little reflection to see that the order of things in which we live does not correspond to this conception of human nature and life. It would be nearer the truth to say that it is society which creates the individual, rather than the individual society. If individuals are the materials out of which society is created, there is a sense in which these materials were, in the first place, of its own creation. Society, like every other organism, is a whole which is ideally prior to its parts. The latter have no reality in which the former is not presupposed. It enters into their very essence, lives and breathes in them ; and they in turn have no moral life which is not due to their action and reaction with the social medium in which they live.

In the first place, each individual nature does not come into existence a mere passive, colourless substance, a blank tablet on which external agencies may write whatever character they will. It has in it not only physical, but intellectual and moral possibilities, which determine the limits within which its future course must be run, and greatly contribute to shape it. Nor are we to think of these inborn capabilities and tendencies as the original endowments of a nature emerging out of nothingness, or dropped full-fledged from the skies. In many ways they can no more be accounted for as an entirely new creation, apart from the anterior life of the family or the nationality from which they spring, than the fruit apart from the tree on which it hangs, or the flower apart from the plant on which it blossoms. Of the transmission at least of *physical* qualities by physical generation, there can, as we have already said, be no question ; and in so far as mental characteristics are conditioned by or correlated to physical, the former are, at least indirectly, an inheritance of the child from the parent. And not from the immediate parents only. The brain and nervous system of the infant born of a civilized race, his whole physical organization and capabilities, differ from those of the child born of a community in a state of barbarism ; but in both cases they are, whether in the way of development or deterioration, the slow result of a process that has been going on from generation to generation ; and every successive age from the remotest past has contributed to, and may be said to live in, the more or less perfect organization of the existing individual. Nor does it involve any concession to materialism to admit that the more or less perfect physical organization carries with it incalculable influences on the mental and moral life. If, therefore, there is any connection between a high or low type of brain and the intellectual and even moral possibilities of a human agent, and if in either type we can trace the inherited product of ancestry and race, it is obvious that the purely individualistic theory will not apply to the very beginning of human life, and that, even at his entrance on his earthly career, the individual is steeped in influences which are due to the past history of his kind.

But, again, the world into which he enters, and in which his spiritual life begins to unfold itself, is not a moral vacuum. From the very outset he is surrounded by an atmosphere charged with moral influences. If we recoil from the notion of directly inherited moral qualities, we are still as far as ever from the absolutely isolated and independent life of the individualistic theory. If not by inheritance, yet by influences—which, as they long precede the age of reflection, are equivalent to inheritance—the mental and moral life of the individual is coloured. The social environment into which he is born, and which is itself the product of a long process of historic evolution, is, in the earlier and more passive stage of human life, the main factor in his moral development. Long before the period of reflection, the self of which he is to become conscious is steeped and suffused in influences, that stream into it from the moral medium in which it lives. Not merely by positive teaching, by the educational discipline to which it is subjected, but also by the more continuous and potent influence of example, by the tone and spirit that prevail in the family or community, by the quick imitative instincts unconsciously reflecting the character, the tone of thought and speech, the very look and bearing of those with whom he is in daily contact, —by the unconscious action of these and similar forces playing on his ductile susceptibilities, the life of society, which is itself the distilled result of the life of the past, enters into and becomes part and parcel of the life of the individual.

Nor does this process cease with the waking up of the individual to self-consciousness and self-determination. The language he speaks, itself the silent growth, the crystallized product of the life of ages, and which is not only the expression of thought, but the mould which shapes and modifies it; the laws, customs, civil and political institutions, the current beliefs and accepted standards of judgment in literature, art, philosophy, and even religion,— these constitute all through life the mould into which the moral and intellectual being of the great mass of men is run, and against the dominating force of which only a few original and exceptional minds, and even they only to a very limited extent, can assert themselves.

It would thus appear that a purely individualistic

conception of human nature and human life runs counter to the most obvious facts of observation and experience. The abstract individual, starting from a position of unconditioned freedom, charged with his own destiny and working it out unaffected by anything outside of his own volition, is a conception which, however much it may seem to be the condition of moral responsibility, is ludicrously inconsistent with the actual moral order of the world. On the other hand, whatever exception we may take to the Augustinian doctrine as an explanation of the origin of moral evil, yet in its recognition of the organic unity of the race, and of the consequent implication of every individual member of it with its past history and its present moral complexion and character, it far surpasses the shallow philosophy which seeks a solution of the problem only by ignoring the stern facts of human history and experience, and it has in it, as a philosophy of life, a depth and significance which the latter cannot claim.

END OF VOL. I.

GLASGOW: PRINTED AT THE UNIVERSITY PRESS BY ROBERT MACLEHOSE AND CO.